WHY MUSLIMS
PARTICIPATE
IN JIHAD

WHY MUSLIMS PARTICIPATE IN JIHAD

An Empirical Survey on Islamic Religiosity in Indonesia and Iran

DICKY SOFJAN

mizan

Why Muslims Participate in Jihad:
An Empirical Survey on Islamic Religiosity in Indonesia and Iran

© 2006 by Dicky Sofjan

Published by
Mizan Pustaka
Jln. Cinambo No. 135 Cisaranten Wetan
Bandung 40294
Indonesia
Ph. 62-22-7834310
Fax. 62-22-7834311
http://www.mizan.com

ISBN 979-433-399-9

Cover design by Andreas Kusumahadi

For Tini, Zahra, Mahsheed, Mahdi and Layla ...

Preface and Acknowledgments

In this present age of terrorism, doing political research on *jihad* is indisputably one of the 'sexiest' occupations. A simple search on the word "*jihad*" using *Google* or *Yahoo!* can easily come up with 15 million entries that encompass websites, news, personal blogs, pictures and an assortment of other Internet-based information as well as disinformation. Although the quality of the information, propaganda and analyses posted in the Internet varies considerably, the sheer number in itself provides us with a hint as to the level of interest the world's virtual community has on the subject of *jihad*, not to mention if one were to do a similar search for "Islam". *Amazon.com*, one of the most popular websites for the virtual community to purchase books online, contains at least 200 hundred titles for sale bearing the title of *jihad* on its cover. Indeed, if the search were to be expanded to public libraries and conventional bookstores, the results may not differ so much. Why is there this *jihad* "fixation", as one author calls it? Did September 11 really change the world *that* much? Or, is it merely the way we look at this world? Or, perhaps, it may simply be a sign of our mounting insecurity and our efforts to scramble for some form of explanation or understanding.

Going into the real world, eyebrows are frequently raised each time my study is disclosed, in particular to those who do not know me so well. "*Jihad*?!", "Are you not afraid?" or "Is that permitted?" Such frantic reactions, in my view, are anything but unusual. For good or bad reasons, laymen tend to become apprehensive whenever the word "*jihad*" is mentioned. The instant stereotypical portrayal inadvertently points to an aggressive, if not violent, religion that is supported and propagated by bearded men and veiled women with medieval mind-sets.

This book is not intended to dispel, more so to manufacture, 'myths' surrounding Islamic *jihad* and its manifestations. Hence, readers looking for references on "Islamic radicalism" or "Muslim fundamentalism" would be thoroughly disappointed. Even more disheartening would be those who expect to obtain in this book further evidence and justification on the existence of a global network of "Islamic terrorists". Such themes, I venture to say, have extensively been written and in fact have become what a Muslim professor-friend in Boston once described a "cottage industry". Unfortunately, while some works of this nature are insightful and highly contributive to our overall understanding of Islam as a sociopolitical phenomenon, most come across as being *a priori*, judgmental and accusative. The production of the latter, I might add, is initiated by opportunistic strategies to advance their own particularistic political standing, guided by sensationalism and based largely on fragmented, popular understanding of the issues at hand.

For all its worth, this book takes a path of deliberate estrangement from the 'conventional wisdom' by taking into account the multiple, often hidden interpretations and subjective meanings that *jihad* participants themselves attach to their sociopolitical action. This stance obviously does not entail the "idolization of *jihad*", as was cautioned to me on one occasion by a concerned senior professor of Indonesian politics. Rather, this book attempts to humbly offer a new analytical perspective in the way we look at *jihad* and Islamic militancy by utilizing empirical survey data on religiosity from Indonesia and Iran. For anyone allergic to numerals and statistical analyses, I have deliberately streamlined and simplified the data presentation to ensure greater comprehensibility and readability.

From my personal viewpoint, the greatest challenge to this study lies in two things: One is data gathering involving one thousand Muslims in Indonesia and Iran, and the other concerns the constantly changing political circumstances that may affect this study, directly or indirectly. First, apart from the difficulty in gathering data on one thousand Muslim respondents, the task of measuring their level of religiosity and willingness to participate in *jihad* is a different ball game altogether. To many, the undertaking may appear impractical, to say the least, given the post-September 11 political landscape, where research on *jihad*, much less Islam, would surely raise some red flags. A colleague from Singapore, working as an assistant professor, even exclaimed, "It is difficult for me to imagine you going around the streets of Jakarta or Tehran asking one thousand Muslims whether or not they were willing to participate in *jihad*." Indeed, as anticipated from the outset, the survey was never meant to be a simple, straightforward task. Out of fear, apprehension and advice from my Indonesian research assistants, a formal notification letter was filed to the Indonesian Intelpam (Police Security Intelligence Division). However, such a gesture proved pointless because apparently the higher echelons in the Police Headquarters did not think it was at all necessary. As was later explained to me, albeit rather unconvincingly, by the security *apparatchiks*, the 1997/8 *reformasi* had changed much of the way they conduct business. The usual security approach mentality and the looming human rights laws had evidently relinquished, *despite* the occurrence of September 11 tragedy and the spate of bombings in various parts of the country. Adding further twist, a sympathetic police intelligence officer attending to my request expressively stated, "I am also a Muslim. And I do not like Westerners constantly accusing *us* Muslims of supporting terrorists! So if you can counter this growing opinion through your research, you would no doubt be doing Indonesia and Islam a great service." Frankly, in the beginning, I failed to see the logic and connection in the officer's statement. After all, like almost all graduate students, I previously regarded my work as a self-aggrandizing mission to purely obtain my Ph.D. degree, and ultimately secure a comfortable academic post. However, as my study began to take shape following numerous interviews with informants, I started realizing why, where and how my research fitted into the larger context and discourse of Islam, Muslim politics, religious nationalism, democracy, globalization and transnational terrorism. The Indonesian data gathering activities, however, were only the first phase of my overall research undertaking.

The next phase of the survey brought me to a fascinating country, where I studied for almost a year during my years as a lost and wandering undergraduate student in the early 1990s. Data gathering activities in Iran were conducted between May and September 2003. However, prior to conducting the survey, a silent approval from the Idore-e Nahod-e Rahbar (Office of the Spiritual Leader) in Qazvin, Iran, was successfully obtained through the mediation of friends. This approval, to me, was extremely vital considering the circumstances dictating the country during the period of my research stint. Coincidently, two important events took place: one being the American invasion and the subsequent occupation of Iraq; and the other, the anti-government demonstrations held by university students across the country in which "foreign agents" had allegedly been instigating. Thus, the strategy to approach the Office was not so much to acquire a *carte blanche*—for that would be almost impossible in a country such as Iran—but rather to attain a certain level of assurance that if the members of the *Pasdaran* (Revolutionary Guards) or the *Basij* (Islamic Volunteer Force) were to question why a *khareji* (foreigner) like myself was interested in surveying the Iranians' politico-religious propensity to participate in *jihad*, I would be readily equipped with some convincing, yet previously constructed, answers. Indeed, anyone familiar with Iran's incessant political upheavals would acknowledge that security assurances for *kharejis* are almost next to none.

The second greatest challenge to completing this study is associated with *jihad*-induced or *jihad*-inducing occurrences that, if entirely ignored, may cause a fissure. Unfortunately, a number of related occurrences took place when this manuscript was in the finalization stage. Of course, not all *jihad*-related events directly affect the main arguments posed in this book, as the various forms and manifestation of politico-religious actions do not necessarily change the essential reason why people would choose to opt for extreme exploits. These occurrences include the spate of bombings taking place in Iraq, Madrid, Jakarta, Bali, London and elsewhere. Not to mention the related events pertaining to the deadly capture of Dr. Azahari, the Malaysian bomb maker, in East Java, Indonesia, the capture of the dethroned Iraqi president Saddam Hussein, the electoral victory of Hamas in Palestine and the current standoff between Western states and Iran on the nuclear issue. In some ways, these occurrences seem to be affecting the intensity and repertoire of the *jihad* activities but hardly add any nuances to the long and relatively stable reasoning why Muslims participate in *jihad*.

During the preparation and finalization of this study, I was very fortunate to receive the generous assistance and support of countless individuals willing to sacrifice their precious time, energy and thoughts to better improve the substantive quality and timeliness of its delivery. To begin with, it would only be appropriate to convey my gratitude to those who provided me with the necessary academic training to pursue this intellectual endeavor and personal guidance to further build my motivation. I am confident to point out that had it not been for these enthusiastic and inspiring individuals, both the research and this book would not have come thus far. These individuals include, but are not limited to, my formal as well as informal advisors in the

National University of Singapore's Department of Political Science. Most notable among them is Hussin Mutalib, who has gone to enormous length in tolerating the plentiful needs and accommodating the strange demands of his ill-disciplined advisee. Apart from Mutalib, the following names need mentioning: Lee Lai To, Cai Yongshun, Suzaina Kadir, Kyaw Yin Hlaing and Yusaku Horiuchi. My heartfelt appreciation also goes to Bilveer Singh, Alan Chong, Kripa Sridharan, Reuben Wong and Ethan Putterman for their tender supervision throughout the period of my Teaching Assistantship at NUS.

A host of other scholars have either helped add value to this book or encouraged me in many inspiring ways. They include: Professor M. Shahid Alam, Professor Anthony Reid, Professor Leo Suryadinata, Professor Denis Sullivan, Professor William Crotty, Aris Ananta, Syed Muhd Khairudin al-Junied, Hiro Katsumata, Adam Tolnay and Irman G. Lanti. Without their input and feedback, I would not be as confident about the subject matter, argumentation and methodology set out in this study, as I would have been otherwise. When conducting my survey research in Indonesia, my good friend and former teacher Teuku Rezasyah, who was then Chair of the Department of International Relations in Universitas Padjadjaran, Bandung, came to offer his sincere help. With his facilitation, I was able to find the likes of Lia, Yais and Ghafur to endure the rigorous demands of being my research assistants. Meanwhile, throughout my research stint in Iran, I am indebted to the directors and staff of the Tehran International Studies and Research Institute (TISRI) such as Ali Abdullah-Khani, Marzieh Kouhi and Agha-ye Moradi. I thoroughly enjoyed their pleasant companionship, and am very grateful for the fruitful research collaboration that was established.

Scores of individuals provided constructive criticisms and beneficial comments, which forced me to rethink about some pertinent issues in this study that had slipped out of my mind. They were mostly derived from my seminar presentations in Singapore both at NUS and at the Institute of Defence and Strategic Studies (IDSS) in Nanyang

Technological University. Numerous other colleagues also lent a hand in many ingenious ways, enabling me to find creative avenues to resolve problems during the course of my research work in Singapore, Indonesia and Iran. They are: Gusri Cahya Iman, Jana Hermawan, Achmad Suhendra, Dahlia Darmayanti, Deni Ramdhani, Kar Yen Leong, Priyambudi Sulistiyanto, Arry Bainus, Shadiq, Supratman, Hasyim, Colonel Agus Herry, Pak Siradjuddin, Mas Agus Surya, Jiang Yang, Ning Zhaoxin, Sukardi Rinakit, Liu Lin, Li Hongxia, Daiki Shibuichi, Stephanie Theng, Oh Yoon Ah, Sol Iglesias, Mas Didi, Pak Cik Sani, Stephanie, Mumtaj, Jamuna, Zawiyah and others whom I cannot mention due to the constraints of space. I will always cherish their friendship and sincerely hope to build upon it to make this life more beautiful and meaningful.

For the publication of this book, I am grateful to have as a mentor-friend, Haidar Bagir, who over the past ten years has provided me with kind advice, persistent wisdom and constant encouragement. In Mizan, I am thankful to Ahmad Baiquni and Putut Widjanarko for their patience and superb work in managing the editorial and printing processes.

I am also indebted to my 'partners in development' in the United Nations Development Programme, who provided me with great opportunity to grasp at the realities and complexities of day-to-day governance in Indonesia. It is in UNDP that I was able to apply my experiential learning to help, in my own little way, the country in its quest to embark on the journey toward deepening democracy. For that matter, some names deserve mentioning such as Bo Asplund, Gwi-Yeop Son, Iwan Gunawan, Nurina Widagdo, Agung Djodjosoekarto, Dodo Djuliman, Lu'lu Muhammad, Rudiarto Sumarwono, Diana Assoufy, Elis Nurhayati, Ewa Wojkowska, Dewi Metyasari, Ann Hardjosoesilo, Inneke Widodo, Graeme Stephen, Gi-Soon Song, Juniar Heryoso, Chris Morris, Gono Aikan, Maria Immaculata Sudarini and Adi Abidin. Two individuals namely Valentinus Irawan and Fredrik Eriksson in fact served as my proof reader. Despite their heavy work burdens, Irawan and Fredrik went so far as to read the manuscript, and devotedly offered thorough recommendations that eventually lessened the extent of misjudgments, grammatical errors and un-necessary, pathetic little arguments contained in the book's pre-printing version.

Of all people, however, my utmost gratitude goes to my loving and uncomplaining wife Tini Rahayu Gantini, who has perpetually proven her love for me despite all the difficulties she had to put up with throughout my long, intermittent absence from home. It is through her that I have been blessed with four of the most delightful creatures on earth namely Nur Aisyiah az-Zahra, Farah Mahsheed al-Jannah, Mahdi Ismail Syariati and Layla Maryam al-Muqaddas. As the main source of my pride, wonder and happiness, it may seem unfair for them to have to bear having an unrelenting 'student' as their father. Lastly, I would like to state how truly indebted I am to my beloved mother Purnama Mazani, father Sofjan Abdurrahman as well as my dear brothers and sisters for their kind support in guiding me through the perils of life. My prayers will constantly be with them wherever they may go.

Jakarta, April 24, 2006
Dicky Sofjan

Table of Contents

List of Figures

Glossary of Foreign Terms

Arabic words preceded by "al-" refer to the definitive form. Indonesianized or Persianized Arabic vernaculars deployed throughout the text are kept in the original form to maintain the feel of the language. (A)=Arabic; (I)=Indonesian; (P)=Persian/Persianized Arabic.

abangan	: (I) Nominal Muslims
Ahl al-bayt	: (A) Literally, People of the House; the Prophet's Household or offspring
Ahl al-sunnah wa al-jamaah	: (A) Ideology of Islamic 'orthodoxy' practiced in most parts of Indonesia and across the Muslim world
ʻalim	: (A) One who is knowledgeable in Islamic scholarship
Allah	: (A) Generic term for God in Islam
Al-Qaidah	: (A) Literally, the Base; the shadowy terrorist network led by Usamah bin Ladin

'amal	: (A) Benevolent act; the praxis of Islam
'amir	: (A) Leader of a community
Ansar-e Hezbollah	: (P) Helpers of the Party of God; Iran-based militant group
Ayatollah	: (P) Sign of Allah; highest religious title used by Shia Muslim clerical class
azas tunggal	: (I) Literally, sole foundation; the doctrine was ssentially to make *Pancasila* the one and only ideology of the New Order, preventing Communism and Islam from taking root
Basij	: (P) Voluntary paramilitary force in Iran; established to safeguard the Islamic revolution and the republic; *Basiji* being its member
bay'at	: (A) Pledge of allegiance to leader; common practice in militant groups
dakwah	: (I) Islamic propagation
dar al-harb	: (A) The abode of war; territories not under Islamic rule
dar al-Islam	: (A) The abode of peace; territories under the Islamic sphere of influence
dawlah	: (A) Confederation, commonwealth; minimally, state
diin	: (A) Way of life; minimally, religion
dwifungsi	: (I) Indonesian military's dual function of combining defense and sociopolitical affairs
entezar	: (P) Messianic Expectation in Shia Islam
Fagheh	: (P) An expert on *fiqh* (Islamic jurisprudence); see entry on *velayat-e fagheh*

fatwa	: (A) Islamic legal opinion; often mistakenly conceived as religious decree
Fedayeen-e Islam	: (P) Literally, Islamic fighters; Iranian religious militant group with left-leaning ideological orientation
fii sabilillaah	: (A) In the path of God
ghaybat al-kubra	: (A) Greater Occultation (of Imam Mahdi)
haraba	: (A) Root word for "*harb*", as in war
haram	: (A) Forbidden; often referred to action, thing or place
hijrah	: (A) Literally, emigration; Islamic calendar year
Hashashin	: (A) Literally, one who smokes hashish; assassin
Hokumat-e Islam	: (P) Islamic government
husn adh-dhan	: (A) Islamic etiquette on thinking positively about others
Ikhwan al-Muslimin	: (A) Literally, Muslim Brotherhood; Middle East-based religious movement
'ilm	: (A) Knowledge; *ilmu* in Indonesian
Imam	: (A) Literally, one who leads; Infallible Leader of the Shia Muslims
iman	: (A) Faith or affectionate love for God
Intifada	: (A) Religious-nationalist movement in Palestine, which started in 1987
Islam	: (A) Peace, submission to Allah
Islam-e vaqi'i	: (P) The essentially true Islam
istimata	: (A) Suicide
istiqamah	: (A) Steadfast

Itsna Asyariyah	: (A) Twelver school of thought in Shia Islam; also called the Ja'fari creed
jahada	: (A) Root word for *jihad*
jahiliyah	: (A) Pre-Islamic period of ignorance
jahit	: (I) To sew
jamaah	: (A) Muslim congregation; (I) see *jemaah*
Jannah	: (A) Paradise; Heaven
Jemaah Islamiyah	: (I) Literally, Islamic Congregation; a shadowy network of militant Muslims operating in Southeast Asia; allegedly linked to al-Qaidah
jihad	: (A) Striving, endeavoring, struggling toward righteousness; colloquially, "holy war"
jilbab	: (I) Muslim women's headscarf
kaaffah	: (A) Totality, wholeheartedness
kafirin	: (A) Infidels; from *kufr*
Khalifah	: (A) Caliph; leader of the Islamic community
Laa ilaaha illallaah	: (A) Literally, "There is no God but Allah; Islamic religious testimony
margbar	: (P) Death; "*Marghbar Amrika!*" therefore means "Death to America!"
maslahah	: (A) Public interest
mujahidin	: (A) People engaging in jihad; singular form, *mujahid*
mullah	: (P) Literally, A man of God; Muslim scholar
munafiqin	: (A) Hypocrites; singular form, *munafiq*

Muslim	: (A) One who professes Islam as his or her way of life; plural form, *muslimin*
mustadh'afiin	: (A) The oppressed
mustakbiriin	: (A) The oppressor
negara	: (I) State
nemaz-e jum'eh	: (P) Friday prayers
Pancasila	: (I) Literally, Five Main Principles; Indonesia's state ideology
pendekatan keamanan	: (I) Security approach; Suharto's main strategy to intimidate the populace
pesantren	: (I) Traditional Islamic boarding school
pesta demokrasi	: (I) Festival of democracy; refers to general elections; an Indonesian phrase coined during the Suharto era
politik kambing hitam	: (I) Scapegoating politics
preman	: (I) Thug; member of a gang of various backgrounds; often deployed for political purposes
qitaal	: (A) Physical fighting
Quraish	: (A) One of the most respectable clans in Mecca, which Muhammad originated from; some the Prophet's staunchest political opponents came from his own clan
Quran	: (A) The holy book of Islam; believed by Muslims to be the Literal Word of Allah
Rahbar	: (P) Supreme Leader of the Islamic Republic of Iran

Ramadhan	: (A) Islamic holy month when able-bodied Muslims are obligated to fast from dawn to dusk
rauza	: (P) Annual event to commemorate the gruesome death of Imam Hussein. Celebrated each year on the 10th of the Muslim month of Muharram
reformasi	: (I) Reform movement
resaleh	: (P) True message of Islam
Shah	: (P) Monarch or king
Shahanshah	: (P) King of kings
Salafi	: (A) Literally, ancestors; Islamic orthodox theology
Santri	: (I) Literally, student of Muslim boarding school
shalat	: (A) Prayers; generally divided into two: obligatory and commendable prayers
Shia	: (P) Ideology of Muslims in Iran, majority part of Iraq, Lebanon and the Gulf states; of the aggregate world Muslim population, Shias constitute around 10 per cent
Shirk	: (A) Polytheism
Sufi	: (A) Gnostic; Muslim dervish
sunnah	: (A) Muhammad's Prophetic traditions; includes the sayings, deeds and non-verbal omissions
Sunni	: (A) Abbreviated form of *ahl al-sunnah wa al-jamaah*
syahid	: (A) Literally, one who testifies. Colloquially, martyr

syariah	: (A) Islamic system of jurisprudence
syuhada	: (A) Plural form of *syahid*
tahajom-e farhangi	: (P) Western cultural imperialism; a rallying cry used by Muslim revolutionaries
taqiye	: (P) Religious prudential dissimulation with the aim to salvage Islam from annihilation
tolabeh	: (P) Muslim seminarian
ukhrijat li an-naas	: (A) The best among peoples; derived from the Quran
ulama	: (A) Scholar-teachers; singular form, *'alim*
ummah	: (A) Muslim community
velayat-e fagheh	: (P) Guardianship of the Jurist; politico-religious foundation of the Islamic Republic of Iran
wayang	: (I) Javanese art of puppetry

Glossary of Abbreviations and Acronyms

ABRI   : Angkatan Bersenjata Republik Indonesia (former name of the Indonesian Armed Forces); now TNI (Tentara Nasional Indonesia)

CIA   : Central Intelligence Agency

DDII   : Dewan Dakwah Islamiyah Indonesia (Indonesian Islamic Propagation Council)

DI/TII : Darul Islam/Tentara Islam Indonesia (Abode of Islam/Indonesian Islamic Soldiers); an Indonesian Islamic movement striving for a confessional state

FPI   : Front Pembela Islam (Islamic Defenders' Front)

GAM   : Gerakan Aceh Merdeka (Aceh Independence Movement)

Golkar : Golongan Karya (Functional Group); previously, Suharto's political machinery

Hamas   : Harakat al-Muqawamah al-Islamiyah (Islamic Resistance Army)

HTI   : Hizbut Tahrir Indonesia (Indonesian Party of Liberation)

ICMI	:	Ikatan Cendekiawan Muslim Indonesia (Indonesian Muslim Intellectuals' Association)
JIL	:	Jaringan Islam Liberal (Liberal Islam Network)
KISDI	:	Komite Solidaritas Dunia Islam (Committee on the Solidarity of the Islamic World)
KMM	:	Kumpulan Militan/Mujahidin Malaysia (Malaysian Militant /Mujahidin Group)
LJ	:	Laskar Jihad (Jihad Soldiers)
MKO	:	Sazman-e Mojahedin-e Khalq-e Iran/Mojahedin-e Khalq Organization (Organization of the People's Holy Warriors of Iran). A Marxist religious terrorist group, having bases in Iraq, France and the U.S.
MMI	:	Majelis Mujahidin Indonesia (Indonesian Council of Mujahidin)
MTV	:	Music Television
MUI	:	Majelis Ulama Indonesia (Indonesian Council of Ulama)
MUIS	:	Majlis Ugama Islam Singapura (Singapore's Islamic Religious Council)
Nasakom	:	Nasionalisme, Agama dan Komunisme (Nationalism, Religion and Communisme)
NII	:	Negara Islam Indonesia (Islamic State of Indonesia). Once a Muslim clandestine movement to bring about an Islamic state
NU	:	Nahdlatul Ulama (Revival of the Ulama); Indonesia's most influential Islamic mass-based socio-religious organization
PA	:	Palestinian Authority; the formal governing body in Palestine
PAN	:	Partai Amanat Nasional (National Mandate Party)
PAS	:	Partai Islam Se-Malaysia (Malaysian Islamic Party)
PD	:	Partai Demokrat (Democratic Party)

PDI-P   : Partai Demokrasi Indonesia-Perjuangan (Indonesian Democratic Party of Struggle)

PKB   : Partai Kebangkitan Bangsa (National Awakening Party)

PKMS   : Pertubuhan Kebangsaan Melayu Singapura (Singapore Malay National Organization)

PLO   : Palestine Liberation Organization; now turned into PA

PPP   : Partai Persatuan Pembangunan (United Development Party)

RMS   : Republik Maluku Selatan (Republic of South Maluku); a defunct separatist movement in the Maluku Islands, located in the eastern part of Indonesia

SAVAK   : Sazman-e Etala'at va Amniyat-e Keshvar (National Security and Information Organization). SAVAK was the feared and omnipresent political machination of the Shah of Iran to intimidate the populace

SES   : Socioeconomic status

SFLI(K) : Students Following the Line of Imam (Khomeini)

TNI   : Tentara Nasional Indonesia (Indonesian Armed Forces)

UMNO   : United Malay National Organization

1

The Elusive Phenomenon Called Jihad

This is a holy struggle, not a depraved one, God willing," claimed the field commander of the October 12, 2002, Bali bomb blasts.[1] The statement by Abdul Azis a.k.a. Imam Samudra seemed rather peculiar to most people. Struggle for what? Against who? What was he referring to? Even more perplexing was how the instant murder of nearly 200 nightclub goers could be claimed as a "holy" affair.[2] Almost a similar pattern of sentiment was voiced in the aftermath of the September 11, 2001, terrorist attack on the United States of America, killing almost three thousand people and subsequently instilling fear and anxiety in the hearts and minds of people across the globe. Usamah bin Ladin, the assumed leader of Al-Qaidah and accused by the U.S.

---

[1] "*Menguntit pemindahan Imam*" [On trail of Imam's relocation], *Kompas* (Jakarta), published on November 26, 2002. The statement was made when Imam was arraigned in court, which later handed down the capital punishment, together with a few others responsible for the blasts.

[2] For further reading into the thoughts of Azis, see Imam Samudra, *Aku Melawan Teroris!* [I fight Terrorists!] (Solo, Indonesia: Jazera, 2004). The book was written during his time in prison. At the time of writing this manuscript, Samudra's book has already entered its sixth printing.

of masterminding the meticulously planned attack, reportedly said, "It is the duty of every Muslim to fight ... [I]f avenging the killing of our people is terrorism, let history be a witness that we are terrorists."[3] Although his comments fell short of a confession, his 'declaration of war' and the sympathetic support he presently receives indicate a conspicuous discrepancy in perception about the world we all live in. Ironically, this revelation appeared in light of *prima facie* evidence of a threat to humanity's survival as a direct consequence of mass terrorism.

Responding to the September 11 attack and the ever increasing threat of 'religious terrorism', America unleashed its military might and waged the relentless "war on terrorism" against an elusive enemy lurking behind the veils of Islam. In his "Address to the Joint Session in Congress and the American People" delivered on September 20, 2001, President George W. Bush made it clear that "either you are with us, or you are with the terrorists". Indeed, in America's war on terrorism, nations have been left without any opportunity to be neutral. Although Bush and other U.S. high-ranking officials have insisted that the global military campaign is *not* a war against any specific religion, many Muslims still perceive it as an "excuse to attack Islam",[4] if not a pretext "to defuse the light of Islam throughout the world".[5]

In response to the U.S. fury over Afghanistan and Iraq, some Muslims took a militant stance and called for a *jihad*,[6] which they have equated to a devotional act in defense of their way of life.

---

[3] "Osama admits role in WTC attack" in *Daily News* (New York), published on November 11, 2001: 25.

[4] "Khamenei says U.S. uses war against terror as excuse to attack Islam" in *BBC* Monitoring International Reports, published on December 24, 2003.

[5] The assertion was made by a popular Jakarta-based Islamic newsmagazine *Sabili* in which it constantly denounce America's war on terrorism. See *Sabili* (Jakarta) 14 (X), published on November 14, 2002: 8-12.

[6] As *jihad* will be rampantly employed throughout the book, subsequent utilization of the word will not be italicized for aesthetic purposes. A more in-depth discussion on the meaning and application of jihad is provided in the latter part of this chapter.

Although, etymologically, jihad carries an innocuous literal definition (i.e. struggling or striving), the term—like many in the realm of divinity and social sciences—has undergone a series of permutations. Ironically, modern Western stereotypical understanding of jihad as "holy war" bears striking resemblance to the Muslim classical legal interpretation currently being revived by militant Islamic activists across the globe. Nonetheless, thousands of Muslim "foreign fighters" from various nationalities and all walks of life converged in Afghanistan, only to be bombed, killed, captured or forced into waging a guerilla war against the so-called "Coalition of the Willing". In Iraq alone, the initial phase of the American invasion saw between 8,000 and 12,000 number of hardcore "foreign fighters",[7] who entered the country to assist domestic resistance groups in the fight against the perceived occupiers of the 'Muslim land', causing much havoc to the coalition forces spread thinly throughout the country. Daily media reporting on Iraq for the past three years indicates an escalating trend in collective resistance against the U.S.-led occupation *despite* the capture of Saddam Hussein, the holding of democratic parliamentary elections—won largely by the Shia camp—and the establishment of a rainbow government. Planted bombs and guerilla attacks have caused major casualties to the occupying forces as well as the new recruits of the Iraqi armed forces and police, regarded by the insurgents as collaborators.[8] Political developments have also witnessed growing Muslim Shia resentment toward the Americans, who have committed both military and political blunders. This has been led by a charismatic militant cleric named Moqtada al-Sadr, who commands the Mehdi Army.

In view of the above, some pertinent issues come to mind. As this was not the first instance in which Muslims were called to armed struggle, the question lies centrally on the determining factors that encourage Muslims to want to participate in jihad. What is their

---

[7] "U.S. Pushes Upward its Estimate of Iraq Rebels" in *International Herald Tribune*, published on October 23, 2004: 1.

[8] At the of writing, around 2500 American soldiers have perished while serving in Iraq.

rationale? Does it stem from their particular understanding of Islam? Why do they share deep-seated resentment toward America or the West? Why would one be prepared to go through all the trouble to participate in a seemingly unwinnable war? What drives a Muslim to leave his or her world behind and fight shoulder-to-shoulder against the 'infidels'?

Confronting this barrage of questions, some elaboration is required to deal with the elusive and confounding jihad phenomenon. *First,* Muslims have had major grievances against the West (namely the U.S., Europe and Israel) for many decades now, if not centuries. All the while, the legacy of the Medieval Crusade, which was subsequently followed by European imperialism, lingers on in the collective memory and consciousness of the Muslims. Within this purview, one is induced to ask: will history repeat itself with religionists battling one another in the name of God? Or, is it a mere beginning of what Huntington (1993 and 1996) predicted to be "the clash of civilizations"?[9] *Second,* jihad is firmly embedded in the teachings of Islam, "the fastest growing religion" in the world, including in the U.S. In the Quran, the term jihad and its derivatives are mentioned 41 times. A quick glance at the state of affairs in contemporary Muslim societies would confirm that jihad is far from being an anachronism. In almost all conflict areas, militant Muslims often insist that their armed struggle or participation in jihad is a religious duty stipulated in the doctrines of the holy Quran and endorsed by numerous Prophetic traditions. Thus, from the militant Muslims' viewpoint, the American war on terrorism is a mere pretext to cause harm to their brethren and undermine the Islamic faith. As Hussein Umar, Secretary General of DDII (Indonesian Islamic Propagation Council), noted, 'The established international opinion on terrorism is part and parcel of a "grand design" to ensnare Islam

---

[9] "The Clash of Civilizations?" appeared initially in *Foreign Affairs*, 72 (3) Summer 1993: 22-49, which was later extended and published as a book [see Samuel P. Huntington, *The Clash of Civilizations and the Remaking of the World Order* (London: Touchstone, 1996)]. Here, the author argues that following the fall of the Soviet Union, Islamic and Confucianist civilizations by virtue of their cultures will have some common causes and inevitably clash with the West's Judeo-Christian civilization led primarily by the U.S.

and the Muslim world. And it is borne out of the forces that are anti-Islam.'[10]

Third, contemporary practice of jihad has been instrumental for militants to rally moderate Muslims to support their political agenda. Their main objectives are normally set at three distinct levels. One is to determinedly struggle against political repression adopted by many secular governments. The aim is to attain some degree of freedom and autonomy in running their own affairs, which may or may not insist on the imposition of the *syariah* (divine-inspired law). In Southeast Asia, three cases quickly come to mind, notably the Acehnese (in northwestern tip of Indonesia),[11] the Moro (in southern Philippine) and the Patani (in southern Thailand) rebellions. The next level involves a greater goal of 'Islamicizing' the state by way of instilling Muslim doctrines, values and ethics into the political system. Such cases can be found in Egypt, Turkey, Algeria and Indonesia, whereby Muslim politico-religious groups have been continuously asserting themselves and pushing for the Islamicization of the country either via peaceful, constitutional means or, if necessary, armed struggle and collective violence. The last objective takes the form of a regional or global effort by Muslims to create a 'superstate' or more precisely to reestablish the "*Pax Islamica*".[12] It revolves around romanticizing the once powerful institution of the Caliphate or Imamate.[13] Transnational Islamic movements such as Al-Qaidah and

---

[10] Derived from personal interview with the author on November 29, 2002, in Jakarta.

[11] As will be discussed in more detail in Chapter 4, the Free Aceh Movement or GAM signed a peace deal with the Government of Indonesia in August 2005, effectively ending the long struggle for secession.

[12] For an elaboration of the concept, see David George, "Pax Islamica: An alternative new world order?" in Abdel Salam Sidahmed and Anoushiravan Ehteshami, *Islamic Fundamentalism* (Boulder: Westview Press, 1996).

[13] Although both terms can be interchangeably used, they mean totally different things. Muslims from the *Ahl al-sunnah wa al-jama'ah* (abbreviated hereon, Sunni) school of thought are usually more familiar with the former notion of politico-religious central authority than the latter. Meanwhile, the Shia Muslims are politically and religiously inclined to support the latter, which coincides with laying the groundwork for the re-advent of the Imam al-Mahdi (The Rightly Guided One). This issue will be further discussed in Chapters 3, 4 and 5.

Hizb at-Tahrir (Liberation Party) in the Middle East as well as the recently exposed Jemaah Islamiyah (JI) in Southeast Asia provide good examples. Although the three agenda may overlap, or perhaps even interact with one another, the dynamic framework is nonetheless instrumental as an entry point to comprehend the diverging politico-religious goals and orientations of different Muslim subcommunities in various parts of the world.

Fourth, violent reactionary movements are often regarded as byproducts of poverty and dispossession, rendering the destitute class to be amenable to delusions of overcoming, if not reversing, the unfavorable sociopolitical circumstances. As a logical corollary, such a case fosters an emotional bond among the 'underdogs of society' to prescribe to a particular form of ideology and sociopolitical action that would supposedly resolve their immediate problems. As an illustration, for the impoverished Palestinian Muslims living in the squatters of the Gaza strip or the West Bank, joining the Islamic Resistance Movement or Hamas (Harakat al-Muqawamah al-Islamiyah) against Israeli occupation and repression becomes an almost irresistible option.[14] Furthermore, it is highly conceivable that the high level of willingness among Palestinian Muslims to engage in Intifada, or become active members of Hamas, Islamic Jihad or Al-Aqsa Martyrs Brigade, is arguably related to their unfortunate socioeconomic status.[15] Such political inclination is reinforced by the role of these organizations, which often play as a surrogate mother for the Palestinians by providing a vast network of welfare services such as schools and clinics as well as providing food subsidies and cash. According to a poll held in mid 2002 by Bir Zeit University in Ramallah, Hamas' popularity rose considerably due to its seemingly altruistic manner in serving the

---

[14] For more on Hamas' ideological outlook, read Khaled Hroub, *Hamas: Political thought and practice* (Washington, D.C.: Institute for Palestine Studies, 2000).

[15] Empirical studies on political participation have mostly relied on the SES (socioeconomic status) model as a primary frame of analysis. See, for instance, Jan E. Leighley, "Attitudes, Opportunities and Incentives: A field essay on political participation" in *Political Research Quarterly*, 48 (1) 1995.

Palestinian destitute populace regardless of political affiliations.[16] It was no wonder then that Hamas was able to secure an electoral victory in the Palestinian occupied territories over the late Yasser Arafat and Mahmoud Abbas' Al-Fatah faction, which pre-dominated the so-called Palestinian Authority. Hamas' victory will obviously and significantly transform the political configuration both in Israel and throughout the Middle Eastern hemisphere. In response to the victory by Hamas, considered as a "foreign terrorist organization", the U.S. and the European Union have decidedly turned to economic embargo as a way to 'choke' the Palestinian government and, at the same time, penalize the Palestinians for its 'wrong' choice of leadership.

Lastly, jihad as a political rhetoric has had a mixture of successes and failures. The questions to pose are as follows: why is the call for jihad sometimes effective and other times not? Could it be that mass propaganda plays a role in determining the fate of the call for jihad? If so, could it be that Western (namely American) propaganda against "Islamic fundamentalism" have reached a point beyond toleration, thereby causing alienation among the majority Muslims and further radicalizing the minority? Or, is it perhaps the other way around? With the immense wealth of Bin Ladin and the effective use of politico-religious propaganda, Al-Qaidah was merely bent on recruiting suicidal militants and employing mass terrorism to widen the traditional cleavage between Western (Judeo-Christian) and Islamic civilizations?

In light of the above, this study sets out to answer the following question: *why do Muslims participate in jihad?* The timing of this study could not have been better, as both government security officials and social scientists scuttle to find an explanation on what truly determines the willingness or unwillingness on the part of Muslims to participate in jihad. Judging from its often coordinated calls and widespread involvement, jihad cannot be simply categorized as a random act of collective violence, nor could it easily be dismissed as

---

[16] See "*Hamas* exploits Robin Hood image to its benefits", *The Straits Times* (Singapore), published on August 2, 2002: 17.

being senseless. Is there then some form of logic behind the Muslims' participation in jihad? Is the determination largely based on perceived grievance, rationality, culture, personal and collective identity or religious expression? Can the SES model tell us something about the profiles of the participants and possibly predict the individual's level of willingness to participate in jihad? How crucial is religiosity in determining a Muslim's choice of action in this regard? If crucial, which "dimension of religiosity" is the most important in explaining Muslim participation in jihad?[17]

To meet the objective that has been laid out, this study employs methodological individualism as its main approach in answering why Muslims participate in jihad. This entails that social explanations and descriptions are grounded in facts about the individuals, while assuming that "social entities" are "nothing but ensembles of individuals in various relations to one another".[18] In this case, descriptions and observations are gathered from an individual level survey on 'Muslims on the streets' of Indonesia and Iran. Combining both qualitative and quantitative methods, this study endeavors to demonstrate the role of Islamic religiosity in determining Muslim participation in jihad. Here, religiosity refers to a person's level of devoutness or, as Simmel (1997) puts it, "a quality of spiritual being".[19] In the more practical and mundane terms, religiosity is basically a measure of one's "commitment to religion".[20] By defining it so, "religion stands juxtaposed to religiosity, which is in itself a *state* or a spiritual rhythm lacking any object" [original emphasis].[21] In this study,

---

[17] Among numerous work on the multidimensional conception of religiosity, see Gordon F. De Jong, Joseph E. Faulkner and Rex H. Warland, "Dimensions of Religiosity: Evidence from a cross-cultural study" in *Social Forces*, 54 (4) June 1976: 866-889.

[18] Daniel Little in David Marsch and Gerry Stoker (editors), *Theory and Methods in Political Science*, Basingstoke (Hampshire: Macmillan, 1995), 183.

[19] Georg Simmel, *Essays in Religion* (New Haven, Connecticut: Yale University Press, 1997), 209.

[20] Philip E. Secret, James B. Johnson and Audrey W. Forrest, "The Impact of Religiosity on Political participation and Membership in Voluntary Associations among Black and White Americans" in *Journal of Black Studies*, 21 (1) The Emerging African American Environment, September 1990: 87.

[21] Simmel, op. cit., 165.

religiosity is composed of three dimensions: knowledge of Islam, ritual practices and religious affection.[22]

The implication of this study is threefold. *First*, a whole range of new opportunities in empirical political research, relating to the effects of religiosity on participation in, more specifically, politico-religious forms of collective action would hopefully be opened. In stating so, it is expected that future studies will be undertaken without necessarily resorting to the conventional explanation of the SES model and rational choice. According to Euben (2002), such predisposition as described above is "the newest expression of scientism" and "informed by a set of oppositions between science and religion, rational and irrational, modern and pre-modern in terms of which messy and multiple histories are pressed into a dominant narrative about the emergence of a modern West".[23] *Second*, while state of the art research on religiosity have mostly centered on "American religious traditions",[24] studies of a similar nature on other religions should indeed be welcomed. Thus, offering an operationalizable framework on Islamic religiosity would not only be essential but also instrumental in empirically measuring the level of religious commitment among Muslims. *Third*, in spite of the congested interest in Islam, jihad and "religious terrorism",[25] any creative venture in political research rising above the preoccupation on judgmentalism will expectedly counter the present-day conventional 'wisdoms'. The current trend in global Islamic militancy obviously needs to be further explained. Such benign intention, however, should be preceded by firstly *understanding* these phenomena. In this regard, the present author is in no way persuaded to succumb to strict dicho-

---

[22] Detailed elaboration on the measures and operationalization will be discussed in the latter part of this chapter.

[23] For more, see Roxanne L. Euben, "Killing (For) Politics: Jihad, martyrdom, and political action" in *Political Theory*, 30 (1) February 2002: 7-8.

[24] Brian Steensland, Jerry Z. Park, Mark D. Regnerus, Lynn D. Robinson, W. Bradford Wilcox and Robert D. Woodberry, "The Measure of American Religion: Toward improving the state of the art" in *Social Forces*, 79 (1) September 2000, 291-318.

[25] The term was borrowed from Mark Juergensmeyer, *Terror in the Mind of God: The global rise of religious violence* (Berkeley: University of California Press, 2000).

tomization of traditions between "explanation" and "interpretation", which to a significant degree has been institutionalized in political science research. Though it may be viewed as somewhat eclectic, from the methodological viewpoint, it is almost imperative that when it comes to religion and politics, mechanisms and actions are too often acutely intertwined with symbolisms and rituals.

The general hypothesis of this study is as follows: religiosity matters when considering Muslim participation in jihad. More explicitly, the level of willingness to participate in jihad is significantly determined by religious affection, which denotes Muslim identity, affinity, solidarity and sense of attachment to the universal Islamic body politic or the *ummah*.

Theoretical Terrain

The reservoir of literature on jihad is filled with inspiring works by Muslim theologians, historians, jurists and activists. All the while, political pundits and media gatekeepers simply covered the subject of jihad under the blanket of "religious fundamentalism", "Muslim radicalism" or more recently "Islamic terrorism".[26] This partiality unfortunately has too frequently generated myopic viewpoints, even among the most thoughtful scholars. In effect, the utter confusion and subsequent rush to attach meaning to the heartrending episode of September 11 permitted some level of sheer tribalism. In that sense, the U.S. could have learned a lesson or two instead of merely viewing the terrorist attacks "through the prism of selected images that are being played up *ad nauseum* on our television screens".[27] What is more important, for social scientists, is that September 11 has confirmed that religious, identity-seeking movements are here to stay.

---

[26] For an excellent review on the Western critical view of jihad, see Fida Muhammad, "Jihad as Terrorism: The Western media and the defamation of the Qur'an" in Jeff Ferell and Neil Websdale (editors), *Making Trouble: Cultural constructions of crime, deviance, and control* (New York: Aldine De Gruyter, 1999).

[27] M. Shahid Alam, *Is There an Islamic Problem: Essays on Islamicate societies, the US and Israel* (Petaling Jaya, Malaysia: The Other Press, 2004), 105.

To obtain a respectable degree of objectivity,[28] this study is inclined to treat the subject matter (jihad) similar to any other sociopolitical phenomenon, whereby participation becomes amenable to what Schwartz (1984) describes as "multisubjective interpretation".[29] The approach taken in this study with regard to the notion of participation would hopefully serve the interest of preempting any propensity to criticize or valorize jihad. Judgment should be made on the basis of, what Henry James suggests, "irreducible and stubborn facts".[30] Thus, to equate *all* forms of jihad with terrorism is not only outright subjective but also counterproductive, especially if one's desire is to understand. On this matter, Daniel Little maintains that:

> [A]ll social action is framed by a meaningful social world. To understand, explain, or predict patterns of human behavior, we must first penetrate the social world of the individual—the meanings he attributes to the environment (social and natural), the values and goals he possesses, the choices he perceives, and the way he interprets other individuals' social action. Only then will we be able to analyze, interpret and explain his behavior.[31]

Likewise, to categorize jihad under "weapons of the weak" nomenclature may well trivialize the devastation and human suffering that such sociopolitical action may entail.[32] With respect to the jihad participants, this study is therefore committed to the familiar adage that: "*one man's terrorist is another man's freedom fighter*". Juer-

---

[28] The present author concedes that scholars and scientists from within any realm of discipline, especially the arts, social sciences and humanities, cannot in anyway be entirely objective. Even the choice of topic may prove to be significantly biased toward a researcher's socioeconomic status, belief system, ideological leaning and an array of other determining factors.

[29] Joel D. Schwartz, "Participation and Multisubjective Understanding: An interpretivist approach to the study of political participation" in *Journal of Politics*, 46 (4) 1984: 1117-1141.

[30] Alfred North Whitehead, *Science and the Modern World* (New York: Free Press, 1967), 3.

[31] Marsch and Stoker, op. cit., 85.

[32] James C. Scott's influential work provides many insights as to how the weak (in this case, Malaysian peasants) conduct subtle forms of insurgencies against hegemonic local power structures. See Scott, *Weapons of the Weak: Everyday forms of peasant resistance* (New Haven, Connecticut: Yale University Press, 1985).

gensmeyer (2001) took a similar path in discussing religious violence by stating, "The designation of terrorism is a subjective judgment about the legitimacy of certain violent acts as much as it is a descriptive statement about them".[33] In observing such neutrality, I intend to deal with the subject matter at hand in an impartial manner. To answer the question posed earlier, relevant theories pertaining to participation in collective action will be elaborated.

Participation in Collective Action

What really constitutes participation? Conventional usage of the word in political science has for the most part been equated with formal political participation. A standardized definition by Verba and Nie (1972) limits the meaning to "those activities by private citizens that are more or less directly aimed at influencing the selection of governmental personnel and/or the action they take".[34] Huntington and Nelson (1976) later refined the definition to denote "activity by private citizens designed to influence governmental decision-making".[35] Clearly, the above definitions are overly restrictive and biased toward advanced democracies because they assume the existence of peaceful and legal channels open to all private citizens to meaningfully redress their grievances or to simply put forward their everyday concerns.

No doubt, liberally classifying jihad under political participation would also prove disingenuous. Unlike voting—commonly used as a measurement of political participation in advanced democratic states—jihad is a complex manifestation of politico-religious action, as it involves aspects such as objectification of faith, collective 'bad' memory, emotional sentiments and identity politics. However, looking at it from the perspective of the doers, jihad is a form of participation. Drawing upon Iran's 1978/9 "Islamic revolution", Schwartz (1984) sees Muslim

---

[33] See Juergensmeyer, op. cit., 9.

[34] Sydney Verba and Norman H. Nie. *Participation in America: Political democracy and social equality* (Chicago: University of Chicago Press, 1972), 2.

[35] Samuel P. Huntington and Joan M. Nelson, *No Easy Choice: Political participation in developing countries* (Cambridge, Massachusetts: Harvard University Press, 1976), 4.

participation as "performing the activities laid down in Islamic law ... a sacred ideal in the world of the profane".[36] He further writes, "[I]nsofar as [the Muslim] religion holds that secular laws must be aligned with the higher law of the Koran, he cannot fully participate in the city of God, to use Augustine's language, until his heavenly Father rules over the city of man."[37]

Based on Islamic jurisprudence, two levels of religious obligations exist: the individual duty (*fardh al-'ain*) and the collective duty (*fardh al-kifayah*). Zawati (2001) categorizes jihad as being a "collective religious duty".[38] It therefore brings forth the collective action problem.[39] Sandler (1992) defines collective action plainly as "activities that require the coordination of efforts by two or more individuals. As such, collective action involves group actions intended to further the interests or well-being of the members".[40] It is thus a cooperative venture requiring more than one individual to undertake. Tarrow (1994), a social movement scholar, has this to say:

> Collective action takes many forms—brief or sustained, institutionalized or disruptive, humdrum or dramatic. Most of it occurs within institutions on the part of constituted groups who act in the name of goals that would hardly raise an eyebrow. It becomes contentious when it is used by people who lack regular access to institutions, act in the name of new or unaccepted claims and behave in ways that fundamentally challenge others ... They have power because they challenge opponents, bring out solidarities and have

---

[36] Schwarts, op. cit.

[37] Ibid, 1129.

[38] Hilmi M. Zawati, *Is Jihad a Just War?: War, peace and human rights under Islamic and public international law* (Lewiston, New York: E. Mellen Press, 2001).

[39] If Muslim territory is invaded, the law on jihad shifts from being a collective to an individual obligation. According to Article 15 of the Hamas Charter, "When an enemy usurps a Muslim land, then jihad is an individual religious duty on every Muslim." Hroub, op. cit., 276.

[40] Todd Sandler, *Collective Action: theory and applications* (Ann Arbor: University of Michigan Press, 1992), xvii.

meaning within particular population groups, situations and po-litical cultures".[41]

Concealed in the above description, collective action hinges on rationality and logic. First generation literature on collective action basically derived its structure of argument from Olson's (1971) *Logic of Collective Action*.[42] The main logic presupposes the individual to be a rational actor, who is predisposed to utilitarian motives and con-stantly seeking higher returns on investment. As it follows, every action an individual person, party, group or state makes is expected to bring benefits that are tangible and measurable. In view of the incentive structure, the individual becomes motivated and focused on attaining the objective. The two most important contentions, which will be discussed at greater length in the next chapter, relate to "public good" and "selective incentive" in which all forms of collective action must guarantee in order for the group of rational individuals to reasonably function.

However, a shift is occurring within the domain of political science. Expressive choice model, which involves identity and sense of attach-ment are on the verge of becoming a counter explanation to the highly instrumental way of thinking about collective action. Instead of focusing much attention on the costs and benefits of collective action, expressive choice model recently developed by Schuessler (2000) centers around the notion of *who they are* and the need to attach oneself to a col-lective, which most appropriately represents them.[43] In that sense, participation in any form of collective action principally serves as a reaffirmation of the self and the collective that the individual wish to

---

[41] Sydney Tarrow, *Power in Movement: Social movements, collective action and politics* (New York: Cambridge University Press, 1994), 2-3.

[42] Mancur Olson, *The Logic of Collective Action: Public goods and the theory of groups* (second printing) (Cambridge, Harvard University Press, 1971). To learn more about second generation model of rationality, read Elinor Ostrom, "A Behavioral Approach to the Rational Choice Theory of Collective Action" in *American Political Science Review*, 92 (1) 1998: 1-22.

[43] See Alexander A. Schuessler, *A Logic of Expressive Choice* (New Jersey: Princeton University Press, 2000).

be associated with.[44] Unlike the rational choice schema, which solely depends on cost-benefit calculations, expressive choice relies heavily on what Padgett (2000) dubs "solidary incentives", derived from "social solidarity and identification".[45]

Conceptualizing Jihad

Before venturing any further, jihad, as the subject matter of this study, needs to be conceptualized and contextualized. This is to avoid any confusion and misunderstanding derived from arbitrariness in opting for specific, if not selected, meanings attached to jihad.[46] What exactly is jihad? Why is it still relevant in this day and age? As previously stated, popular media usage of the term has spurred a major onslaught to the notion of jihad. This is not to say that the misperception and misconstruction of jihad are entrenched merely among non-Muslims or that they are solely the product of Western political and cultural biases. I will argue that ignorance is also prevalent among many Muslims. The convoluted debate on jihad prevails not only at the historical and conceptual levels but, most profoundly, at the application of the doctrine. Islamic classical texts and modern references point to a rich and diverse interpretation of jihad. Muslim scholars unanimously agree that the word itself is etymologically derived from Arabic root word of *jahada*, which denotes struggling, striving or endeavoring to achieve something good. The literal meaning itself has no direct correlation with the notions of war or battle, which would normally be represented by the words *haraba* (which refers to war) or *qitaal* (which denotes physical fighting).[47]

---

[44] A deeper elaboration on the choice model will be provided in Chapter 2.

[45] Stephen Padgett, *Organizing Democracy in Eastern Germany: Interest groups in post-Communist society* (Cambridge: Cambridge University Press, 2000), 99.

[46] It may also be useful to know that the term jihad in the Quran is frequently attached to the phrase *fii sabilillaah* ("in the path of Allah"), which for all intent and purposes should be deemed as an early warning signal to those who misuse and abuse the religious injunction.

[47] For a more expanded discussion, see Bernard Lewis, *The Political Language of Islam* (Chicago: University of Chicago Press, 1988).

Nonetheless, any discussion on jihad is never complete without due consideration of the popular ideology that Egyptian Sayyid Qutb (1906-1966), whom Armstrong (2000) qualifies as "the founder of Sunni fundamentalism",[48] developed during his 15 years of imprisonment for being involved in militant activities of the Ikhwan al-Muslimin (Muslim Brotherhood). Famed for his pamphlet entitled *Ma'alam fii al-Thariq* (Milestone),[49] Qutb laid out the work plan (*manhaj*) for the inevitable victory of Islam, which for decades has inspired Muslim activists and Islamic movements throughout the world. Another important figure in the development of both the theory and praxis of jihad is Abul A'la Maududi (1903-1979), a renowned Pakistani Muslim journalist-turned-activist. Maududi (1980), who founded the Jamaat-e Islami, explains jihad succinctly in the following manner:

> Jihad means struggle to the utmost of one's capacity. A man who exerts himself physically or mentally or spends his wealth *in the way of Allah* is indeed engaged in jihad. But in the language of the *Syariah* [Divine-inspired system of law] this word is used particularly for the war that is waged solely in the name of Allah and against those who perpetrate oppression as enemies of Islam ... Jihad is as much a primary duty of the Muslims concerned as are the daily prayers or fasting. One who shirks it is a sinner. His very claim to being a Muslim is doubtful. He is plainly a hypocrite who fails in the test of sincerity and all of his '*ibadat* [religious acts of obedience] and prayers are a sham, a worthless hollow show of devotion.[50]

Through the passage of time, jihad has somewhat undergone substantial permutations, attaching itself more progressively with less innocuous undertakings. What has then become of jihad? Is jihad the only recourse to defending Islam and the Muslims? According to the widely cited *Al-Faridah al-Ghaybah* (The Neglected Duty)—

---

[48] Karen Armstrong, *The Battle for God* (New York: Alfred A. Kopf, 2000), 239.

[49] Seyed Qutb, *Ma'alam fii al-Thariiq* [Milestone] (Himpunan Belia Islam, undated).

[50] See Abul A'la Maududi, *Towards Understanding Islam* (Beirut: IIFSO, 1980), 140-141.

regarded as one of the most influential handbooks for militant Muslims aside from Qutb's *Milestone*—the answer would be a resounding yes.[51] For author Abd al-Salam Faraj, "jihad of the sword" is not only a potential common denominator among Muslims, but also a perfect litmus test to distinguish between the true believers (*muslimin*) and the hypocrites (*munafiqin*) or the unbelievers (*kafirin*). Faraj's view is based mostly on classical-legal references that essentially divide the world into *dar al-Islam* (the "abode of peace") and *dar al-harb* (the "abode of war"). The logic is alluringly simple: as Muslims are God's 'chosen few'—having been bestowed the final revelation, the Quran—it is consequently their religious obligation to invite all of humanity to respect and abide by the rule of Allah, if need be by waging a jihad. In view of this logic, Muslims are inclined, if not obligated, to proselytize their religion in the hope of expanding the *dar al-Islam*. This must be achieved even if it means resorting to war. Only then, according to this line of thinking, can Divine justice prevail and God's blessing be placed upon the whole universe.

However simple and alluring as the above logic may seem to offer, a more nuanced analysis beyond the binary logic is definitely required in order for Muslims to rise above the *minna wa minkum* (us and them) mentality. Moderate scholar Hasyim Muzadi, chairman of Nahdlatul Ulama (NU)—Indonesia's largest Islamic socio-religious mass organization—, argues that 'Muslims are forbidden to act aggressively. There is no such thing as "preemptive strike" in Islam. Only *musuh nyata* (real enemies) can be fought against. Thus, the principle remains that you can wage war *only if* war is waged upon you.'[52] Ali

---

[51] Johannes J.G. Jansen (translation), *The Neglected Duty: The creed of Sadat's assassins and Islamic resurgence in the Middle East* (New York: Macmillan, 1986). This work has been the primary source of inspiration behind the Egyptian-based Islamic Jihad movement, which in the early 1980s was responsible for the 1981 assassination of President Anwar Sadat, who was accused of blasphemy for signing the Camp David Accord with Israel.

[52] Derived from personal interview with the author held in Tehran on June 10, 2003. At the time, the *Rahbar* (Leader of the Islamic Republic) Ayatollah Ali Khamenei invited an NU delegation headed by Muzadi to forge closer ties between the religious establishment and its Indonesian counterpart.

Syariati (1933-1977), Iran's most celebrated modern Muslim intellectual and ideologue, takes a statist view on the subject and contends, "The various means employed by an Islamic state to spread Islam are called jihad."[53] Meanwhile Noorani (2002) cites two dimensions of jihad, which most Muslims are dearly accustomed to: one being "the individual's struggle for piety"; and the other, "the society's struggle for justice".[54] While the former denotes the exercise of achieving higher spiritual goals, the latter form can take various manifestations—as one reliable Prophetic tradition informs us—from "conveying the message of truth before a tyrant" to armed struggle.

A disparaging view on the subject asserts that jihad is basically "a code of murder and rapine disguised under a thin coating of religious verbiage".[55] Meanwhile Watt (1961), making a clear distinction between the early Muslim struggles, notably the *razzias*, during the period of Prophet Muhammad's persecution in Mecca and the religiously sanctified forms of jihad during Islam's political ascendancy in seventh century Arabia, describes jihad plainly as "the action of a religious community against non-members of the community".[56] Another critique comes from a prominent Muslim futurologist Ziauddin Sardar, who chastised contemporary Muslims for their retrogressive approach to understanding jihad. He argues:

> Jihad has now been reduced to the single meaning of 'Holy War'. This translation is perverse not only because the concept's spiritual, intellectual and social components have been stripped away, but because it has been reduced to war by any means, including terrorism. So anyone can now declare jihad on anyone, without any

---

[53] In William Montgomery Watt, *Islamic Fundamentalism and Modernity* (London: Routledge, 1988), 52.

[54] A.G. Noorani, *Islam and Jihad: Prejudice versus reality* (Reading, U.K.: Global Issues, 2002), 46.

[55] Suhas Majumdar, *Jihad: The Islamic doctrine of permanent war* (New Delhi: Voice of India, 2001), 67.

[56] W. Montgomery Watt, *Muhammad: Prophet and statesman* (Oxford University Press, 1961), 109.

ethical or moral rhyme or reason. Nothing could be more perverted, or pathologically more distant from the initial meaning of jihad.[57]

From the above elaboration, jihad can manifest into a multitude of actions and characterizations. However, it should be mentioned here that if otherwise stated, the term jihad in this study relates to the classical meaning of collective armed struggle.[58]

In this study, Muslims will be treated as a community sharing some form of collective identity, defined here as "cultural representations and social norms involving names, narratives, symbols, verbal styles, rituals and so on".[59] Clarification should be made at this stage with regard to the usage of terms such as "Muslims" and "militant Muslims". From the linguistic viewpoint, the latter follows the adjective-noun subordination principle in the English language. To say "Asian American" is to mean that one belongs to a racial category of people born with Asian heritage but at the same time possessing formal American citizenship. Ironically, when it comes to religion, the English language is somewhat favorable to religionists. It is almost imperative that one is called an "American Muslim" or "Indian Muslim" and not "Muslim American" or "Muslim Indian". Similarly, the author is not using "Muslim militants" but rather "militant Muslims" to denote Muslims who happen to be militants and not militants who happen to be Muslims. In this instance, I am also not inclined to employ the customary use of adjectives such as traditionalists, conservatives, modernists, neo-modernists, liberalists, scripturalists, etc. For the most part, these adjectives are mere superficial constructions established by social scientists obsessed with categorizations, typologies and taxonomies, which have all

---

[57] Sohail Inayatullah and Gail Boxwell (editors), *Islam, Postmodernism and Other Futures: A Ziauddin Sardar Reader* (London: Pluto Press, 2003), 31.

[58] For a comparative reading on the subject, see Rudolf Peters, *Jihad in Classical and Modern Times: A reader*, (Princeton, New Jersey: Markus Wiener, 1996) and Reuven Firestone, *Jihad: Origin of holy war in Islam* (New York: Oxford University Press, 1999).

[59] See Francesca Polletta and James M. Jasper "Collective Identity and Social Movements" in *Annual Review of Sociology*, (27) 2001: 284-285.

contributed meagerly to the understanding of the Muslim mindset. For the sake of conceptual simplicity and lucidity, Muslims simply represent those who regard Islam as their *diin* or way of life.[60] This implies a generic category of people who look toward Islam for guidance and cue in life. Nominally, they identify themselves as being Muslims, who in principle accept the *syahadah*—the Islamic religious testimony: "*I witness that there is no god but Allah and Muhammad is His Messenger*"—as truth regardless of whether they are for or against the implementation of the *syariah*. These people are distinct from the militant Muslims who prescribe to jihad as their way of life. For the militants, their lives revolve around jihad. Studying, traveling, putting aside a thorn from the street and even engaging in intimacy with their lawful wives can be regarded, according to their standards, as subtle manifestations of jihad. To these people, their hearts and minds are focused on imposing God's law on earth. Thus, every activity, in their view, should be made for the benefit of expanding the *dar al-Islam*. More often than not, the militant Muslims are prone to adopting a radical politico-religious outlook to the extent that certain militant groups do not regard moderate Muslims as true believers. This is largely based on Faraj's earlier notion that refusing to participate in jihad would constitute a grave dereliction of religious duty. This form of politico-religious thinking is most profound in closely-knit groups such as the Egyptian-based At-Takfir wa al-Hijra (Denigration and Flight). In the eyes of Takfir members, those beyond their collective are considered as unbelievers, providing them with justification to spill the blood of *the others'*. Nonetheless, looking at the bigger picture of the *ummah*, those who are seemingly fixated with jihad are more likely to be the exception rather than the rule.

---

[60] In the Islamic lexicon, the Arabic word "*diin*" cannot be equated with the common Western notion of religion, as the term denotes a comprehensive system of living, transcending the conventional understanding of spirituality.

Methodology of Study

As mentioned earlier, the methodology employed in this study essentially combines methodological individualism and multisubjective interpretation, utilizing empirical data gathered in Indonesia and Iran. Qualitative data were gathered through library research that encompassed books, journal articles, monographs, and conference papers as well as media publications. Throughout the period of research, the author also conducted in-depth, open-ended interviews with Islamic leaders, activists, seminarians, university students and jihad participants both in Indonesia and Iran. Quantitative datasets were derived from a sampling survey on Muslims on the streets, which employed face-to-face, interview technique. Meanwhile the statistical analyses involve chi-square tests, crosstabulations, correlations and binary logistics regression.

Statistically speaking, the survey population in this study comprises the aggregate number of Muslims in Indonesia and Iran,[61] which amounts to somewhere in the neighborhood of 270 million or about one fifth of the total Muslim population throughout the world. The sample size stands at 996, consisting of 738 Muslims from Indonesia and 258 from Iran. Selectivity of the respondents rests upon the religion (in this case, Islam) that the subjects profess.[62] The Indonesian survey was conducted in the last quarter of 2002 (in the aftermath of the Bali bomb blasts) in the cities of Jakarta, Bandung (West Java), Solo (Central Java), Surabaya (East Java), Bandar Lampung (Lampung)

---

[61] It is important to acknowledge the fact that the survey was not conducted in any Arab countries. The decision was based on practical as well as substantive considerations. The latter was led by the assumption that racial differentiation between Arab and non-Arab Muslims would pose little effect on the respondents' willingness or unwillingness to participate in jihad. To confirm such a hypothesis, I will leave other scholars to take on this challenge and to prove me wrong.

[62] The specific targeting of respondents was based on an even-odd chance, which was determined from the outset of the survey by way of coin tossing. Before any interviews were done, I decided that "heads" were for odd numbers and "tails" for even. This required my band of interviewers to pick prospective respondents from the flowing crowds from different directions in accordance to either odd or even number. Whenever the subject turned out to be a non-Muslim, the interview was immediately halted and annulled.

and Pontianak (West Kalimantan). The Iranian survey was conducted in Tehran, Qazvin and Esfahan during the post American invasion and subsequent occupation of Iraq in mid 2003. Venues for the survey were purposively selected to include cities with no distinctive or significant religious centers. Hence, in the case of Iran, no "holy cities" (for example, Mahshad and Qum) were duly incorporated, as it may somehow skew the outcome of the survey in ways that are predictable. The survey itself was based on heterogeneity sampling, or sampling for diversity, to guarantee the attainment of ordinary Muslim respondents. Most of the survey activities were carried out either at city squares or their vicinities. The questionnaire—prepared and posed in the local languages of Bahasa Indonesia and Farsi—,[63] was divided into three sections, comprising demography, religiosity and participation. Demographic characteristics and attributes involve standard features of the SES model such as gender, age, marital status, employment, income and educational levels. In addition, racial/ethnic identity and political affiliation—translated as one's level of identification and activism in politics—were also included.

As depicted in Figure 1, the main independent variable in this study is religiosity. The dataset on religiosity was derived from separating three religious dimensions into 12 different measures.[64] The questionnaire was subdivided in accordance to the three cited dimensions. The partitioning of the main independent variable was based on Islam's intrinsic notion of religiosity, which usually entails the compartmentalization of: 'ilm (religious knowledge), 'amal (ritual practice) and iman (faith/affection).[65]

---

[63] See Appendices 1B and 1C.

[64] De Jong et. al. contend that multidimensional conceptualization of religiosity requires "oblique methodology", and that "most researchers have concluded that religion cannot be conceived as a single, all-encompassing phenomenon" (op. cit., 866).

[65] In the basic teaching of Islam, the ordering is usually made in line with the level of significance of each aspect. Therefore, 'iman, 'ilm and 'amal is the correct priority list. For the purpose of this research, however, the author deliberately tinkered the ordering to give a sense of flow and continuity in the questionnaire.

Figure 1: Hypothesized model of relationship

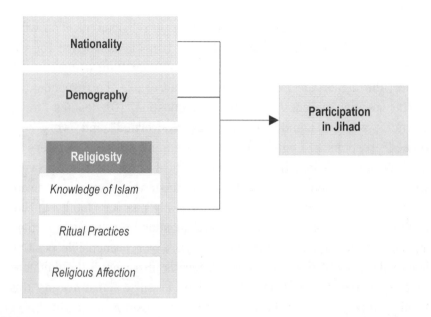

To set the boundaries straight, a description of each dimension and measure is briefly provided: Knowledge of Islam covers aggregate period of Islamic studies both formally and informally, Quranic recitation, number of religious books read, quantity of Islamic media subscription as well as exposure to Islamic preaching or propagation. The measure of ritual practices incorporates daily prayers, weekly visits to mosque and frequency in alms giving. Lastly, religious affection dimension signifies politico-religious identity, affinity, solidarity and sense of attachment to the *ummah*, which is measured against three things: religious sacrifice, self-sacrifice and solidarity. The dimension on religious affection was operationalized using the following questions:

* Some people would give up their lives for the defense of Islam and/or Muslims. How do you feel toward this attitude?

* Would you be willing to sacrifice your *own* life for the sake of Muslims and/or Islam?

♦   How do you feel toward the plight of Muslims in Palestine, Bosnia and Iraq?

Like many of the others, the questions on religious affection were accompanied by a Likert Scale coded as {0}, {1} and {2}.[66] For the first two questions, coding was made to denote level of agreement. Hence, the higher the number, the more agreeable the respondent is to the question posed. As for the last question, {0} denotes "indifference", while {1} and {2} represent "concerned" and "very concerned" responses. Logic was used to supply possible answers to this specific question. In the methodological sense, it is to prevent what is often called "response bias". For instance, it would be inconceivable for a Muslim respondent to honestly answer "totally unconcerned" or "unconcerned" for the third question on religious affection, as this would render the person in a morally reprehensible position before the eyes of the interviewer. There is also very little likelihood that respondents would actually answer in such a manner, as this would entirely exhaust the credibility of the person as a Muslim.

Following demography and religiosity, respondents were then asked the fundamental question: *Would you be willing to participate in jihad?*[67] This constitutes the operationalization of the dependent variable.[68] The main function of this question is to measure the level of willingness to participate in jihad as a politico-religious form of collective action. In this instance, the author is fully aware that queries may surface with respect to the notion of intended willingness, as it may not necessarily be followed up by *actual* participation. Hence, respondents who claimed they were willing to participate in jihad (by

---

[66] For the survey's full scale coding system, see Appendix 1A.

[67] The exact wording for the Indonesian survey is: *Apakah Anda bersedia untuk berpartisipasi dalam jihad?* For the Iranian one, the question posed was: *Ayaa dar jehad-e Islami syarkat mikoniid?* For the complete wording of the questionnaire, see Appendices 1B and 1C.

[68] As expected, some respondents did question more or less: "What kind of jihad are you talking about?" In the face of such response, the interviewers simply explained that it was referring to "jihad of the sword" or "jihad as armed struggle". The number of respondents who did this, however, was not more than 20 respondents out of the 996, making it almost negligible.

answering "*ya*" or "*baleh*") do not automatically mean that they will actually do so when the opportunity avails itself. Similarly, respondents who answered "no" or "unsure/don't know" may in fact due to some circumstances or reason be eager to participate in jihad. An almost comparable issue is found in pre-elections polling to gauge the level of support for each candidate and/or party. The question frequently raised is: which candidate or party do you intend to choose in the upcoming elections? The assumption of such polling will never assume that respondents will necessarily tell the truth or that they will ultimately commit to their choices when voting day arrives. Is it still useful? Indeed, because although the outcome will never be precisely the same as the actual vote tabulation, the polling results will provide a preliminary basis for action and analysis on the part of the contesting candidates and/or political parties. A more realistic scenario is that while respondents may be eager to participate in jihad, they may not get the chance to do so.

Organization of Chapters

Chapter 2 is a critical overview of the literature related to the subject matter of participation in collective action, while elaborating on the two major social theories, namely rational and expressive choice models. Chapter 3 looks at Islam as a tool of resistance for the militants. While the first part delves into the politico-religious mindset of the militant Muslims, the latter part of the chapter discusses the role of political identity and its corollaries. Chapters 4 and 5 deal separately with the issue of Muslims in Indonesia and Iran. The two chapters venture into areas such as sociopolitical history, the place of Islam within the respective states as well as a discussion on various jihad groups. In the second half of each chapter, survey findings conducted in these two countries are analyzed. Chapter 6 sheds light on the empirical findings based on the aggregate dataset from Indonesia and Iran. Similar to the previous two chapters, Chapter 6 incorporates narratives and statistical analyses such as chi-square tests, crosstabulations and a binary logistics regression. Chapter 7 brings this study to a conclusion and correlates the findings to the overall framework on participation in politico-religious forms of collective action. Implications and limitations of the research are finally discussed with hopes to contribute, if not improve, future work on the subject matter.[]

2

Subjective Notion of Participation

Man simply is. Not that he is simply what he conceives
himself to be, but he is what

he wills, and he conceives himself after already existing—
as he wills to be after that leap

toward existence. Man is nothing else but that which he
makes of himself.[1]

Participation, as previously stated, denotes actions by individuals or a collective to influence a given polity or system. In this study, participation is framed using the multisubjective interpretative approach, whereby it is viewed broadly, if not loosely, and can encompass any type of sociopolitical activities consciously developed to influence the polity, whether they are direct or indirect, legal or illegal, peaceful or violent. More importantly is how participants themselves view their involvement, no matter how disruptive or destructive the consequences of their actions

---

[1] Jean-Paul Sartre, *L'Existentialisme est un humanisme* (1948, translation) in Morton White, *The Age of Analysis: 20th Century philosophers* (New York: Mentor Books, 1956), 124.

may be to the overall system or structure that they intend to change. This essentially means that the nature of the collective action being investigated here, namely jihad, will be considered as a valid, but not necessarily legitimate, form of participation, at least from the academic viewpoint. As Schwartz (1984) contends, 'Participatory acts are not "brute facts" ... that have an objective ontological status "in the world"'.[2] He further writes that political scientists 'must define participation internal to the conceptual universe of the "actors" studied if there is to be any hope of understanding the "acts" that they are engaged in'.[3] The notion of participation will hence be based on how participants, or prospective participants for that matter, regard their actions or rather intended actions. The reason for this, more than anything, is common sense. Participants who are involved in various identity-seeking movements and politico-religious groups hold "privileged access to their intentions and beliefs" and therefore "the presumption must be that their characterizations of their actions and their accounts of why they are performing them are the correct ones".[4] Furthermore:

> Such a presumption must prevail until evidence is advanced either to show that they are lying, or to show an alternative set of characterizations and reasons unknown to the [participants], accompanied by an explanation—supported by further evidence—of why they think they are doing something else, why they fail to see the real reasons for their actions and beliefs.[5]

Drawing lessons from philosophers such as Martin Heidegger and Hans Georg Gadamer, Euben (1999) prefers to describe the process as a "dialogic model of interpretation".[6] In her perspective:

---

[2] Schwartz, op. cit., 1124.

[3] Ibid.

[4] Roy Wallis and Steve Bruce, *Sociological Theory, Religion and Collective Action* (Belfast: Queen's University, 1986), 19.

[5] Ibid.

[6] Roxanne L. Euben, *Enemy in the Mirror: Islamic fundamentalism and the limits of modern rationalism* (New Jersey: Princeton University Press, 1999).

> [U]nderstanding emerges from a dialogue in which participants attempt to cross divide meaning by acknowledging and appropriating their own prejudices within a language that evolves to accommodate and ultimately transform disparate understandings into mutually intelligible meanings ... Learning from others means learning from the past and present, but being open to future interpretations that may benefit from experiences and observations not yet available to present understandings. This underlies the notion of "inexhaustibility" of the meaning of texts, and the challenges to the possibility of an objectively valid interpretation.[7]

In simple terms, what Euben attempts to convey is that participants should have some say in what they do and the reasons for why they do it. This, I believe, is the key to explaining and ultimately understanding the whole episode on modern day jihad. In the absence of any dialogic interpretation, Muslim participation in jihad thus becomes easily exhaustible amid the current oversupply of analyses offered by government officials and hordes of dubious 'international terrorism experts'. In most cases, their analyses hardly go beyond the obvious fact that terrorism is "against civilization",[8] and the so-called "terrorists" are "people who hate freedom".[9] Rationalization of the jihad phenomenon typically entails accounts about 'mentally-ill terrorists' and 'pathological suicide bombers' rampaging through the streets while engaging in wanton killing. Another explanation finds economically deprived men of jihad resorting to extreme exploits, making it seem that jihad is a kind of "poor people's social movement".[10]

Such superficial rationalizations, however, does neither justice to the subject matter nor does it provide new ways of looking at the

---

[7] Ibid, 37.

[8] 'Bush calls on the world to act with "moral clarity"', *White House Bulletin*, published on September 23, 2003.

[9] "Bush Stresses Anti-Terror Resolve" in *Washington Post*, published on October 15, 2002: A16.

[10] See Melvin F. Hall, *Poor People's Social Movement Organizations: The goal is to win* (Westport, Connecticut: Praeger, 1995).

phenomenon. In the case of Iran, Muslim revolutionaries consider their militant actions as participating in a seemingly exclusive polity that does not allow for much access. In their own view, '[W]e are creatures of Allah and are performing our assigned "parts" only when we obey Allah's laws'.[11] Hence "to the revolutionary, individuals participate only when they bend their will to the dictates of the Koran, as interpreted by the *mullahs*: they participate *as* Muslims (the part) *in* Islam (the whole)" [original emphasis].[12] Thus jihad, for all intent and purposes, is a participatory act, which militant Muslims believe to be the only plausible alternative to correct the perceived wrongs in society. From the militants' perspective, jihad is a way of participating in the world drama where only a select number of actors are invited to participate. As will be illustrated in the subsequent sections, the militant Muslims will go to great lengths and risk while running the ultimate cost to be able to participate in the world 'drama'.

When dealing with the notion of participation, one should also appropriately consider the given sociopolitical context and circumstances private citizens confront on a daily basis. In other words, to influence a system, its policies, its structure and processes, participants may not necessarily find formal, legal or peaceful strategies as viable options for the simple reason that they are neither effective nor can they make much impact on the intended target. Admittedly, some forms of participation are riskier than others, and jihad is one that operates beyond the boundaries of mainstream politics. What is more important, the principal decision underlying such actions may well be applied to other modes of participation, at least in terms of the intent to change or influence the form and nature of any given polity. In view of the above, there is much less inclination to agree with oversimplified assertions that religious militants do what they do because they merely try to get "a place on the table".[13] The

---

[11] Schwartz, op. cit., 1130.

[12] Ibid.

[13] Simon Reeve, *The New Jackals: Ramzi Yousef, Osama bin Laden and the future of terrorism* (Boston: Northeastern University, 1999).

reservation is borne out of the logic that participating on the table—though it may serve some specific purposes and provide direct benefits to participants—is really not an end in itself, at least in the minds of militant Muslims. After all, from the militants' line of argument, participation in jihad supplies the only recourse to undo the Muslims' fate in current history. Unfortunately, in carrying out their task, they are rarely troubled with the prospect of justifying their ends using violent means and cruel methods, as witnessed in the unprecedented event of September 11.

This is not to advocate that one should take the participants' subjective notion of jihad at face value, as this would undoubtedly forestall any scholarly attempt at critical analysis or interpretation. It is also not the intention of the present author to insist that jihad be equated and grouped together with other established and conventional modes of participation such as voting, lobbying and contacting found in advanced democratic states.[14] The main contention is that applying a strict model of political participation without due consideration will rule out much of the participatory nature of politics within the Third World context, which for the most part is not necessarily formal, legal nor peaceful. The primary reason for this relates to boundaries that define what mainstream politics should and should not be. These boundaries help political actors comprehend where they can or cannot operate. In an authoritarian country, for example, voting rarely depicts the true level of citizens' participation, as it frequently represents a regime's capacity to mobilize constituents in its attempt to disguise

---

[14] See the classic work by Verba and Nie op. cit. on participation in America. Contemporary empirical studies on such formal participation have largely focused on electoral turnout as the measure of political participation. For further reading, see for instance: Stephen Ansolabehere and Shanto Iyengar, *Going Negative: How political advertisements shrink and polarize the electorate* (New York: Free Press, 1995); Kim Fridkin Kahn and Patrick J. Kenney, "Do Negative Campaigns Mobilize or Suppress Turnout? Clarifying the relationship between negativity and participation" in *American Political Science Review*, 93 (4) 1999: 877-889; Jan E. Leighley and Arnold Vedlitz, "Race, Ethnicity, and Political Participation: Competing Models and Contrasting Explanations" in *Journal of Politics*, 61 (4) 1999: 1092-1114; Benjamin Radcliff and Patricia Davis, "Labor Organization and Electoral Participation in Industrial Democracies" in *American Journal of Political Science*, 44 (1) 2000: 132-141.

and compensate for the lack of political legitimacy. In such an instance, participation becomes nothing more than a manipulative tool of the authoritarian regime to cling onto power. And while participating in the system may do citizens some good, consciously or not, they in effect strengthen the position of the authoritarian government. In turn, this leads to two possibilities: one, as state repression intensifies, the risk of going against the state is heightened, and people will choose to lie low and opt for non-participation; the other is the opposite. The appeal to resort to non-mainstream politics may increase, as the state is perceived to be unresponsive and not providing any peaceful or legitimate options.

The next section attempts to elaborate on the reasons why people participate in jihad. It is followed by highlights on rational and expressive choice models.

Why Bother to Participate in Collective Actions

There is almost a perennial question when it comes to collective action. The question, often hidden beneath assorted wordings, relates to the choices actors make in deciding whether to work cooperatively in a collective or to 'go it alone'. As mentioned previously, the substance of the debate centers around the reason(s) *why* a course of action is taken and *what* determinants shape a decision. Some of the ensuing questions may illustrate this point: why do some states choose to become members of a regional or multilateral organization, while others do not? Why do some societal organizations come together and form interest groups when others simply choose to work in solo? Why does a person want to actively participate in staging a protest while a large number of people do not see the wisdom behind the drive? Why would some Muslims engage in terrorist acts, while the majority does not? The bottom line to all the above questions is that while some actors, whether states, societal groups or individuals, choose to participate in collective endeavors, others do not necessarily feel, think and act in the same manner. Despite its seemingly simple logical structure, this is exactly what makes such studies puzzling. It is puzzling primarily because the society is more accustomed than not to search for conformity and patterned behaviors. As King et. al. (1994) put it, "[H]uman beings are very good at recognizing patterns but not very good at recognizing non-patterns."[15] Consequently states, groups and people are often forcibly grouped into superficial categorizations *as such* that they are assumed to inevitably take similar courses of action, provided that the internal and external determinants are held constant.[16]

A range of innovative works on collective action and why people participate in collective efforts is widely available. While many studies focus on traditional subjects such as peasants,[17] students,[18] workers and union members,[19] others highlight contemporaneous ones such

---

[15] Gary King, Robert O. Keohane and Sydney Verba, *Designing Social Inquiry: Scientific inference in qualitative research* (New Jersey: Princeton University Press, 1994), 21.

[16] The holding of such determinants in the real social world is obviously hypothetical, as no human experience can ever be replicated precisely and experimented inside political laboratories. The closest possible manner in holding the effects of variables is via the use of statistical tools.

[17] James C. Scott, *Moral Economy of the Peasant: Rebellion and subsistence in Southeast Asia* (New Haven, Connecticut: Yale University Press, 1977); Samuel L. Popkins, *The Rational Peasant: The political economy of rural society in Vietnam* (Berkeley: University of California Press, 1979); Scott 1985; Daniel Little, *Understanding Peasant China* (New Haven, Connecticut: Yale University Press, 1989); Charles D. Brockett, "The Structure of Political Opportunities and Peasant Mobilization in Central America" in *Comparative Politics* (1991): 253-274; Gi-Wook Shin, "The Historical Making of Collective Action: The Korean peasant uprisings of 1946" in *American Journal of Sociology*, 99 (6) 1994: 1596-1624; Mark I. Lichbach, "What makes Rational Peasants Revolutionary?: Dilemma, paradox, and irony in peasant collective action" in *World Politics*, 46 (3) 1994: 383-418.

[18] Craig Calhoun, *Neither Gods Nor Emperors: Students and the struggle for democracy in China* (Berkeley: University of California Press, 1995); Dingxin Zao, "Ecologies of Social Movements: Student Mobilization During the 1989 Pro-Democracy Movement in Beijing" in *American Journal of Sociology*, 103 (6) 1998: 1493-1529 and "State-Society Relations and the Discourses and Activities of the 1989 Beijing Student Movement" in *American Journal of Sociology*, 105 (6) 2000: 1592-1632.

[19] Carol Conell and Kim Voss, "Formal Organization and the Fate of Social Movements: Craft association and class alliance in the Knights of Labor" in *American Sociological Review*, 55 (2) 1990: 255-269; Marsha Priptein Posusney, "Irrational Workers: The moral economy of labor protest in Egypt" in *World Politics*, 46 (1) 1993: 83-120; Stephen Crowley, "Barriers to Collective Action: Steelworkers and Mutual Dependence in the Former Soviet Union" in *World Politics*, 46 (4) 1994: 589-615; Kim Voss, "The Collapse of a Social Movement: The

as nongovernmental organizations and civil society.[20] Although a lot can be derived from these studies, emphasis has persistently been on the actors' calculations of perceived costs and benefits to participation in the collective action.[21] The logic is based on a simple assumption that when benefits exceed costs, people are willing to participate. In contrast, when costs are higher than the perceived benefits, individuals are more likely to opt for non-participation. While this line of academic work has in many ways significantly contributed to the increasing range of literature on rational choice, the approach undermines the salience of inner attributes, identities and values of actors engaged in various forms of collective action. In view of this, more studies on personal and collective identity should be pursued to further our understanding on non-instrumental models of collective action. From the socio-psychological viewpoint, this collective identity can be imagined or concrete. It involves perceptions and construction as well as discovery of pre-existing bonds, interests and boundaries.[22] As such, studies on lesbians and gays,[23] African-Americans and the

---

interplay of mobilizing structures, framing, and political opportunities in the Knights of Labor" in Doug McAdam, John McCarthy and Mayer N. Zald, *Comparative Perspectives on Social Movements: Political opportunities, mobilizing structures, and cultural framings* (England: Cambridge University Press, 1996); Bert Klandermans and S. Goslinga in McAdam *et. al.,* 1996.

[20] Mara Loveman, "High-Risk Collective Action: Defending human rights in Chile, Uruguay and Argentina" in *American Journal of Sociology,* 104 (2) 1998: 477-525; Gerard Clarke, *The Politics of NGOs in Southeast Asia,* (London: Routledge, 1998); Kim Sunhyuk, *The Politics of Democratization in Korea: The role of civil society* (Pennsylvania: University of Pittsburgh, 2000).

[21] While game theorists preferably employ terms such as payoffs and sanctions, public policy analysts and economists are in favor of using incentives and disincentives. This pattern of studies, however, is distinct from those that focus on interpretative values. Scott's (1985) work, for instance, highlights the subtle, moral and cultural forms of everyday peasant resistance.

[22] Polletta and Jasper, op. cit., 298.

[23] Kenneth D. Wald, James W. Button and Barbara A. Rienzo, "The Politics of Gay Rights in American Communities: Explaining anti-discrimination ordinances and policies" in *American Journal of Political Science,* 40, (4) 1996: 1152-1178; Mary Bernstein, "Celebration and Suppression: The strategic uses of identity by the lesbian and gay movement" in *American Journal of Sociology,* 103 (3) 1997: 531-565.

Civil Rights movement,[24] women and racial minority[25] and Indians[26] can all provide profound insights into how these categories of people *shape* or are *shaped by* their political identities either by their biological, racial, cultural or sexual behavioural attributes.

However, gaps still abound. Most, if not all, of the above studies of this nature apparently pay little attention to one of the essential ingredients to identity, which is religiosity,[27] which, as defined earlier as one's "commitment to religion".[28] Some studies, however, have been undertaken to investigate the effects of religiosity on political participation and behavior,[29] political process and legitimation[30] as

---

[24] Doug McAdam, *The Political Process and the Civil Rights Movement* (Chicago: University of Chicago Press, 1982); Laura A. Reese and Ronald E. Brown, "The Effects of Religious Messages on Racial Identity and System Blame among African Americans" in *Journal of Politics*, 57 (1) 1995: 24-43.

[25] Belinda Robnett, "African-American Women in the Civil Rights Movement, 1954-1965: Gender, Leadership, and Micromobilization in *American Journal of Sociology*, 101 (6) 1996: 1661-1693; Debra C. Minkoff, "Bending with the Wind: Strategic Change and adaptation by women's and racial minority organizations" in *American Journal of Sociology*, 104 (6) 1999: 1666-1703; Cheryl Hercus, "Identity, Emotion and Feminist Collective Action" in *Gender and Society*, 13 (1) Special Issue: Gender and Social Movements (Part 2) 1999: 34-55.

[26] Alison Brysk, "Turning Weakness into Strength: The Internationalization of Indian Rights" in *Latin American Perspectives*, 23 (2) Ethnicity and Class in Latin America, 1996: 38-57.

[27] The author is fully aware at this stage that some less thoughtful authors would interchangeably utilize the notion of religion with ethnicity and race. To avoid this confusion, I offer two simple logical propositions that may help to resolve it: 1) while religion can be altered, ethnicity and race cannot; 2) while religiosity can be measured to some degree, ethnicity and race are immeasurable.

[28] Refer back to the section on "Research questions, objectives and hypothesis" in Chapter 1.

[29] Philip E. Secret, James B. Johnson and Audrey W. Forrest, "The Impact of Religiosity on Political Participation and Membership in Voluntary Associations Among Black and White Americans" in *Journal of Black Studies*, 21 (1) 1990: 87-102; John C. Green, James L. Guth and Kevin Hill, "Faith and Election: The Christian right in congressional campaigns 1978-1988" in *Journal of Politics*, 55 (1) 1993: 80-91; Fredrick C. Harris, "Something Within: Religion as a mobilizer of African-American political activism" in *Journal of Politics*, 56 (1) 1994: 42-68; Geoffrey C. Layman, "Religion and Political Behavior in the United States: The impact of beliefs, affiliations, and commitment from 1980 to 1994" in *Public Opinion Quarterly*, 61 (2) 1997: 288-316; Jeff Manza and Clem Brooks, "The Religious Factor in U. S. Presidential Elections, 1960-1992" in *American Journal of Sociology*, 103 (1) 1997: 38-81.

[30] Rhys H. Williams and N. J. Demerath III, "Religion and Political Process in an American City" in *American Sociological Review*, 56 (4) 1991: 417-431; Dwight B. Billings and Shaunna L. Scott, "Religion and Political Legitimation" in *Annual Review of Sociology*, 20, 1994: 173-202.

well as value priorities.[31] From the variations of the dependent variable in the above-mentioned studies, it is apparent that scholars have yet to agree on how exactly religion or religiosity influences people's worldly outlook, political behavior and actions. What can be derived though from this line of research is an underlying assumption that certain levels of religiosity tend to move people toward a particular position in politics. For instance, a high level of religiosity is likely to move people to a more conservative political stance, and make them less inclined to endorse liberal issues such as women's right to abortion, same-sex marriages or clear cut separation between the church (religion) and the state (politics). It should be noted that in the Muslim context, the latter issue often invites contentious politics. In the context of Indonesia and Iran, the contention is traditionally between those who are in support of a religious or clerical state and those against it. To discuss the divergence of the models, the author will first review rational choice and then go on to the expressive choice model.

Rational Choice Model

In conducting their affairs, human beings are often regarded as a *homo economicus* (economic man) possessing innate characteristics such as logical, calculating, utilitarian, incentive driven, risk averse,[32] etc. Meanwhile politicians (or the *homo politicus*) are typically described as self interested, gain conscious, instrumental rationalists, goal seekers, and—when operating within a democracy—"vote maximizers".[33] All of these jargons and labeling point to a single underlying assumption that man (as species, not gender) is a rational being, calculating each

---

[31] Shalom H. Schwartz and Sipke Huismans, "Value Priorities and Religiosity in Four Western Religions" in *Social Psychology Quarterly*, 58 (2) 1995: 88-107.

[32] For further reading, see John Rawls, *Theory of Justice* (Cambridge: Harvard University Press, 1971).

[33] The notion of vote maximizers was borne out of English utilitarian thinking advanced by proponents such as Jeremy Bentham (1748-1832), James Mill (1773-1836) and John Stuart Mill (1806-1873).

and every step of his way by employing a measure akin to cost and benefit analysis. Self interest guides his instinct and intuition to the extent of forfeiting others'. In a crude manner of speaking, his vulgar, hedonistic mind is bent on "maximizing pleasure and minimizing pain", a notion dating back to Greek Epicurean philosophy on the ultimate recipe for happiness.

The extension of this assumption is that any and all actions undertaken by man are attached to some specific identifiable values, and assessed using rational valuations. Any risk is therefore measured against the necessity of an action and the benefits that one accrues from the undertaking. Thus, the imagery that emerges is that of an actor, who instinctively calls upon his basic arithmetic skills to decide whether to go ahead with the planned action despite the costs and risks involved or to abandon the idea altogether. When it comes to interest or utility of members within a collective, the model becomes convenient and assuring. This, I would argue, is one of the most compelling strengths of the rational choice theory. Furthermore while this theory, which often revolves around the payoff-sanction game theoretical structure, is indeed convincing, it is somewhat restrictive. Nevertheless, since Olson's (1971) seminal work was published,[34] studies showcasing a variety of groups, organizations and movements have been looked at to provide more rigorous nuances to the so-called "logic of collective action". Yet, in all of the exhaustive research on collective action, two intertwined subjects never escape its fundamental logic: "collective good" and "selective incentive".

The main contention is that although participants may participate in a collective action for the sake of accruing benefits, they are likely to serve the collective interests of the group, whether consciously or not. The interest fulfillment of the other actors is basically what collective good represents. A classic illustration of this can be found in a business association, which acts in the name of an industry

---

[34] Olson, op. cit.

within a state. Its basic function is to pressure the government to essentially push for policies beneficial to that specific industry, which can take the form of tax reduction, import subsidies or wholesale industry deregulation. The product of the collective (for instance, the textile association) can therefore be a policy to reduce taxation for the purposes of export. In such a case, the state policy is the collective good that can be enjoyed by firms within the industry to further their primary interest, which is twofold: one is to reduce distributional cost to attain higher competitiveness or profitability, while the other is to globally expand the business with both parties (the industry and the state) coming out as ultimate winners. However, even at the outset, Olson (1971) had already acknowledged the basic problem in his own model. The problem is situated in the question of who exactly benefits from the collective good, and who exactly pays for the cost. The logic is summed up as follows:

> Though all of the members of the group therefore have a common interest in obtaining this collective benefit, they have no common interest in paying the cost of providing that collective good. Each would prefer that the others pay the entire cost, and ordinarily would get any benefit provided whether he had borne part of the cost or not.[35]

To resolve this problem, Olson (1971) offered the solution of exclusivity and inclusivity, especially in regard to the accrued benefits. Thus textile firms that opted not to participate in the collective endeavor should logically be barred from accruing benefits as a result of the association's lobbying or pressuring of the government simply because they did not participate in cost reduction. A similar logic applies to cooperatives, where dividends are selectively distributed to members only. In such case, non-members (in this case, the general public as well as the customers) have no right to receive dividends from the profit sharing scheme. Hence, the "free-rider problem"

---

[35] Ibid, 21.

rises to the occasion. A free-rider is a beneficiary who opts to exploit positive spillovers from collective endeavors by non-participation. The sole intent is to eliminate the cost of participation on the actor's part. This has been known to be the classic collective action problem. The core of the problem rests on the fact that even non-participants can still accrue benefits from the active participation of others. Thus if actors know that by non-participation they can accrue benefits similar or almost similar to those who *do* participate, then why participate at all? Would not then the participating individuals have to bear the cost of participation for the sake of others? In filling this fissure, Olson (1971) introduces "selective incentive", whereby benefits can only be accrued by those actively participating in the collective, while strictly barring non-participants and bystanders who constantly seek for free rides. In his words:

> [G]roup action can be obtained only through an incentive that operates, not indiscriminately, like the collective good, upon the groups as a whole, but rather selectively toward the individuals in the group. The incentive must be "selective" so that those who do not join the organization working for the group's interest, or in other ways contribute to the attainment of the group's interest, can be treated differently from those who do.[36]

With this, participation (or nonparticipation, for that matter) then becomes logically fitting. Individuals, firms or states, knowing for sure the costs and benefits of participation, can then decide whether or not to cooperate in the collective endeavor.

For many, however, the concern over free-riding does not wither away with the persuasion of the selective incentive argument. The ensuing question often posed is the following: What if everybody else thought similarly? What if individuals only consider their personal returns and ignore the collective interest? Wouldn't it then render the number of participants as indistinguishable from zero? This issue

---

[36] Ibid, 51.

is especially pertinent to those involved in studies on voter turnouts. The question is why, despite the seemingly low level of benefits that can be accrued, do people still go out and vote? According to prominent political scientist Dahl (1963), the answer lies in "civic duty".[37] He views that if everybody did indeed think in a similar fashion, and assuming that everyone is rational, hardly anybody would take the trouble of participating in elections, considering the costs involved. However, the fact remains that people *do* go out and vote, although still perhaps not to the extent desired by the government. Yet, Dahl (1963) believes that people, more precisely citizens, have a sense of duty or responsibility when they go out to vote during election times. Politicians too seem to frame the activity of voting in terms of res-ponsibility and moral obligation to the state. For this purpose, it is probably prudent to refer to the famous calculus for returns-to-par-ticipation utility model offered by Riker and Ordeshook (1968),[38] which takes the form of:

$$R_i = pB_i - C + D$$

where:

R_i : individual returns to participation

pB_i : benefit of participation derived from probability in deter-mining the outcome of elections

C : cost of participation

D : civic duty

As it follows, individuals will only participate if and only if:

$pB_i + D > C$ (rendering R_i to a positive value)

Conversely, individuals will *not* participate if:

$pB_i + D < C$ (which will then render R_i as a negative value)

---

[37] Robert A. Dahl, *A Preface to Democratic Theory* (Chicago: University of Chicago Press, 1963).

[38] William Riker and Peter Ordeshook, "A Theory of the Calculus of Voting" in *American Political Science Review*, 62 (1) 1968: 25-42.

Despite its elegance, limitations to the model are plentiful. It is evident that when Olson (1971) laid down his logic of collective action, what he had constantly in mind was "organizations with a significant economic aspect", which are "*expected* to strive for the higher interests of the members" [original emphasis].[39] He conceded that his theorem might not be particularly useful or even endure scholarly criticisms if the logic were to be applied to communal groups, religious and philanthropic organizations or identity-seeking movements.[40] In other words, applying Olson's (1971) model of rationality may not be useful in explaining or understanding the actions undertaken by individuals with entrenched religious predispositions. The main difficulty is that "communal groups"—as Max Weber labels non-instrumentalist individuals who form collectives—, may well define terms such as costs and benefits differently from the more rational group of individuals.

A simple example of this would be membership in a church congregation. One assumes from *a priori* knowledge that Catholics and Christians alike participate in church gatherings to attain spiritual enlightenment, if not religious escapism from the severe confinements of the modern secular and nihilistic world. However, more mundane reasons can be to seek practical advice from the priest, to meet friends and neighbors or simply to be around people who share similar religious belief.[41] Either way, the basis for participation in the congregation does not necessarily originate from the outcome of their cost-benefit calculations. Even if one were to insist that church services also cost participants the traveling expenses to the venue or alms and contributions paid to the congregation, faithful members of the church would not see it so much as 'cost'. Similarly it would be dubious to argue along the lines of material benefits that one accrues from

---

[39] Ibid, 6.

[40] Ibid, ft.6, 6.

[41] Contemporary sociologists would argue that most people trust or like to be with others who are similar to them in terms of habits, thinking, ideology, nationality or even more biological attributes such as race or ethnicity.

participating in church activities. This is not because there is an absence of an incentive structure, but rather the form of incentive itself is supple, immaterial and perhaps unintelligible. An almost comparable case concerns jihad. It is difficult to conceive that Muslims who participate in jihad do so due to the material benefits accrued from such high-risk undertaking. Even if a materialistic incentive structure were to be attached, the worldly benefits would not go directly to the participant but rather to his or her next of kin, something which pure individualistic rationalists would have a major problem with. This form of incentive structure can be found in the way blood compensation schemes are used to entice Muslim suicide bombers, whereby the sponsoring organization, group or movement would supply cash to the martyr's families. In a way, the compensation scheme resembles that of a conventional insurance plan. The major difference lies in two aspects: *first*, the absence of obligatory premiums; *second*, unlike conventional insurance schemes, the higher the risks, the better for both parties i.e. the insurer and the insured. To conceive this logic and to better understand the value participants put in their weaponization of death, a variable akin to an "afterlife consumption motive" should be included in the equation,[42] giving benefit of the doubt to participants on the prospects of their direct admission into Paradise.

Thus if one were to strictly go by Olson's (1971) schema on rational decisions actors make in deciding whether or not to participate in collective action, the next question to ponder is: to what extent are people rational? How far can rationality take us? And in relation to participation in jihad, why is it that some people may find an action to be rational, while others do not? This is equivalent to stating that a group of people may find X as a rational action, while Y is not. Alternatively, another group of individuals may justifiably see things in a diametrically opposite perspective, whereby X is considered utterly irrational, while Y becomes a reasonable, if not most viable, option.

---

[42] See Euben op. cit, 22.

In writing about *Collective Behavior*,[43] Turner and Killian (1987) suggest, 'All conscious human behavior involves some sort of cognitive process or reason no matter how "unreasonable" other people's "reason" may seem to us.'[44] This relativity or subjectivism in defining rationality is especially relevant when considering politico-religious forms of collective actions or faith-based social movements. As the authors contend:

> The belief that death in the service of one's religion is the highest value inspired the followers of Ayatollah Khomeini during and after the Iranian revolution to risk death without consideration of what their martyrdom might accomplish. To many Western observers their behavior appeared not just reckless but fanatical and "irrational", but losing their lives was not a "cost" to them. In every situation, what may be cost to one actor may be a gain for another—one's rationality may be madness to the other! [original emphasis][45]

One method to resolve such confusion, employed commonly in political journalism, is to simply apply *ad hominem* labeling to 'the other'. This line of thinking is the essence behind the principle of rejection by denigration, which is equivalent to denouncing people because of who they are or what they represent. As subjective as this may seem, it is the most convenient manner to make judgments on a people, group or collective. The late Edward W. Said, in his *magnum opus* entitled *Orientalism*, also dealt with such blatant subjectivism, if not "obscurantism", by deconstructing subconscious Western stereotypes of "the strange Oriental people" (specifically, the Arabs and Mus-

---

[43] The study on collective behavior was founded essentially by sociologist Robert E. Park. His inspiration was derived from previous works previously conducted by Gustave LeBon, Scipio Sighele, Pasquale Rossi and Sigmund Freud, who applied various labels such as "crowd psychology", "collective psychology" or "group psychology".

[44] Ralph H. Turner and Lewis M. Killian, *Collective Behavior* (3rd edition) (New Jersey: Prentice Hall, 1987), 14.

[45] Ibid.

lims).[46] This 'othering', according to Said (1978), is generated essentially by the brute forces of imperialism in their quest to possess, dominate and inherit 'the other'. In the process, the other is then portrayed as irrational beings, which have neither mental nor intellectual capacity to govern their own affairs.

Another quandary with respect to participation in collective action relates to what has become known as the "paradox of participation". To put it simply, if individuals are cognizant of their participation that merely contributes a minutiae effect on the whole process (of elections, for instance), why participate at all?[47] This unquestionably raises many concerns regarding the main assumption that individuals are outcome-oriented. After all, despite the politicians' frequent campaigning to convince electorates that "each vote counts", it would still make sense to ask how one vote can mean anything amid a hundred million other votes. Take for instance the case of Indonesia, arguably the third largest democracy based on the sheer size of the voters. Voter turnout in each of the 1999 and 2004 general elections reached around 100 million, constituting more than 75% of the overall electorate. For argument sake, each individual vote in the Indonesian general elections would thus amount to: 0.00000001 (a figure almost indistinguishable from zero), which can hardly be considered as having any meaningful significance to the overall outcome of the elections. This phenomenon is even more salient if the 2004 direct Indonesian presidential elections, where one person truly translates into one vote and one value, are put to the test. For pure instrumentally rational individuals, this certainly does not make any sense because the cost of participation—namely time, energy and transportation fee

---

[46] See *Orientalism* (London: Penguin, 1978). Another of Said's seminal work on postcolonial erudition focuses on the relationship between embedded Western cultural legacies and the Occidental's views toward the East. For further reading, see *Culture and Imperialism* (London: Chatto & Windus, 1993).

[47] Kay Lehman Schlozman *et. al.* found that other forms of "gratification" can be derived from participation in collective action. See Schlozman, Sidney Verba and Henry E. Brady, "Participation's Not a Paradox: The view from American activists" in *British Journal of Political Science*, 25 (1) 1995: 1-36.

expended to go to the electoral booth—will not yield the necessary effect to make any worthwhile difference on the outcome.[48] Yet, despite this logic, people still go to the booth and generally believe that their votes *do* count. The fact that in some countries voting is made obligatory and that the state legally imposes fines to individuals to deter nonvoters, the paradox still stands. The reason lies in the fact that individuals can easily apply countervailing measures to avoid state sanction by going to the booth without actually voting, and hence, reducing significantly or even eliminating the high cost of non-participation. In Australia as well as in a number of other countries, for example, voting has been made compulsory since 1924. Any individual choosing not to vote without good reason will be fined in the amount of A$50, a relatively high amount of money compared to the actual cost of participation. The scheme has resulted in overwhelming voter turnout over the decades.

With regard to the rationalists' claim on the salience of civic duty, I am of the viewpoint that the argument would be more convincing if applied to the expressive needs of the electorates, as will be explained later. Due to the above limitations of the rational model, one is then left with doubt as to what really drives people to participate in various forms of collective actions, especially those that are grounded on politico-religious principles. In the next section, the author will elaborate on a totally different model, which centers on a non-instrumental approach to participation in collective action.

Expressive Choice Model

Why do people really participate in collective actions? Why do individuals associate themselves with political groupings, social movements, revolutions or militant religious organizations? While various theories may point to a wide range of determinants, which places heavy emphasis on rational instrumentalism, one line of reasoning focuses on the expressive needs or identity of the participating individuals. These

---

[48] See Lichbach, op. cit.

expressive needs posit on two levels: the personal and the societal. Thus, expressive choice is about the conveyance of attributes by individuals to assert or reaffirm their personal status to themselves individually and socially. A proponent of the expressive choice model, Schuessler (2000), argues that this explanation is applicable in the political, cultural as well as economic realms. According to him, "[I]n all of these realms individuals often are motivated by a desire to express their tastes, or preferences, because such expression has direct influence on *who they are* or on their identity."[49] Political activists, electoral voters, mass consumers and even sports or music fans participate in various events, activities and groupings to primarily assert their symbolic attributes. For them, participation is about the need to convey who they are and also to reaffirm their attachment to a collective that they feel is either like them or appropriately representing them. Using electoral voters as an illustration, Schuessler (2000) maintains:

> If participant motivation is not instrumentally rational, outcome-oriented, or rooted in the domain of Doing, then again it should be considered grounded in the expressive domain of Being. Rather than viewing individuals' participation in elections as means to selecting their favored (assume Democratic) candidates, we might additionally view participation as individuals' expression of their "Democrat-ness," or of their *becoming* Democrats.[50] [original emphasis]

As stated in the previous section, another issue that rationalists often raise concerns the civic duty argument. However, my view on civic duty is that although rational choice may be able to accommodate the argument as an additive element in the equation,[51] it is clearly more appropriate when applied to the individual's expressive choice. The reason behind this is that while civic duty is defined more or

---

[49] Schuessler, op. cit., 3.

[50] Ibid, 17.

[51] Refer back to the section on "Rational choice model" in this chapter, 40.

less as an individual's moral obligation to the state, it actually informs us more of the individual's emotional attachment to the country. For an individual American voter, who chooses to go to the booth—despite knowing its high cost and minor impact on the overall outcome—may do so because he or she feels that it is probably the right thing to do. This is akin to giving back to state and society for all the opportunities and services that had been rendered to the individual throughout his or her lifetime. In short, an individual participates in elections because it is the right thing to do *as* a 'good' American citizen. From this perspective, general elections serve as a way to instil civic morality to the mass populace by providing delusions of contributing to the future of the state and society. By extension, voting offers personal gratification to voters, as the action provides a sense of fulfilment. In contrast, those who opt for non-participation would be more fittingly regarded as being callous, if not irresponsible, citizens.

If the above elaboration holds true with individual voters—considered to be intermittent politicians at the very least and astute political activists at best—the grounds for expressive choice would then be comparatively stronger in groups, organizations or movements whose primary purpose is to make individual members 'to become somebody' rather than 'to do something'. Therefore, it follows that identity-seeking movements or politico-religious forms of collective actions are driven by individual participating members, who are in turn motivated by their need to become someone or to be affiliated with something. Hence, for instance, individuals who join groups such as the anti-Christian fundamentalists[52] and Black Muslim movements[53] are primarily prompted by their anti-Christian fundamentalist*ness* and Black Muslim*ness*. The activities of the collective (within

---

[52] See Louis Bolce and Gerald De Maio, "Religious Outlook, Culture War Politics, and Antipathy Toward Christian Fundamentalists" in *Public Opinion Quarterly*, 63 (1) 1999: 29-61.

[53] See Oliver Jones Jr., "The Black Muslim Movement and the American Constitutional System" in *Journal of Black Studies*, 13 (4) 1983: 417-437; Christopher E. Smith, "Black Muslims and the Development of Prisoners' Rights" in *Journal of Black Studies*, 24 (2) 1993: 131-146.

'the doing domain') are thus relegated to a secondary status. This can also be extended to individuals engaging in ethno-nationalist movements or politico-religious groups such as the Irish Republican Army, the Basque, Hamas, Al-Qaidah, Jemaah Islamiyah, Ansar-e Hezbollah, etc. In such cases, the weighing of the costs and benefits of membership become somewhat irrelevant. Even if such process were to be internalized, the notion of incentive or disincentive would prove to be distinctive from the one understood by the pure instrumental rationalist. As Turner and Killian (1987) previously pointed out that for some people, even the event of death may not necessarily be perceived as cost. One explanation for this is that some people perceive the event of death as a prerequisite to attain the maximum returns to participation i.e. entry into Paradise. From this perspective, it is likely that death will be construed as a desired goal in life, as propagated by all proponents of the ideology of martyrism. Consider a motto, stated in Article 8 of the Hamas Charter:

> God is its goal;
> The Messenger is its Leader;
> The Quran is its Constitution;
> Jihad is its methodology, and;
> Death for the sake of God is its most coveted desire.[54]

Consequently, because of the nature of jihad as a "religious collective duty",[55] the so-called calculus for returns-to-participation utility must be adjusted. The modification I offer focuses primarily on the substitution of C (cost in the direct, tangible and 'secular' sense) in the expressive choice utility model. The 'secular' nature of the cost in the model is based on the assumption that cost means different things to different people, especially when put in context with differential values assigned by the rational instrumentalists *vis-à-vis* the expressive non-instrumentalists. The reason, as implied

---

[54] Hroub, op. cit., 267-291.
[55] Refer back to Chapter 1, ft 30, 6. See Zawati, op. cit.

above, is that the cost to participation, as militant activists perceive it, is far different from how rational actors apply it to their cost-benefit calculations. Cost (with a capitalized C) therefore in politico-religious forms of collective action is replaced by a negative value of transcendental benefit (as earlier implied by Turner and Killian) plus residual cost (with a lower case c). The assignment of the negative value to the transcendental benefits is due to the mirroring effect, which originates from life's twin perspective as seen by the religionists. It represents how benefits to participation in non-instrumental forms of collective action are perceived by the secular, rational mind. Furthermore, the internal logic with respect to benefits in the face of C (and not c) remains the same, meaning that the higher the costs, the higher the benefits in both the secular and transcendental terms. In the rational model, the curves represent marginal benefit and marginal cost, where the intersection is treated as the equilibrium. Any overextension will either lead to diminishing returns or inefficiency. The following illustration can probably provide a better explanation:

Figure 2: Secular vis-à-vis transcendental benefits of participation in politico-religious forms of collective action

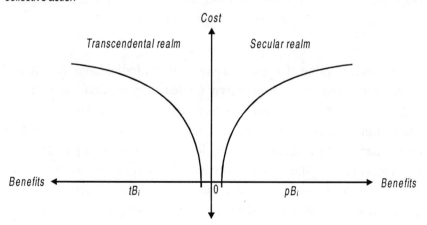

Another alteration put in place in the model is the transformation from civic duty to religious duty, which for all practical purposes, will remain to be coded as D. The individual returns-to-participation formulae found in the rational model, when applied to the expressive choice model, should thus look something like this:

$$R_i = pB_i - C + D, \text{ where } C \text{ is: } (-tB_i + c)$$
$$R_i = pB_i - (-tB_i + c) + D$$
$$R_i = pB_i + tB_i - c + D$$

where:

R_i : individual symbolic returns to participation

pB_i : benefit of participation derived from probability in determining the outcome of collective action

tB_i : transcendental benefit of participation

c : residual cost of participation in the secular sense

D : religious duty

The predictive value of the individual's symbolic returns to participation (R_i) is then obtained from the abstract equation below:

$$R_i \Rightarrow pB_i + tB_i + D > c \text{ or } pB_i + tB_i + D < c$$

A positive value of R_i therefore denotes an individual's willingness to actively engage in expressive modes of participation, while a negative one conversely signifies a tendency to refuse being a part of the collective action. The sum of zero indicates neutrality or failure on the part of the individual to decide on the question of participation. Corresponding to the above abstraction, a happy, decent and risk-free life would never be envisaged as an ideal way of living. The presupposition is reinforced by the religionists' reading of history whereby "the chosen few" are constantly subject to enduring persecution by the Godless proponents of the status quo.[56] Participants in politico-religious forms of collective action will therefore find the Epicurean secular philosophy with its egocentric hedonistic tendencies, which values happiness and pleasure as the ultimate good in life, as abhorrent. In the technical sense, Schuessler (2000) contends that:

> Because the value of participation emerges not from its outcome but from the process of participation itself, free-riding is no longer possible. In economic terms, whereas outcomes or states of the world are "public goods," expressive or symbolic returns to participation are "private goods".[57]

The non-existence of free-riding in the expressive choice model can thus be explained by the inherently personalized incentive structure, where the question, from the viewpoint of participants, lies in the Shakespearean domain of 'to be or not to be'. If this were truly the case, the cost reduction consideration, attained via free-riding, defeats the purpose of participation itself. In other words, individuals participating in politico-religious forms of collective actions may look forward to paying the ultimate cost. This seeming anomaly can be explained thoroughly by way of reasoning that the 'cost' in such endeavor, according to the Quranic precept as well as Prophetic traditions,[58] is in itself a true form of benefit. Consequently, for the individual jihad participant, being a *mujahid* means being a holistic Muslim, and neglecting "to fight in the path of Allah" is equivalent to a major dereliction of duty *as* a faithful believer in Islam.[59]

It is no wonder then that jihad participants (the suicide bombers, for instance) can see no downside to the weaponization of death. To

---

[56] For a more detailed discussion on the mindset of militant religionists, see Chapter 3.

[57] Schuessler, op. cit., 17.

[58] The Quran 4:74 states: "Let those who fight in the way of Allah who sell the life of this world for the other. Whose fighteth in the way of Allah, be he slain or be he victorious, on him We shall bestow a vast reward". In addition, the Prophet Muhammad once asserted: "Whosoever fights in order to make the Word of God supreme is someone who (really) fights for God's cause."

[59] Revert back to Faraj.

the participants as well as their co-sponsors and endorsers, the act of blowing oneself up in an enemy territory is an act of politico-religious sacrifice. Two possible explanations emerge to help us understand this increasingly common phenomenon. For one, a veneer of rationality may be at play, affecting how individuals decide whether or not to participate. The other relates to the intrinsic religious outlook that stresses personal as well as collective identity. For the former, the residual cost (c) placed upon the doer of jihad—should the individual ultimately die in a tour of duty—is the thought of leaving behind his or her beloved family in this world. Though this consideration over residual cost may offset the level of willingness to participate in suicidal forms of jihad, the predicament can be quickly resolved by the customary disbursement of monetary compensation to the martyr's family by the community or organization responsible for the training and preparation of the fatal undertaking. If the prospective candidate for the deadly task were unemployed and perhaps come from a poor socioeconomic background, which may not necessarily always be the case—as will be proven in subsequent chapters—, disbursement of the 'blood money' to his or her family may in turn prove to be a positive intervening variable to the individual's level of willingness. Here, the 'cost', as earlier mentioned, can in effect turn out to be a prospective gain on the part of the candidate for having been able to contribute to the family income in real terms. As for the 'benefits', selective incentive applies in both the transcendental realm of the Hereafter (in the form of direct entry into Paradise) as well as in the secular realm of this world, manifested in the boosting of his or her reputation in society as a true Muslim and martyr for the cause of Islam.

The next reason is centered on the philosophical belief that true existence lies *not* in this world but in the Hereafter. Such an assertion is repeatedly regurgitated during Friday sermons as well as various other religious functions, notably during Muslim death ceremonies. This conviction is of course not exclusive to Islam. The belief in the imminence of the Hereafter is found in almost all major religions of the world, and is dearly held by those participating in what scholars would call "millenarianism" or "apocalyptic movements".[60] Although variations occur in the way Heaven and Hell are depicted, Islam, Christianity and Judaism have more or less similar notions about God's Day of Reckoning. It is this entrenched belief in the Hereafter that partly renders the instrumental model inadequate when applied to religious individuals. However, it is precisely this kind of (mis)-understanding that has prompted writers to define jihad as "a code of murder and rapine disguised under a thin coating of religious verbiage".[61] This particular choice model is indeed relevant, especially when applied to identity-seeking movements or politico-religious forms of collective action. The problem, however, is that considerations on the need for one to express him or her self are often treated as given. After all, if the logic of expressive choice maintains that individuals partaking in events, activities and collectives merely desire to express themselves, what would then become of non-participants? Arguably, those who choose *not* to participate are expressing their inner attributes either intentionally or otherwise by excluding themselves from the consequences of personal identity and collective affinity. Thus, individuals opting for non-participation in gay-lesbian rallies may intentionally avoid involvement altogether not necessarily because they disagree with the participants' right to choose their own partners but rather out of fear of being labeled a non-straight person or a decadent libertine. So the expressive need that determines participation may also in fact mold the choice of non-participation.

The subsequent chapter looks at the issue of religiosity and jihad in the context of the current world 'disorder'. It delves into various facets of modern day challenges for both Muslims and their

---

[60] For a good discussion on the subject, see Thomas Robbins and Susan J. Palmer, *Millennium, Messiahs, and Mayhem: Contemporary apocalyptic movements* (New York: Routledge, 1997).

[61] Suhas Majumdar, *Jihad: The Islamic doctrine of permanent war* (New Delhi: Voice of India, 2001), 67.

militant brethren such as modernization and the structure of international political economy. Such an elaboration will hopefully provide further contextualization on the subject matter of jihad.[]

3

Resistance, Militancy and Politico-Religious Mindset in Islam

Time and again, religion has become a tool of resistance against the *status quo*. Arguably, the three great Semitic religions of the world—Judaism, Christianity and Islam—all rose at specific historical junctures as a powerful force of defiance against raging godlessness, supposedly stimulated by society's hedonistic, materialistic and nihilistic ways of living.[1] The irreligious societies' all-out efforts to circumvent spiritual development became the standard justification for the defiant attitude by the often persecuted, marginalized religious few. It is this typical feature in human history that has made religion in some ways an ideology of the oppressed. This spirit of resistance against perceived injustice, entrenched in all monotheistic religions of the world, originates from the theological notion of the dispensation of Divine justice on earth. In understanding this religious-based politics of contention, it is said that:

> Opposition has always been a most effective basis for a religion.
> Opposition offers a direction, a mission and a role. It offers self-

---

[1] Almost following the same line of thinking, see Asghar Ali Engineer, *Religion and Liberation* (New Delhi: Ajanta Publications, 1989).

importance and palpable achievement. It offers comradeship and organization. Above all, it offers a definite value system against which to judge each action.[2]

Reinforcing this line of reasoning, George Santayana, a renowned 20th century philosopher, asserts that religion, by virtue of its systematic creed and transcendent legal dogmas, "makes absolute moral decisions" on virtually all aspects of life.[3] This instills in the believers a sense of mission to propagate *the* truth, which in turn buttresses the confidence among them on the righteousness of their politico-religious cause.

Yet, conceivably Islam is somewhat unique when it comes to the idea of building a 'perfect society'. What sets Islam apart from other major religions is its insistence on radical changes to sociopolitical structures, norms and practices. In this regard, Max Weber's sociological distinction between "exemplary" and "ethical prophets" may be useful.[4] According to Weber, being an ethical prophet, the Prophet Muhammad was "a figure of radical social change" and can be distinguished from the more conservative figures of the exemplary prophets.[5]

In his quest to spread the 'Word of Allah' and simultaneously countering economic blockade, political aggression and physical harassment by the infidel Meccans, Muhammad initially laid out the strategy of flight (*hijrah*) as opposed to fight. The tactical forms employed included political quietism, religious dissimulation and, at one critical juncture, physical emigration. It was only after the *hijrah* period when the early Muslim community grew exponentially stronger both

---

[2] Writing on the *Happiness Purpose*, Edward de Bono proposed a "new religion" to be inducted to provide man with a more self-fulfilling purpose in life. In doing so, he asserts his readers on the effectiveness of religion as a tool for opposing the *status quo*. See de Bono, *The Happiness Purpose* (Harmondsworth, Middlesex: Penguin, 1990), 1.

[3] In Morton White, *The Age of Analysis: 20th century philosophers* (New York: Mentor Books, 1956), 59.

[4] Robin Gill, *Theology and Sociology: A reader* (London: Cassell, 1996), 36.

[5] Ibid, 37.

in number and political leverage that Muhammad taught his first generation companions about the art of contentious politics to counter-measure the hostilities generated by the Quraish-dominated system. Here, Islam arguably offered a potent ideational platform of opposition, which in essence provided the necessary foundations for cognitive liberation from the almost barbaric nature of the *jahiliyah* (pre-Islamic, ignorant) society. The Islamic religious pronouncement of *"Laa ilaaha illallaah"* (there is no God but Allah) in itself supplied the basic repudiation against the sociopolitical schema of the idol worshipping Meccan society. In describing Muhammad's pursuit to convert the Pagans of Arabia, Davidson (1998) asserts:

> During his twelve years as prophet in Mecca, Muhammad was cast in the role of a rebel. He stood against the traditional authority in his native city and called for a revolution in both morals and politics. Throughout the subsequent history of Islam, even to the present day, this model of Muhammad the rebel has lent legitimacy and respectability to other Islamic reformers working toward a more just and pious society. Indeed, many contemporary Islamic fundamentalist activists see themselves in this light.[6]

As such, Muslims ideally strive to emulate the Prophet not only in terms of his ascetic ways of living but also in his socio-religious outlook and political activism. This can be one of the laten why per-haps many Muslims are inclined to resort to direct actions in protesting against what they perceive as an unjust, or rather ungodly world order. The internalization of this desire to emulate the Prophet generates among Muslims an attitude and mindset in which Armstrong (2000) cleverly dubs "militant piety",[7] a common platform for any religious fundamentalist movement. However, this sort of pietism was in actual fact anathema to the "conservative spirit" that was the main hallmark

---

[6] Lawrence Davidson, *Islamic Fundamentalism* (Westport, Connecticut: Greenwood Press, 1998), 5.

[7] Armstrong, op. cit.

throughout the period of Islamdom. Much of "fundamentalism", still according to Armstrong, is a result of a backlash to the painful transition from the Muslim society's conservatism to Western-oriented modernist ethos.[8]

As religious conversion multiplied and political leverage intensified in favor of Muhammad's community, jihad quickly became an irresistible tool of justification to wage war on the 'enemies of Islam'. In practice though, anyone or any tribe that got in the way or opposed the *Khalifah* was subjected to the principles of jihad then governed by the state. In this context, Militant Muslims would quickly defend this stance by insisting that Islamic jihad by the state had always been guided by the sacred religious laws and ordained by the '*ulama*. One Indonesian jihad participant insisted, "It is impossible for jihad to be misused and abused, as it required *ilmu* (more specifically, knowledge of the sacred law) to administer it".[9] This stance obviously assumes the infallibility of historical actors who administered the process and gave blessings to the application of the religious injunction. Following the demise of the Prophet in 632 AD, jihad campaigns became an almost permanent feature of the newly established 'Islamic state'.[10] These campaigns, however, were often obscured by the policies of the political caliphs, who were desperate in securing and augmenting their positions by waging jihad against their own insurgent brethren. Such policies indeed caused major internal rifts among Muslims, which later led to the crystallization of ideological divisions within the *ummah*, most notably between the Sunnis and the Shias. From the external viewpoint, the propensity for jihad resulted in a swift expansion in the political, religious and military fields, covering virtually all parts of the Arabian Peninsula, North Africa, Persia and to a large extent the Indian subcontinent. The Islamic glory even brought southern Europe into the fold of Islam, which forced Muslims and the 'white

---

[8] Ibid, 33.

[9] A statement made to the author in late 2002.

[10] Refer back to Syariati's statist view on jihad in Chapter 1.

infidels' to interact with and learn from one another, initiating various kinds of politico-religious and cultural repercussions. By this time, Islamdom had already reached its zenith. As Lewis (2004), a prolific writer on Arab and Muslim history, argues:

> In the period which European historians see as a dark interlude between the decline of ancient civilization—Greece and Rome—and the rise of modern civilization—Europe, Islam was the leading civilization in the world, marked as such by its great and powerful kingdoms, its rich and varied industry and commerce, its original and creative sciences and letters. Islam, far more than Christendom, was the intermediate stage between the ancient East and modern West, to which it contributed significantly.[11]

As a direct consequence to the Muslims' extraordinary rate of success in expanding the *dar al-Islam*, and driven by their zeal for jihad, a deep sense of complacency quickly settled in. At this juncture, they were finally convinced of the inevitability of the Muslims' victory over the infidels. However, ensuing chapters of the Muslim history had somewhat proven them wrong. Until now, Muslims are far from being successful in their bid to bring the whole world into the fold of Islam, as many had earlier expected. Nevertheless, the belief in the notion of Islam's inevitable victory remains almost constant, notably among militant and revivalist Muslims. Muslim activists and intellectuals from around the world still hold the belief that the Western (read, Judeo-Christian) civilization would not have thrived without the massive body of knowledge, scientific achievements and sophisticated artistries imparted by generations of Muslim geniuses. This unexaggerated belief would then be typically followed by statements to indicate how various fields of modern sciences namely mathematics, medicine, physics, chemistry, astronomy, literature, metaphysics and philosophy were once the epitome of the Muslim civilization. Although

---

[11] Bernard Lewis, *The Crisis of Islam: Holy War and Unholy Terror* (New York: Random House, 2004), 4.

many have misgivings about the extent of Islam's contribution to the advancement of human civilization, only a few would go as far as stating that the golden age of Islam was a mere "myth",[12] an invented tradition to boost Muslim confidence and standing of the *ummah* amid the current flood of social anxiety over the future of Islamic civilization. Conversely, Muslim ideologues persistently employ the above historicism as a basis for the 'Islamic alternative' argument. This line of argument would normally read like the following: in view of the failure of secular ideologies (notably Socialism, Communism, Nationalism and Capitalism) in truly fulfilling the lives of people across the world, Islam—offering a universal, yet definite value system—is the most readily available and logical solution to humanity's relentless search for the well-balanced and just society. It is on this ground that militant Muslims ardently believe that "Islam *is* the solution!" While the militants do the chanting, the majority of Muslims do earnestly, albeit quietly, share the same sentiment. However, contrary to the militants' insistence in pushing for the political agenda, the majority realizes its incapacity and hopelessness, if not powerlessness, to submit any real set of alternatives to advance their own societies. As a result, many Muslims become entrapped in their seemingly medieval mindset, which presupposes "the unchangingness of the static world".[13]

> This unchangingness of human nature, as they see it, justifies Muslim scholars in asserting the finality of the rules and laws for human conduct, which are expressed in the Quran and the Sunna of the Prophet. Since human nature does not change, there can in essentials be no new problems, and therefore no need for any fundamental revision of the Shari'a.[14]

For centuries, the stifling of the Muslim mindset has turned the Islamic *ummah* into a withdrawn entity that is socially, politically

---

[12] See "The Myth of the Golden Age" in Sidahmed and Ehteshami, op. cit.

[13] Watt, op. cit.

[14] Ibid, 4.

and economically retrogressive. As much as the European industrialization and modernization during the Renaissance period astounded
Muslim societies, it also rendered them to passivity, causing them to
be positioned as mere spectators in the unfolding drama. Thus while
Europe was struggling its way through to emerge out of the 'Dark
Ages' during the 17th century, the Muslims came down with an overwhelming inertia, leaving their societies vulnerable and weak, politically, economically, culturally and militarily. Lewis (2001) attributes
this general decline of the Muslim civilization to "a simple lack of
freedom",[15] leading inevitably to "the crisis of Islam".[16] It was then
that the Muslims began to gaze at their former nemesis in Europe
with envy, as they watched in despair the white infidels, slowly but
surely, claiming the position they had once occupied. As a response,
some from within the Islamic quarter responded almost impulsively
by branding the process of industrialization and modernization as
anti-Islamic or even ungodly. Such pattern of thinking has been persistent for centuries, and is now inherited by the militant Muslims.

Quo Vadis? Muslims during Post-Independence

Assessing the social history of the *ummah*, Ahmed (2003) asserts,
"It is not a good time to look at Muslims. The earlier breadth of vision,
tolerance and self-assurance are missing. A new element of hysteria,
shrill and discordant has entered."[17] The extent of the civilizational
decay alone brought about new challenges to the traditional Muslim
societies in the Arabian Peninsula, Persia and North Africa, which
came under the fold of European and Russian imperialism. By this
time, Europe was already surpassing Muslim societies in virtually
all aspects of life, be it in governance, education, socioeconomic development and the art of war. Even the recently Islamicized societies in

---

[15] Lewis' main argument on this point was elaborated in *What Went Wrong? Western impact and Middle Eastern response* (Oxford: Oxford University Press, 2001).

[16] Lewis 2004, op. cit.

[17] Akbar Ahmed, *Discovering Islam: Making sense of Muslim history and society* (London: Routledge, 2003), 8-9.

Southeast Asia (namely the Indonesian archipelago, the Malay Penin-sula and the southern parts of the Philippines) had their fair share of the colonial experience. The psychological outcome, as a result of over three centuries of colonialism, was that Muslim confidence became utterly ravaged, "creating in them and of them an image of childlike helplessness".[18] Inadvertently Muslim societies became mentally, intellectually, politically and economically dependent on their colonial masters, whose beliefs and ways of life they once abhorred. This experience undoubtedly paved the way to social numbness and atmos-phere of defeat felt by Muslims worldwide. The final blow came in the early 20th century when the last, surviving Muslim empire, the Turkish Utsmani Sultanate, was subjected to political and military capitulation by the British imperial forces. With the disintegration of the Sultanate in 1924 and the rise of liberal Kemalists, the last of the Islamic bastion finally succumbed. During this climate of defeat, Muslims had little choice but to tread along the agonizing, if not humiliating, path of Westernization. Together with it, Muslims had to arduously come to terms with the dreaded scheme on the privatization of religion, whereby Islam would be kept segregated from politics, for better or worse.

With the downfall of the Islamic center of gravity, a burgeoning of movements across the Muslim world emerged, purportedly aimed at revitalizing the Islamic caliphate. For instance, in the Middle East, the Ikhwan al-Muslimin was established in 1928 by Hasan al-Bana of Egypt, who attempted to keep alive the spirit of the *Pax Islamica*.[19] The Ikhwan al-Muslimin was established initially to fill in the noticeable vacuum of power in the Islamic world, while simultaneously taking on the responsibility of being a surrogate mother for the Muslims in the Middle East, much like how Hamas is to the Muslims in the Palestinian occupied territories.[20] Meanwhile in Southeast Asia, the

---

[18] Ibid, 117.

[19] Refer back to George in Sidahmed and Ehteshami, op. cit.

[20] "*Hamas* exploits Robin Hood image to its benefits", *The Straits Times* (Singapore), published on August 2, 2002: 17.

gap was filled by the traditionalist NU, which capitalized on its vast network of *pesantrens* (Islamic boarding schools) throughout Java.[21] At first, most of these pre-independence organizations maintained an internationalist outlook and orientation. Decidedly, most resorted to cultural grassroots approach and employed non-political strategies in the national arena primarily due to the classic colonial policy of state repression, which saw any and every form of political or religious consciousness as a dangerous prelude to Nationalism. In the aftermath of the two devastating World Wars and the subsequent decline of the traditional form of colonialism, many newly independent nation-states emerged in various continents. The Muslims, whose societies had been managed and ruled by the Europeans for some centuries, indeed saw this as an opportunity to make claims on self-determination.

The worldwide movement for independence, however, did not only bring them contentment but also caused political confusion and socioeconomic problems. From the outset, Muslims were never truly comfortable with the framework as stipulated in the 1215 *Magna Carta* (Latin, Great Charter) on the requirements of a nation-state. This was mainly due to the unfamiliarity on the part of Muslims in discerning why there should even be a nation-state in the first place; and how it would fit in to their idea of an 'Islamic world government', which they aspire to reestablish. In that sense, Muslims have persistently been used to the idea of a single Islamic body politic ruled by a Muslim *khalifah*, *imam*, king or sultan. As such, governance would be left to the philosopher-king, who would ostensibly impose, protect and dispense Allah's laws. This is in accordance with the Islamic doctrine on the sovereignty of Allah over all affairs including law, politics, ethics and governance.[22] One of the distinctive features of

---

[21] NU today comprises thousands of autonomous *pesantrens*. With almost sixty million loose members throughout Indonesia, NU is probably the largest Muslim organization in the world. It was previously headed by former president Abdurrahman Wahid, who is a grandson of Syaikh Hasyim Ashari, the revered founder of NU.

[22] Among various Quranic verses that support this notion, one stands out in particular 67:1: "Blessed is He in whose hand is the sovereignty, and He is able to do all things".

this kind of system is that territorial boundaries are less relevant, as membership of the polity is conferred on the basis of the faith that individuals professed. Thus, never before did they anticipate that sovereignty be bounded by nationality or territoriality, much less international law that governs the interaction among states. In fact, many from within the Muslim quarters, arguably until now, view the Magna Charter as a man-made invention that is against the true teachings of Islam. The argument goes that the Quran neither mentions "states" nor "nation-states". Even the term "*dawlah*", which is part of the doctrine on the inseparability of 'religion and politics' (*diin wa dawlah*), is said to be non-existent in the holy text of the Quran. Instead, it favors the notion of a universalistic and integrated Muslim body politic called the *ummah*. In relation to this, while others tend to see states divided into nations, many Muslims tend to see their nation, the *ummah*, being divided into states. Clearly, this political logic is highly problematic in a world dictated by nation-state politics.

Due to this inverted logic, Muslims conceivably regard Nationalism as being "anathema to Islam".[23] The contention between the two ideologies dates back to the early establishment of the nation-states. The question, however, remains whether or not love for one's country is part and parcel of *iman* or the Islamic faith.[24] Theologically, it begs the question of whether defending and sacrificing one's body and soul for the 'country', 'state' or 'nation-state' is tantamount to polytheism (*shirk*) or not. Clearly, the majority Muslims today may not necessarily approve of this denunciation. Nevertheless the ideal political system still entrenched in their consciousness rests upon an archaic notion of the 'Islamic state', whereby membership (or rather, citizenship) is made inclusive to all Muslims regardless of race, ethnicity or socioeconomic status. Anyone who thus professes Islam should in principle become a member-citizen of the state by default, as the laws

---

[23] Inayatullah, Sohail and Gail Boxwell (editors), *Islam, Postmodernism and Other Futures: A Ziauddin Sardar Reader* (London: Pluto Press, 2003), 82.

[24] This assertion was based on an Arab proverb: *Hubb al-wathon min al-iman* (love for the country is part and parcel of the articles of faith).

of Allah transcend any artificial, man-made geopolitical boundaries or even national territories. As it follows, loyalty and solidarity should thus be directed toward the *ummah* and not to any artificial, man-made nation-states.

This notion, however, stumbled upon a new challenge, as scores of Third World countries, barely surviving from centuries of political bondage, rode on the wave of Nationalism. This was brought on by Muslim maverick leaders such as Egypt's Gamel Abdel Nasser and Indonesia's Sukarno, who later initiated the Non-Aligned Movement, which was to get on board as many newly-independent or still colonized nations to remain politically neutral in the then bipolarizing world. What later transpired from this global trend was that Nationalism became a new force to be reckoned with vis-à-vis capitalism, Communism and Islam. It was at this particular juncture that Islam and Nationalism came to be seen as inevitable, yet reluctant, partners in emerging Muslim populated countries such as Indonesia, Iran, Malaysia, Pakistan, Egypt, Libya, Morocco and others. Hence, the notion of Islam and the state became intrinsically connected. The experiences of these societies had in many ways molded a new ideological framework for latter-day Muslim activists throughout the Islamic world.

Domestication of Muslim Politics

Within the context of the emerging nation-states, Muslims became increasingly politicized than their previous generations. They saw their priorities change, and confined their political activities within the state territory, while still reminiscing the golden days when 'Muslims ruled the world'. This era was marked by the mushrooming of Islamic-oriented political parties in various Muslim as well as non-Muslim dominated countries, which by this time had already begun operating within the state's domestic secular, constitutional realm. The ultimate objective was to 'Islamicize' the state and politics by way of instilling or imposing, whichever suits the conditions, Islamic doctrines and values into the state's governing structures, legal frame-work and political ethics. In a way, this was to ensure that Muslims actively participate in the political process and that Islam would not be left out in the cold. If need be, Muslims would use the democratic process to 'capture the state' and transform it into an Islamic one. Much of this political thought and consciousness among Muslim activists and politicians have resulted in the flourishing of numerous socio-political and religious movements, which largely focused on advancing the Islamic cause at the domestic level.

In the Middle East, such a development was evidently marked by the increasing influence of the Front Islamique du Salute in Algeria, Ikhwan al-Muslimin in Egypt, Jordan and Morocco. In the case of Iran, Muslims were fused into the nationalistic political party led by Prime Minister Mohamed Mossadegh. However, due to his sponsorship of the planned nationalization of the Anglo-Irani Oil Company, Mossadegh was subsequently deposed by a political conspiracy spearheaded by the American CIA. Until now, the political wound is still felt and remembered by Iranians, especially those under the sway of the clerical regime.

Almost a similar experience reverberated throughout Southeast Asia. Indonesia, for instance, saw a number of Muslim-based political parties during the heydays of liberal democracy in the early 1950s such as NU, Masyumi, Syarikat Islam, etc. In Malaysia, Parti Islam Se-Malaysia (PAS) became the political umbrella for the strict, conser-vative Muslims, who insist on the establishment of a purist Islamic state. Its existence until today is often at odds with the United Malay National Organization (UMNO), which takes pride in championing the predominance and preeminence of the Malay ethnic majority. Even in Singapore, where the Malay-Muslims constitute a mere 14% of the aggregate population, an ethno-religious political party was set up calling itself the Singapore Malay National Organization (PKMS). The purpose of the PKMS was supposedly to channel the political aspiration of the Muslim minority group in the hopes to ultimately reunite with their Malaysian brethren.[25]

Despite the increasing tendency for Muslims to participate in mainstream politics of the secular state, most view their participation as a transitory one. For some, it was a necessary evil, a pre-requisite to ultimately setup what became progressively known as the "Islamic state" (or "*Negara Islam*" in Indonesia or "*Hokumat-e Islam*" in Iran). While the objective of both entities is essentially similar—i.e. to build a 'Muslim nation-state' as a precursor to reinstating the global caliphate or imamate—they are distinct in terms of their theory and praxis. This strategy admittedly demands the *syariah* to make incessant incursions into the realm of state and politics until it becomes the established law of the land. However, as witnessed and experienced by various countries, the quest for the Islamicization of the state has time and again failed. According to Roy (1994), there lies "the failure of political Islam" in which the Islamicization project serves as a mere camouflage to conceal what he called the "politicization of religion". [26] Roy (1994) further elaborates by saying:

> Today, any Islamist political victory in a Muslim country would produce only superficial changes in customs and law. Islamism has been transformed into a type of neo-fundamentalism concerned solely with reestablishing Muslim law, the *syariah*, without inventing new political forms, which means that it is condemned to serving as a mere cover for a political logic that eludes it—a logic in which we ultimately find the traditional ethnic, tribal or communal divisions, ever ready to change their discourse of legitimization, hidden beneath the new social categories and regimes.[27]

---

[25] Singapore and Malaysia once merged as a single federal state in 1963. The political merger, however, proved too much for both sides to cope with, resulting in their separation two years later.

[26] Olivier Roy, *The Failure of Political Islam* (translation) (Cambridge, Massachusetts: Harvard University Press, 1994), 23.

[27] Ibid, ix.

Making an almost similar assessment, Esposito (1997) asserts:

The failures of increasingly discredited secular forms of Nationalism—from Arab Nationalism to Muslim Nationalism—streng-
thened new voices who appealed to an Islamic alternative, calling
for the Islamization or re-Islamization of society ... Within some
countries, contending voices and groups have vied for power in the
name of Islam. Moreover, the appeal to Islam has also served as a
two-edged sword. Those who wield it run the risk of being judged,
strongly challenged, or even toppled by that very same Islamic
yardstick.[28]

On the whole, Muslim participation in mainstream politics has
neither offered tangible benefits to the Islamic community at large
nor has it brought greater leverage for the Muslims at the international
level. The trappings of *realpolitik* have made Muslim politicians no
different from their secular counterparts. In fact, some benefited from
the corrupt practices of a regime, which was more often than not
willing to co-opt them. In turn, this *quid pro quo* politics increases
"the magnitude of the dilemmas posed by working within a system
that is not itself based on impersonal principles".[29] These various
contradictions and dilemmas have all contributed to the great
disenchantment on the part of Muslims toward mainstream politics,
leading some to resort to extreme forms of participatory actions.

From Disenchantment to Resurgence and Militancy

One of the major downsides to participating in mainstream politics
lies in the ability of governments to co-opt and corrupt social, not
least religious, groups in society. Furthermore, democracy has a
tendency to make weak states and unstable societies highly penetrable
and prone to foreign interference, intervention and domination. In

---

[28] John L. Esposito, *Political Islam: Revolution, radicalism, or reform?* (Boulder, Colorado:
Lynne Rienner, 1997), 2.

[29] Ibid, 22.

the post-World War II and during an extended period of the Cold War, a number of states experimenting with democracy were sabotaged by the same Western powers that practice and preach democracy. Many such examples exist where fledgling democracies and newly independent states were sabotaged politically to prevent and preempt power falling into the hands of the Communists or far right Nationalists. In doing so, pro-Western military juntas were provided support and dictators were propped up for the sole purpose of serving the needs of the Western powers in its bid to win the Cold War. This effort in "deterring democracy", as Chomsky (1991) terms it, is by no means confined to the Muslim experience, as many Latin American countries were also subjected to similar political machinations.[30] For the Muslims, the most conspicuous and hardest hit in the string of political sabotages by the West were notably Iran and Indonesia. This of course is not to mention the relentless problem of Palestine in which Arab Muslims consider themselves to be a victim of an international conspiracy between Western nations (notably, Britain and the U.S.) and the Zionists. Ever since the 1948 Balfour Declaration, which paved the foundation for the establishment of Israel as a Jewish state, three wars had been waged involving Israel and its neighboring Arab countries.[31]

Hence the great disenchantment on the part of the Muslims swelled, which understandably made them less trusting toward democracy both in principle and in practice. Some went to the extreme, and found refuge in totally rejecting all things Western. As Anderson (1997) writes, "For a significant number of Islamist leaders, the reciprocal rejection of Western influence was absolute, and notions of popular sovereignty, majority rule, and pluralistic democracy were equated with exploitation and lack of authenticity."[32] For the politically

---

[30] For further reading, see Noam Chomsky, *Deterring Democracy* (London: Verso, 1991).

[31] The Arab-Israeli wars took place in 1948, 1967 and 1973.

[32] Lisa Anderson, "Fulfilling Prophecies: State Policy and Islamist Radicalism" in Esposito 1997, op. cit., 26.

conscious Muslims, the entrenchment of the nation-state posed a clear and present danger to their politico-religious ideals. They had learned that participation in the secular political processes has apparently not yielded the kinds of results they had initially hoped for. Meanwhile those who participated in mainstream politics were in reality gullible enough to think that by sheer majority, they somehow have a "constitutional right" to make *syariah* the law of the land.[33] According to their logic, democratic process is a necessary evil to be undertaken with the sole purpose of carrying out *amr al-ma'ruf wa nahiy an-munkar* (imparting good and preventing evil). General elections, for that matter, merely serve to reinforce the constitutional rights of Muslims. In Machiavellian phraseology, the end justifies the means. As in the case of Egypt, Baker (1997) explains this phenomenon as follows:

> While the militants fire away, their allied Islamic moderates, mouthing slogans of pluralism and democracy, undertake the systematic subversion of civil society, hoping to reach power through the ballot box so that the election that brought them to power will be the last. Faced with this pincer movement, the regime has no choice but to slow the move to democracy in order to contain the Islamic threat and preserve the democratic option for the long haul.[34]

A related issue concerns political expediency. Meaning, if democratic elections were in place in Muslim-populated states, there is never a guarantee that Islamic political parties may end up as the winners. As seen in the cases of Indonesia, Malaysia, Pakistan and others, the so-called 'Islamic political parties' can hardly triumph over their more secular or nationalist counterparts. Again, such development creates

---

[33] Derived from a statement made by Fauzan al-Ansari, head of MMI data and information division, at a religious gathering (*Tabligh Akbar*) in Bandung, Indonesia, on November 2, 2002, where the present author attended. He further stated, "As the *syariah* is the Muslims' constitutional right as citizens, no Muslim should oppose the institutionalization of the *syariah*."

[34] Raymond William Baker, "Islam in Egypt" in Esposito 1997, 118-119.

even deeper frustration among the militant Muslims. For the growing number of these disenchanted Muslims, having been disheartened by the 'normal' processes of recent history, three options became available to them:[35] *Loyalty*, which means to remain in mainstream politics, while confronting the likelihood of being either corrupted or co-opted by the state; *Voice*, to undertake political insurgency and demonstrate the power of Muslim solidarity either through ballot casting or pressure tactics; and finally *Exit*, to abandon mainstream politics altogether and participate in extreme actions against the state and all its perceived agencies.

In the Middle East, the great disenchantment gave an incentive to many disgruntled Muslims to engage in various forms of collective endeavors. While those choosing the soft approach dealt with collective action at the political, cultural and socioeconomic levels, others took the hard approach, and engaged instead in more direct, reactionary and violent forms of collective action. For Muslims choosing the latter option, resorting to armed struggle and becoming members of a militant separatist groups, radical clandestine movements or even terrorist organization become highly conceivable, if not understandable. It may be useful at this stage to consider Scott's (1985) distinction between "the men of words" and "the men of action" when dealing with various everyday forms of resistance. Arguably, there may well be a lot of young and restless Muslims, who fantasize about joining the *mujahidin* rank and file, and going to the battlefields of Bosnia, Afghanistan or Iraq. The reality, however, shows otherwise because evidently those who *actually* participate in these direct actions are always in the few. In other words, most would dream of or only begin to imagine their participation in these extreme endeavors.

Hence, the Middle Eastern disenchanted Muslims would be seen actively participating in groups such as the then Palestinian Liberation

---

[35] The model was derived from Albert O. Hirschman, *Exit, Voice, and Loyalty: Responses to decline in firms, organizations and states* (Cambridge, Massachusetts: Harvard University Press, 1970).

Organization (PLO) and its affiliates namely Fatah and al-Aqsa Martyrs Brigade; Hamas (Palestine); GIA (Algeria); Hezbollah (Lebanon); Ikhwan al-Muslimin (the one in Jordan and Morocco); and Takfir wa al-Hijra (Egypt). In Iran, the manifestation of the exit option came in the form of the Fedayeen-e Islam, Students Following the Line of the Imam (Khomeini) and the Mojahedin-e Khalq Organization (MKO). In many of these cases, governments would come down harshly on these groups by incarcerating their leaders and militant members for supposedly engaging in subversive activities against the state.

In Southeast Asia, an almost similar trend occurred during the same period. In each of these cases, Southeast Asian governments responded swiftly and heavy-handedly. In Indonesia, the Muslim armed insurgency problem was spurred by the so-called DI/TII (Abode of Islam/Indonesian Islamic Soldiers),[36] which garnered support from pocket areas in the sprawling archipelago namely in West Java, West Sumatra, Aceh and South Sulawesi. Faced by mounting pressures, Sukarno, a leading nationalist figure in the Third World, eliminated the 'Islamic threat' by promptly opting for the military solution, knowing that the institution is the country's bastion of Nationalism and satiated with anti-Islam sentiments. Regionally, the Philippines had to deal with the Moros on the southern island of Mindanao, the Thai government with the Patanis and the Malaysians with their brethren in the north with the majority being affiliated with the Islamic opposition party, PAS. Although these militants failed to gain the political foothold they long desired for, their ideological legacies continue until today. Remnants of these mostly defunct movements have either splintered into smaller groups or are still spreading their ideology surreptitiously via exclusive religious classes or a network of tightly knit *usrohs* ('religious families'). Later, these elements evolved into various Islamic militant, revivalist groups that were largely created to forge a common identity, solidarity and destiny with the main intent to reconstruct

---

[36] Remnant of the group, which now comprise many splinters, is called *Negara Islam Indonesia* (NII).

the *ummah.* This development in the late 1970s and 1980s was mainly spurred by at least two major world events, which in turn triggered rising expectations among Muslims. The first relates to the victory of the Islamic revolution of Iran, while the other was prompted by the Soviet Union's invasion of Afghanistan. These events had seemingly attracted and encouraged militant Muslim individuals and groups worldwide to consolidate and mobilize themselves to participate in the project to revitalize the *Pax Islamica.*

No doubt, a tremendous hype and optimism swept across the Islamic world when Ayatollah Ruhollah Khomeini (1901-1989), the Iranian revolutionary cleric, succeeded in overthrowing the despot Shahanshah Reza Pahlevi in February 1979. For a vast number of Muslims, the Iranian triumph was thought to be the ultimate cue for the long-awaited Islamic revivalism. After all, "the success of the Iranian revolution gave an enormous boost to the Islamist political cause, seeming to serve as proof of both the righteousness and feasibility of imposing religious standards in politics".[37] It was no wonder that when Khomeini began to "export the revolution" to all corners of "the oppressed world",[38] the initial response was overwhelming. The once little-known Shia Islam became a hot topic of discussion within various Muslim religious circles, attracting notably the young and restless. Khomeini's politico-religious doctrine on *Velayat-e Fagheh* (Governance by the Jurist) became widely read and popular.[39] It was only much later that questions pertaining to the replicability of the revolution were raised, especially among the Sunni Muslims, who began to suspect it as something uniquely associated with the Shia ideology.

---

[37] Anderson, op. cit., 23.

[38] For more on Khomeini's politico-religious idealism, see Ruhollah Khomeini, *The Last Message: The political and divine will of His Holiness Imam Khomeini (S.A.)* (The Imam Khomeini Cultural Institute, Tehran-Iran, 1992).

[39] To further understand the framework, see Ruhollah Khomeini, *Hokumat-e Islam* (translation) (Tehran: Institute for the Compilation and Translation of Imam Khomeini's Work, 2002).

Meanwhile, across the borders of Iran, the Soviet military invasion and occupation of Afghanistan turned out to be a *cause celebré* for militant Muslims worldwide. It was, so to speak, a re-entry point where Islamic militant groups were able to make themselves relevant once more. An account from one of the jihad veterans probably illustrates the sentiment among Muslim jihad enthusiasts that the Afghani-Soviet war (1979-1989) "reminded them of the glorious old days, hundreds of years ago, when the Muslims were fighting the infidel".[40] It became clear that it was in Afghanistan that the Muslim men, who served on various tours of duty started to learn the tools of trade in the war against the infidels. Apparently these *mujahidin* did not only equip themselves with the combat skills necessary for the battlefields, but they also drenched themselves in a militant ideology suited only for the rough and rugged terrain of Afghanistan's flimsy colonial politics. It was at this specific juncture that Muslims from around the world united under the banner of Islam, and participated in the waging of jihad against a common enemy. Although the Soviet Union finally ended its occupation of Afghanistan, the U.S.-backed *mujahidin* were a highly fractious and peevish lot, triggering a long drawn out civil war among ethno-linguistic tribe men, causing famine, poverty and devastation to the country's social infrastructures. The chaos and total lawlessness that prevailed throughout the country later prompted the harsh and purist Taliban regime to gain control of Afghanistan, and turned it into what Ahmed Rashid (2001) describes as "the hub of a worldwide terrorist network".[41]

From these two major world events emerged a new brand of militant Islam, which exposes and exploits the plight of Muslims around the world. In most, if not all, cases the protagonists would call upon Islamic solidarity with the aim of encouraging Muslims to participate in jihad. For them, jihad is a means to achieve ultimate victory in all these provinces of war.

---

[40] Juergensmeyer, op. cit., 189.

[41] *Taliban: The story of the Afghan warlords* (Oxford: Pan Books, 2001), preface, viii.

The Mindset of Militant Muslims

What makes an individual Muslim a militant? And what defines a militant Muslim? The above questions are pertinent when one begins to explain why Muslims do the things that they do; and why militants engage in actions they feel are necessary. The key to answering these questions should not rest solely on what an individual have or have not committed to doing. Nor should it be based solely on *post-factum* analyses, which often do not supply further reach of understanding. Besides, such analyses are easily and quickly exhaustible. Efforts should thus be directed at providing some kind of elaboration on the mindset or mental configuration of the militant Muslims, which would then enable us to anticipate and understand their likely choices of actions. For the purposes of this study, let us first provide an inventory list of common assumptions held by militant Muslims relevant to this study. They comprise a mixture of truths, half-truths and myths. While some claims and assumptions originate expressly from religious Scriptures i.e. the Quran and/or Prophetic traditions, others are based on the militant Muslims' perception of political reality. In effect, elements of time-honored prejudices, stereotypes and hyperbolic accounts are easily detectable.

Assumption 1: *The world is heading to a moral abyss*

Significance: This generic assumption is the one sure thing that unites all religious conservatives and militants from all religions, denominations and belief systems, possessing and embracing an ingrained system of ethical codes. The rampant spread of the nihilistic and pleasure-seeking "*MTV* culture", in Barber's (2001) phraseology,[42] is seen as a major indicator of this increasingly decadent world. Through cable television and satellite dishes, the *MTV* channel is broadcast without rest for 24 hours daily, seven days a week. To many militant Muslims, such blatant propagandizing of Western decadence is anathema to their religious sensibility and moral codes.

---

[42] See Barber, op. cit.

Furthermore, it is perceived as the Iranians would say a form of *tahajom-e farhangi* (Western cultural imperialism). Having 'half-naked women dance in public',[43] according to their ethical standards, is offensive and goes against their notions of modesty and common decency. In addition, militant Muslims tend to view the *MTV* culture as a Western construction for the sole purpose of diluting the Muslim faith, and taking away the will to fight among the young believers. Its hidden utility lies in destroying the Islamic identity and way of life.

*Assumption 2: **The fact that Islam "ruled the world" for 14 centuries goes to show how Allah has bestowed His blessings upon the Muslims***

Significance: Muslims maintain that Islam was once the compass of the world. It was Islam that essentially brought great heights to human civilization, and helped ushered in the modern scientific industrial revolution. To their understanding, without the discovery of the Islamic civilization by the Europeans, "they would still be living in mud houses".[44] For the more militant Muslims, the argument is stretched further. An Indonesian Muslim provincial parliamentarian once involved in the Komando Jihad movement in the 1970s, said, "Look, all of modern sciences were derived, if not stolen, from the Muslims. It is high time that we reclaim it."[45] This line of thinking leads to the strong conviction held by militant Muslims that the golden age of Islam is inevitably restorable. And once achieved, it would prove once more how Allah favors the Muslims over the rest of humanity. This assertion is supported by a Quranic precept that claims that Muslims are the *'ukrijat li an-naas* (the best among peoples).[46]

---

[43] This phrase is a standard ethical point often lamented by Muslims preachers.

[44] This was once conveyed to me by an American Muslim university professor teaching in Boston, Massachusetts.

[45] Derived from personal interview with Daud Gunawan in October 2002 in Bandung, West Java.

[46] See Quran 34:90.

Assumption 3: **Islam is a religion of peace and the imposition of the syariah should not in any way be a cause for apprehension**

Significance: Militant Muslims maintain that Islam is first and foremost a comprehensive ideology that provides man with Divine inspiration to mend all shortcomings of this world. As elaborated earlier in the chapter, Islam *is* the solution to all sociopolitical, economic, cultural and environmental degradation that man himself had created. The assumption indeed verges on Muslim utopian thinking where peace on earth would ultimately reign once the whole world accepts Islam. Up to this stage, there is no divergence of views between the militants from the Sunni and Shia schools of thought. However, in the case of the Sunnis, the mode of thinking is reinforced with the militants' mostly artificial knowledge of Islamic history to which they claim that "whenever Muslims gained power, they never persecuted anyone, least of all the religious minorities".[47] The reason for this supposed magnanimity is due to their perception that Islamic politics is governed by the will of God and the sacred laws enshrined in the *syariah*. Clearly, no human failings are factored in the equation. It follows that because of the magnanimous nature of the Muslims, the *syariah* should not in any way be a cause for apprehension among non-Muslims.[48] Also, still according to them, Islam's impressive expansion to Asia, Africa and southern Europe should not be looked upon as a martial conquest but rather a legitimate and peaceful form of *da'wa* (religious propagation). Interestingly, for the Shias, the historical narrative is almost diametrically opposite, as they regard themselves being the quintessential victim of the usurpers of power, who use Islam to get hold of earthly desires. The illegitimate caliphs and their stooges were the ones to blame for the Shia Muslims' despondent position in society. Even until today, religious scholarship within the

---

[47] Statement told to the author by an anonymous Sunni jihad participant.

[48] The negative sentiment that non-Muslims usually have toward the *syariah* is caused mainly by the seemingly fearsome punishments that Islamic law often entails. The most dreaded is the cutting off of limbs of those who steal and the stoning to death of married individuals who commit adultery.

Shia Muslim world still shoulders the historical baggage of being the persecuted minority.

Assumption 4: *The Jews and Christians are out to undermine the Muslim faith*

Significance: This assumption is borne out of the religious conviction on the following Quranic doctrine: "And the Jews will not be pleased with thee, nor will the Christians, till thou follow their creed."[49] For militant Muslims, this doctrine would be insufficient without the supplementary observations on the growing number of Muslims converting to Christianity. Of course, one of the ambiguities in this assumption is that "Judaism is not a faith that is chosen. One is a Jew by birth, whether one likes it or not ... [Thus, unlike Christianity] conversion has not usually been encouraged."[50] This is often spiced up by descriptions on the kinds of method used from the subtle 'food-for-soul' exchange to a systematic program of impregnation of Muslim women in the hope that victims would adopt the faith of the newborn's father by way of *fait accompli*.[51] The highly subjective view on the issue also entails the denial of the fact that Islam is one of the fastest growing religions in the world, not least in the U.S. and Britain.[52] An even more extreme conjecture than the above posits a worldwide Judeo-Christian global conspiracy to harm the Muslims, and "defuse the light of Islam throughout the world".[53] The justification for such conspiratorial line of thinking is found in the interests Muslims have in daily media reportage about the continuous plight of Muslims in Palestine, Bosnia, Chechnya, Albania, Afghanistan, Iraq and now Iran. Militant Muslims maintain that the seemingly unbreakable alliance

---

[49] Quran 2:120. One jihad participant interviewee invoked this verse when asked about why he thought it was necessary to wage war against the infidels.

[50] See Keith Ward, *Religion and Community* (Oxford: Clarendon Press, 2000), 12.

[51] This conveyed to the author by a Muslim activist working for a Jakarta-based movement against Islamic apostasy sometime in mid 2003.

[52] Refer back to the issue elaborated in Chapter 1.

[53] See *Sabili* (Jakarta) 14 (X), published on November 14, 2002: 8-12.

between the U.S. (as a Christian state) and Israel (as a Jewish state) embodies this malicious conspiracy. The standpoint on the inevitability of the Judeo-Christian alliance, however, has never remained the exclusive rights of militant Muslims. As briefly mentioned in Chapter 1, even Huntington, a Harvard professor of politics, believes in the inevitability of the clash of civilizations,[54] adding somewhat a twist to the above assumption. From my own personal observation, where the above assumption is held at face value, an individual is likely to develop negative opinions about 'the other'.

Assumption 5: *Jews are a deceitful, treacherous and domineering lot, seeking only to control the world*

Significance: Antipathy toward the Jews is a widespread phenomenon among militant Muslims, especially during street demonstrations in Jakarta, Kuala Lumpur, Tehran, Karachi, Cairo and elsewhere. More often than not, "anti-Semitism" proves to be a powerful rallying cry, almost like a knot that ties militant Muslims of all creeds and nationalities. Yet this antipathy attains much credence in the Islamic world because Muslim leaders from Khomeini to Malaysia's former prime minister Mahathir Mohamad encourage it. A statement by Mahathir that "Jews rule the world by proxy. [And] they get others to fight and die for them"[55] provides a lucid illustration of the kind of attitude some Muslims have toward the Jews.[56] The assumption is further bolstered on a daily basis by media reportage on the relentless Arab-Israeli conflict, which frequently depicts the constant defeat and humiliation suffered by the Palestinian Muslims. The main problem

---

[54] See Huntington, op. cit.

[55] "Omnipotent West suffers denial syndrome" in *New Straits Times* (Kuala Lumpur), published on October 23, 2003, 12. The statement, which apparently referred to the Iraqi debacle, was made in a meeting of the Organization of Islamic Conference attended by many Muslim leaders.

[56] By stating this, I am not in any way categorizing the former prime minister of Malaysia Mohamad as being a militant Muslim. It simply illustrates that such a sentiment sometimes prevails among Muslim leaders and within the elite circle, in spite of the common dictates of political correctness.

of this assumption, however, lies in the fact that most militant Muslims fail miserably in distinguishing between the Jews and the Zionists. To them, the "Protocol of the Learned Elders of Zion"—an alleged 19th century transcript documenting a vision of world domination—is considered as an authentic proof of the Jews' desire to purportedly control the world and enslave all nations. The Jewish world conquest would supposedly be accomplished by way of political subversion, economic domination and cultural annihilation.[57]

Assumption 6: All injustices that currently prevail in the world would eventually be abolished and rectified by the Mahdi

Significance: Both Sunni and Shia Muslims have faith in the re-advent of the 'Messiah'. However, differences transpire with respect to the question of *who* exactly will occupy this venerated position. While Sunni Muslims attach less importance on the role of the Mahdi in redeeming the world, their Shias' politico-religious thinking revolves around it, rendering the latter more inclined to take an active role in eliminating all forms of injustices and exploitation. At any rate, Shia Muslims are fully conscious that their struggle would still be incomplete so long as they are in the period of messianic expectation (*entezar*). Thus, in the absence of the Mahdi, only defensive jihad is permitted. In other words, until and unless the Mahdi re-emerges from the spiritual to the physical plane will the *dar al-Islam* reign supremely in the world, ensuring peace, equity and justice for all mankind.

As stated earlier, the above list of common assumptions held by militant Muslims vary in terms of its degree of truthfulness and reliability. I would argue, however, that every militant Muslim would to some extent have faith in most, if not all, of these elements. Again, this is not to say that ordinary Muslims do not share the

---

[57] The current spate of bombings and terror campaign occurring in Indonesia had also prompted militant Muslims to accuse the U.S. and its "Zionist allies" of being behind the attacks. See "Indonesia calls on Muslims to drop conspiracy theories" in *The Straits Times* (Singapore), published on August 23, 2004: A3.

above assumptions. What distinguishes them perhaps is that while militants are more likely to act upon these assumptions, the non-militant Muslims may take it with a grain of salt.

Examining closely the above assumptions, it is clear how militant Muslims take their politico-religious identities more seriously than their non-combative brethren. For that matter, I will try to elaborate on the complexity of the Muslim political identity, and its potentially lethal ramifications in the next section.

Muslim Political Identity

If identity refers to "the relatively stable elements of an individual's sense of self",[58] then Muslims are generally conscious of it. The Muslim identity stems mainly from the abundance of community-oriented precepts in Islam. Regrettably, the contemporary world of Islam is marred by political divisions and cultural disorientation. Unlike during the long period of the caliphate up until the era of the Turkish Sultanate, the *ummah* is now injuriously fragmented, leaving Muslim nation-states or Islamic sub-communities to venture into the new, modern world as separate entities with no common destiny and shared vision. If one were to disaggregate the so-called Muslim world, it would make sense to grasp it from the 'regional' perspective. Hence, three sub-communities exist: *First*, the Middle East encompassing the whole of the Arabian Peninsula, North Africa, Sub-Saharan region, Turkey and Persia. *Second*, the Muslim region external to the Middle Eastern hemisphere, which includes the Caucasia, South Asia and Southeast Asia as well as some parts of Africa. They include but not limited to countries such as Azerbaijan, Turkmenistan, Pakistan, Indonesia, Malaysia, Somalia, etc. *Third*, the Muslim minorities scattered in traditionally non-Muslim regions such as in North America, Europe, the Balkans, and elsewhere in Asia and Africa. In some cases, Muslim minorities can makeup a significant

---

[58] Jeffrey R. Seul, "'Ours Is the Way of God': Religion, identity, and intergroup conflict" in *Journal of Peace Research*, 36 (5) September 1999: 554.

portion of the population in the host state. In the U.S. alone, the number of "elusive Muslims" taking root in the country is between 1.2 and 10 million with around 500,000 "indigenous, Black Muslims".[59]

Nonetheless, such division or classification hardly poses any quandaries for Muslims. In their perspective, a Muslim is a Muslim, wherever he or she goes, and whatever background that he or she may come from. For Islam does not discriminate on the basis of either race/ethnicity or nationality. Despite the unfavorable political reality that confronts them, the Muslims' consciousness, imagination and perception of their community transcends any and all formal political boundaries or state territories. To them, no matter what, any and every Muslim is unavoidably a member-citizen of the *ummah*, hence ideally, the individual is expected to share the community's ideals, hopes, desires, aspirations and expectations. A Muslim therefore becomes bounded by the laws, customs and traditions that govern the larger Islamic community. Militant Muslims, for all practical purposes, understand how such a social schema operates within the community. It is this emotional bond, social interconnectedness and religious affinity among Muslims in the community that makes '*fatwas*' of jihad able to reverberate beyond the confines of the Tora Bora caves in Afghanistan or the remote Ngruki Islamic boarding school in Solo, Indonesia. This, in my view, is the primary reason why Muslims tend to possess a strong attachment to their brethren. Muslims often exhibit this affection by showing their concern over the past and current plights of their brethren in different parts of the world. For a Muslim, the urge and need to attach oneself to a collective is therefore fulfilled by the very fact that the individual is a believer in Islam. This does not mean, however, that the issue of Muslim identity can then be laid to rest. Contrarily, because of the requirements in Islam, Muslims more often than not confront a dilemma in asserting their religious identity. The complication faced by a Muslim is to

---

[59] "America's elusive minority: Muslims" in *Christian Science Monitor* (Boston), published on October 7, 2002.

define his or herself in light of the status that one acquires as a result of citizenship and racial or ethnic loyalty. In addition to this intrinsic problem, Muslims have also had to bear with the increasing hostility emanating from the application of prejudicial anti-terrorism laws and draconian measures supposedly to pre-empt Islamic militant activities.

In the U.S., for instance, 'American Muslims' previously focused their attention on changing the American foreign policy toward Palestine, Kashmir, Iraq, etc. However, after September 11, their strategy has been more geared to reconstituting "our identity as American", albeit "under duress".[60] Even as it may seem that such processes are contrived and forced, it is a problem that all Muslims living in a nation-state must confront. The aggravation is well illustrated by one American Muslim, who lamented, "America is our home, we will not become foreigners in our own homeland".[61] Such representation of contemporary Muslim sentiment may not necessarily be similar across the board, especially when compared with those living in Muslim countries. Conducting a study in the Middle East, Shibley Telhami found that "the pre-eminence of Islamic identity in the region varies from country to country".[62] While most Muslim respondents in Egypt and Lebanon identify themselves first and foremost as Egyptians and Lebanese, the people of Morocco, Saudi Arabia, Jordan and the United Arab Emirates view themselves as "Muslims" more so than "Arabs" or citizens of their respective countries.[63] Telhami argues that the war on terror and its subsequent implications in Afghanistan and Iraq "have further intensified identification with being a Muslim".[64]

---

[60] "Rebuilding an identity after September 11" by Muqtedar Khan in *The New York Times*, published on September 9, 2003: 6.

[61] Ibid.

[62] "A Growing Muslim Identity: Increasingly, Arabs define themselves in terms of Islam" in *Los Angeles Times*, published on July 11, 2004: 1.

[63] Ibid.

[64] Ibid.

How then does a Muslim reconcile with his multiple and shifting identities? Or how exactly do these expressions of identity take shape and affect Muslim political behavior and action? Take for example a Javanese-born Indonesian Muslim man. For a person with multiple identities, the problem not only lies in the multiplicity of his loyalties but more so because these multitudes of identities often overlap, interact and compete with one another. In other words, when certain circumstances arise, the individual may have to ultimately ask himself the question of where his chief allegiance lies, whether in ethnicity (Javanese), nationality (Indonesian), religion (Muslim) or gender (man). A similar situation occurs when dealing with an Iranian Shia Muslim woman. Although she may pledge allegiance to her faith (Shia Islam), but her nationalistic predisposition (as an Iranian) or gender bias (as a woman) may obscure her political inclinations, attitudes and behavior. Furthermore, her nationalistic predisposition may also be intruded by her identification as either a Fars or non-Fars.

In his work entitled *In the Name of Identity*,[65] Maalouf (2003) deals with the complexities of identity, and explains the precarious ramifications that frequently manifest out of the "need to belong". After arguing that "every individual without exception possesses a composite identity",[66] the author attempts to prove the correlation between people's need to belong and the propensity to commit atrocious acts against 'the other'.[67] He further contends that identity has "lethal potentialities", which can prompt ordinary men to shift their multiple identities (namely, as a religionist, as a member of a racial/ethnic group or as a citizen of a nation-state) to justify their often-horrendous treatment of their perceived enemies.

> Where people feel their faith is threatened, it is their religious
> affiliation that seems to reflect their whole identity. But if their

---

[65] Amin Maalouf, *In the Name of Identity: Violence and need to belong* (New York: Penguin Books, 2003).

[66] Ibid, 20.

[67] Refer back to Said's notion of 'the othering'.

mother tongue or their ethnic group is in danger, then they fight ferociously against their own co-religionists. Both the Turks and the Kurds are Muslims, though speak different languages; but does that make war between them any less bloody? Hutus and Tutsis alike are Catholics, and they speak the same language, but has that stopped them slaughtering one another? Czechs and Slovaks are all Catholics too, but does that help them live together?[68]

Unlike Gurr's relative deprivation argument, Maalouf (2003) considers identity as being almost sacrosanct. The point was especially made in relation to the religionists' loyalty to the "global tribe", which he defines as societies that stress identity, while at the same time blithely reach across traditional frontiers of the nation-state.[69] Although the formal relationship between the assertion of traditional identity and collective violence was never quite lucidly outlined, the proposition that personal and collective identities somehow affect the political behavior among members of the global tribe still stands. Take for instance the case of Ali Imron, one of the Indonesian perpetrators of the Bali nightclub bombing. In his defense before the court, Imron claimed:

> [T]he Jews led by the U.S. and Israel have already declared war against Muslims ... We did it out of sympathy for oppressed Muslims ... That is why we targeted them. It was payback for U.S. policies on the Palestinian issue and for its attack on Afghanistan.[70]

Although seemingly inconceivable, religious identity, affinity, solidarity and attachment to the *ummah* alone may influence Muslims to commit such heinous acts. What worries the West is that such sentiments are voiced time and again by militant Muslims of all varieties. It certainly begs the question of just how exactly such

---

[68] Ibid, 13.

[69] Ibid, 93.

[70] "Suspect regrets Bali attack 'even though victims mostly white'" in *The Straits Times* (Singapore), August 23, 2003: A3.

religious affection can turn a 'regular' Muslim activist to resort to a bloody and merciless form of jihad. In line with this, it would therefore be interesting to know how much religious affection prevails among ordinary Muslims on the streets and how it affects the level of willingness on the part of Muslims to participate in jihad, as hypothesized in this study.[71]

The next chapter will further explore these issues while focusing on the Indonesian Muslims. The findings of the survey, which will touch upon the effects of religious affection on one's level of willingness to participate in jihad, will be presented and discussed.[]

---

[71] Empirical evidence and statistical analyses on this issue will be provided in Chapters 4, 5 and 6.

4

Islamic Reassertion among Indonesian Muslims

This chapter highlights the Muslims' constant search for identity and political recognition in Indonesia. The analysis delves into the Indonesian Muslims' quest to participate in the sociopolitical schema of things. The Chapter is divided into two sections namely on Muslims of Indonesia and their mode of jihad. The first section is a precursor necessary in explaining the inner profiles of Indonesian Muslims. This encompasses the discussion on the sociopolitical history and place of Islam in the modern Indonesian nation-state. The latter part elaborates on the essential mode of jihad common to the country's militant Muslims. The section includes basic statistical analyses on the Indonesian survey.

Throughout the holy month of Ramadhan, television networks across Indonesia compete to create, remake and broadcast movies, video documentaries and storytelling programs on the early history of Islamic propagation in Indonesia year after year. One of the recurring themes of these programs is the account on the *Wali Songo* or the Nine Saints responsible for the early spread of Islam on the island of Java. Essentially, the setting of the storyline is based on an ascetic group of nine Muslim evangelists in the 13th century, who took the challenge of Islamicizing the island of Java. Prior to the Saints' religious endeavor, the Javanese mostly prescribed to the religions of Hindu, Buddha or their local traditional varieties. However, a significant number of others proscribed to what one would categorize today as either animism or dynamism.[1]

The majority of these saints came to the shores of the archipelago via China, but originated from the Middle East from far places such as Hadramaut (the southeastern part of the Arabian peninsula, now Yemen) and Persia. However, out of all the saints, Sunan Kalijaga was considered to be one of the central figures. Folklore has it that the name *Kalijaga* (literally, *kali* for "river" and *jaga* "to guard") was conceived after he supposedly underwent meditation by a river for a good number of years, hence the name 'Guardian of the River'. One of the reasons behind the centrality of this figure seems to have something to do with his indigenous origins and ordinary background. Still according to folklore, before turning himself into an ascetic and venturing into the business of Islamic propagation, Kalijaga was a scoundrel, who made a living out of robbing and extorting money from village dwellers. Upon his induction into the rank of saints, he was regarded as the most successful preacher in converting laymen, princes and kings alike. His distinctive approach to preaching, said to have contributed to his accomplishment in *dakwah*, was by aligning the teachings of Islam with the established, time-honored local Javanese customs, traditions and culture. Kalijaga's stealthy strategy posited on infusing Islamic morality and ethics in the scripts and plots of his *wayang* (Javanese puppet show) performances. It should be noted that according to most Islamic schools of jurisprudence, three dimensional puppets and dolls are objectionable, if not forbidden. Thus, many modernist Muslims consider Kalijaga's

---

[1] Although neither can be considered as religions, in the conventional meaning of term, elements of both belief systems were able to penetrate into the domains of the 'formal' religions and enriched their eclectic variants.

utilization of *wayang* as a reprehensible form of *bid'ah* (heretical innovation).

Modern historical narratives on the Nine Saints are also saturated with stories about how they were guided by the *Sufistic* (Gnostic) tradition in Islam. This has paved the way to a conceivable argument that the spread of Islam throughout the archipelago relied on trade and peaceful cultural enlightenment as opposed to military expansionism. Through cultural infusion, Islam came to be comfortably interlinked with the then prevailing politico-religious thought, practice and ethos. Predictably, the end result of the process was an 'indigenized' form of Islam that is somewhat hard to equate with the Islam found in the Arab Middle East. Furthermore, what came out of this development was an Islamic religiosity, which accommodated external elements and creative innovations even in the often-sterile realm of Islamic ritualism. As if to concur with this known fact, the New York-based *Freedom House* recently concluded that Indonesia is "the least Arabicized" Muslim country along with Bangladesh, Nigeria and Iran.[2]

Famed for his work on symbolic anthropology in Indonesia and Morocco, Geertz (1960) once categorized Javanese Muslims into two major camps: *abangan* and *santri*.[3] *Islam abangan* is a qualification for Muslims who nominally identify themselves with the religion, and would normally practice religious syncretism. Muslims of this category often engage in or at least have firm belief in Javanese mystical traditions. For most, they find no fault in the contradictions between Islam and their idiosyncratic belief systems. The opposite category is the *Islam santri* or the devout Muslims, who are typically *syariah*-oriented and at times overly conscious of their Middle Eastern religious heritage. They keenly observe Islam as a guide and cue in life. The *santris'* sense of affinity and solidarity also transcends the archipelago.

---

[2] The findings were revealed at the conference on "Islam in Modern Indonesia" held in Washington, D.C. on February 7, 2002. It was co-sponsored by the United States-Indonesia Society and the Asia Foundation.

[3] For further reading, see Clifford Geertz, *The Religion of Java* (Glencoe, Illinois: Free Press, 1960).

To some degree, they regard Arab identity as intrinsically their own.[4] Until recently, Java's history has been about the story of the *abangans*. This is less so in the outer islands of the archipelago with the *santri* culture playing a more significant social and political role than the former. A clear indication of this phenomenon can probably be seen in the manner in which traditionalist NU is more dominant in Java, while the more modern Muhammadiyah has greater reach and influence in the outer islands of Sumatra, Kalimantan and Sulawesi. However, current observations point to an increasing assertiveness among the *santris*,[5] even in the heartland of Java, owing to the burgeoning middle class and wave of urbanization, which seemingly contributes to the decline of influence and belief in traditional Javanese mystical values and traditions. In all, although Geertz's (1960) dichotomization may prove useful in explaining the Muslim dynamic within the context of contemporary Java, its application in other parts of the sprawling archipelago remains questionable.

Islam and the State

Within the framework of the Indonesian state, which is "neither secular nor religious",[6] Islam has traditionally played a central role. This is not merely due to the sheer size of the Muslim populace, but also the political dynamics that govern the country's Muslim community, where public piety is gaining salience and increasingly becoming the social basis for interaction. As previously stated, much too often Islam is believed to be inseparable from politics. However, as Effendy (2003)

---

[4] Geertz's third category, *Islam Priyayi* or Muslim bureaucratic subculture, has been criticized for its inconsistency. The main contention was whether *Islam Priyayi* is a socio-religious category or rather a socioeconomic one. In any case, the present author does not ascribe to the third category, as it is considerably outdated to be brought in context into the discussion on modern Indonesia.

[5] One of the superficial, yet indicative, measures to gauge the increasing religiosity among the Indonesian Muslim middle class is the rise in the number of urban Muslim women wearing the Islamic headscarf.

[6] Arskal Salim and Azyumardi Azra, *Shari'a and Politics in Modern Indonesia* (Singapore: Institute of Southeast Asian Studies, 2003).

asserts, "[T]he political relationship between Islam and the state in Indonesia has been largely a story of mutual antagonism and distrust".[7]

The founding father and first president of Indonesia Sukarno from the start realized the problem in placing Islam in context with his global vision, nationalistic drive and left-leaning politics. Through a process of intellectual blending, Sukarno later came up with an eclectic notion of *Nasakom*,[8] an amalgamation of three major ideologies namely Nationalism, religion (in this case, Islam) and Communism, to expectedly keep Western imperialism and capitalism at bay. Sukarno also had himself believe that through *Nasakom*, the fragmented archipelago can once and for all unite under his leadership. Before long, *realpolitik* intervened, and his vision for a united and progressive nation, glued by an eclectic ideology, was shattered mainly due to the unrealistic and improbable alliance among the three competing national elements. When the ideological battle lines were eventually crossed, all three elements were involved in an all-out attempt to capture the state. History then witnessed the elimination of Muslim separatists, the purging of the communists, and the brutal killings of top military generals, who allegedly planned a *coup d'état* against the civilian government. In the end, Sukarno relented to political pressure, and was deposed. This paved the way for the emergence of the New Order headed by a previously obscure army general named Suharto, who was backed by the American CIA, which grew tired of Sukarno's anti-American, anti-Western demagoguery.

Under Suharto's autocratic and militaristic rule (1966-1998),[9] Indonesian Muslim activists felt they were victimized by his contentious policies toward Islam, particularly during his first two decades in power. Apart from his anti-Communistic stance, many of Suharto's

---

[7] Bakhtiar Effendy, *Islam and the State in Indonesia* (Singapore: Institute of Southeast Asian Studies, 2003), 13.

[8] Indonesian acronym for *Nasionalisme, Agama dan Komunisme*.

[9] See R. William Liddle, "Soeharto's Indonesia: Personal Rule and Political Institutions" in *Journal of Asian Studies*, 58 (1) 1985: 68-90 and Adam Schwarz, *A Nation in Waiting: Indonesia's search for stability* (2nd edition), (Boulders, Colorado: Westview Press, 2000).

policies were apparently geared toward restraining Muslim political activism as well as undermining the rich Islamic heritage that modern Indonesia inherited. One example relates to the issue of Islamic headscarves (locally known as *jilbab*) for Muslim women. During Suharto's tenure in office, *jilbabs* were quietly prohibited in schools, banned in government offices and discouraged in public. Moreover, many Islamic activists were jailed and Muslim politicians were side-lined. In short, they became the state's convenient bogeyman. In extreme cases, outright abuse by security apparatus was employed to essentially 'de-politicize' Islam and the Muslims. A case in point was the 1984 Tanjung Priok incident in North Jakarta, when the military killed over 400 Muslims in an apparent attempt to quell a local anti-government demonstration.

Suharto's attempt in the 1980's to make the state ideology, *Panca-sila* (five main principles), as Indonesia's *azas tunggal* (sole foundation of the state) also drew much criticism from the Muslim camp.[10] Suharto contended that only *Pancasila* could unite Indonesia and resolve the grave problem of ideological division and ethno-religious diversity. In practice, the policy forced all political groups and civic organizations to conform, if not succumb, to Suharto's secularist ideals. Those that did not abide by the rule were categorized as "*OT*" (*organisasi terlarang*) or "banned organization", which gave the state the legal right to clampdown on them. From the perspective of the Muslim chattering class, however, the insistence on *azas tunggal* was seen as the New Order's trump card, if not justification, to undermine Islam, while simultaneously marginalizing Muslim politicians and the *ulama* (religious scholars) from national politics. Beneath it all, there was an attempt to detach the religious elite from its widespread traditional grassroots support.

Undoubtedly such insensitivity on the part of the state stirred deep feelings of resentment and apprehension among the Muslims

---

[10] Pancasila comprises five main principles that include: 1. Belief in the Oneness of God; 2. Humanity; 3. Unity of Indonesia; 4. Democracy by way of consensus; 5. Social justice.

toward the government. The anxiety, frequently lamented by devout and politically conscious Muslims, rests on the dreadful thought that Indonesia was progressively becoming another Turkey. From the perspective of many devout Muslims, Suharto's aggressive anti-Muslim stance was seen as an affront to Islam, giving much credence to the militant Muslims' notion of the 'Christianization of Indonesia', which until today remains a strong point of contention.

All in all, the government's main strategy was to offset Muslim influence, and justify persecution against political dissenters and ethno-religious separatists. More often than not, it was the military that used to do all the dirty work for Suharto. In return, the armed forces (most notably the army) attained vast political leverage and immense power in virtually all sectors of life in Indonesia. Under the pretext of *dwifungsi* (dual function of the armed forces),[11] Suharto was able to bequeath a lion's share of civilian roles, especially the strategic ones, to his uniformed loyalists. This was Suharto's typical way of showing gratitude to the military's unyielding support for his regime, most notably during his first two decades in power. Thus, an implicit *quid pro quo* was at play between Suharto and the military elite, which was more than content to play along. After all, many from the military establishment felt comfortable about being bestowed strategic positions as cabinet ministers, ambassadors, governors, mayors and regents. In addition, many of the top brass were granted business concessions or directorships in major state-owned companies. After years of engaging in this balancing act, the military became quickly adept and sensitive toward every desire of its patron. *Pendekatan keamanan* (security approach) became the established procedure in guaranteeing political stability, economic development

---

[11] The dual function of the military was instated during the early days of the republic's independence, during which the military (notably the army) maintained a significant role in the functioning of the civilian administration. Although the doctrine was initially considered a natural evolution in the military's development and expansion, public discourses on civil supremacy was indeed common among those concerned with democracy, and reject any form of governments resembling military juntas.

and civil order. Unfortunately, the militaristic approach toward nation building unquestionably led to an immense problem related civil liberties and human rights abuses.

The condition, however, was somewhat neutralized around 1990, which saw Suharto's endorsement on the inauguration of ICMI (Indonesian Muslim Intellectuals Association), led by his then most trusted aide Bacharuddin Jusuf Habibie, a German trained aeronautics professor and engineer. During this period of what Liddle (1996) calls the "Islamic turn",[12] Suharto's political support for the Muslims was, if truth be told, a pre-emptive strategy to offset the increasing disquiet from some quarters from within the military establishment, which still considered assertive Islam as its main archenemy that is on par with Communism. During Suharto's era, the main enemies of the state were bundled into two categories: *ekstrim kanan* (extreme right), which denotes the green (Islamic) menace, and *ekstrim kiri* (extreme left) representing the red Communists. As a consequence, Suharto's political realignment with "regimist Muslims", as Hefner (2000) labels them, during his last decade of rule encouraged the burgeoning of Muslim religious identity.[13] With Habibie at the helm of ICMI and Suharto being at the forefront to shift the political pendulum, Muslim groups such as DDII (Indonesian Islamic Propagation Council) and KISDI (Committee for the Solidarity of the Islamic World) together with other highly assertive groups quickly went on board the project to Islamicize Indonesia. In the mean time, others that opted to remain outside the given parameters were trapped in a seemingly fruitless struggle for a confessional state that would secure Islam into becoming the sole, formal basis of the state. For ICMI, an obvious approach to accomplish this was to Islamicize the cabinet, military and government

---

[12] See R. William Liddle, "The Islamic Turn in Indonesia: An explanation" in *Journal of Asian Studies*, 55 (3) August 1996: 613-634.

[13] This phenomenon, however, must also be viewed in the larger political context of globalization, which offers a solid platform for the forging of a common political identity, increasing assertiveness and sense of solidarity among religionists. See Robert W. Hefner, *Civil Islam: Muslims and Democratization in Indonesia* (New Jersey: Princeton Review Press, 2000).

bureaucracy by way of getting like-minded Muslims to occupy these highly strategic positions. The logic was based on Habibie's political formulae of "proportional representation", which simply put insisted that Muslims, comprising almost 90% of the Indonesian population, be reserved to occupy nine in every ten top strategic positions. With this, the building up of a political alliance between the regimist Muslims and the state undoubtedly created problems of its own, as the military and minority groups as well as the mainstream Islamic groups (notably NU) felt they were being systematically marginalized.

However, as the Islamicization project was underway, the 1997 Asian regional economic crisis intervened, exhorting the New Order regime to bow to the democratic forces of *reformasi.* From the Muslim quarters, Wahid of NU and Amien Rais of Muhammadiyah emerged as the chief locomotive pushing the agenda for the popular reform movement that eventually dethroned Suharto.[14] From the nationalist camp, it was obvious that Megawati Sukarnoputri, then chairperson of PDI (Indonesian Democratic Party), came to be the icon for resistance against the Suharto regime. This was especially apparent when Megawati had to bear the July 27, 1996, ordeal where the government and army instigated the ransacking of her party headquarters in Jakarta. Amid mounting political pressure to reform, the autocrat eventually transferred power to then vice president Habibie on May 21, 1998. Unfortunately, Habibie's tenure as president was short-lived, as he was compelled to initiate the democratization process, and make way for the first free and fair elections in almost 50 years. As a result of the 1999 general elections, and owing to Wahid's political shrewdness,[15] the near-blind NU cleric was then elected as the republic's fourth president. Similar to his predecessor, however, his political

---

[14] For a juxtaposed discussion on the two leaders' visions and styles, see Arief Afandi. *Islam Demokrasi Atas Bawah: Polemik Strategi Perjuangan Umat Model Gus Dur dan Amien Rais* [Islamic Democracy High and Low: The polemic over the strategic models of resistance of Gus Dur and Amien Rais] (3rd edition) (Yogyakarta: Pustaka Pelajar, 1997).

[15] Despite his party, the PKB (National Awakening Party), coming third in the elections attaining a mere 18% of the popular votes, Wahid was successful in building a coalition in the Upper House (MPR) to elect him as president.

fortunes did not last long. Wahid's presidential mandate was recanted by the MPR after only 20 months in office for his rather erratic leadership style and the aggressiveness in which he handled the powerful military establishment. As if repeating recent history, Megawati, who was chosen by Wahid as his running mate, was propelled to the office of the presidency.

Similar to the experience of other less developed democracies, democratization not only generates political instability but also spurs ethno-religious secessionism.[16] For a country like Indonesia—having more than 17,000 islands spread in three different time zones with 350 ethno-linguistic groups—the challenge to preserve the country's intactness becomes particularly daunting. The most well known case that caught worldwide attention relates to the debacle in East Timor, which ended the Republic's 23 years of 'annexation'.[17] The East Timorese process of secession was backed by a United Nations-sponsored referendum held in late August 1999 with the consent of then president Habibie. The decision clearly angered the ultra nationalist elements in Indonesia, most notably the military, which had throughout more than two decades conducted numerous military operations in the 'province'. For many from within the Islamic community, however, it was seen as an international conspiracy to undermine Indonesia, being a large and potentially powerful Muslim country. The case of East Timor, seen and regarded as a Catholic province, only convinced them of the soundness of their argument.

Nonetheless, the war on terror has provided justification for the military to fully reassert its role in securing and defending the country's territorial integrity. After all, since the downfall of Suharto, the Indonesian military has been battling strenuously in the political arena against both the civilian government and civil society that have

---

[16] For further reading, see Larry Diamond and Marc F. Plattner (editors), *Nationalism, Ethnic Conflict and Democracy* (Baltimore: Johns Hopkins University Press, 1994).

[17] With Western support during the height of the Cold War era, Indonesia invaded East Timor in 1975 and subsequently made it into the country's 27th province. This was done following the brutal civil war that broke during the decolonization process from the Portuguese.

demanded it to return to the barracks. However, contrary to the expectations of the civilians, the 'professionalization of the military' has led to a major deterioration of domestic security, which now lies on the shoulders of the police force.[18]

Another case lies on the western tip of Indonesia, where GAM or the Free Aceh Movement had been persistently trying to secede from Indonesia. The 'Special Region of Aceh', as it had been formally named, is rich in natural resources and possesses one of the largest oil and gas deposits in Indonesia. The secessionist movement was essentially aimed at putting an end to the exploitation of its riches and long suffering caused by human rights abuses by the military. However, latest developments have shown significant strides in the peace process following the August 15, 2005, signing of a Memorandum of Understanding between the government of Indonesia and GAM.[19] The MoU apparently incorporates a "reintegration package", which will serve as basis for "economic facilitation" for all GAM demobilized combatants and "political prisoners". Indeed the MoU signals the government's seriousness in conferring to the staunch Acehnese Muslims greater autonomy to develop their region, even to the extent of institutionalizing the *syariah* into its legal framework as of 2001. This has entailed the return of public floggings for various criminal acts such as gambling and adultery.

Another challenge that confronted Indonesia post-*reformasi* involves the drastic change in the sociopolitical and religious configura-

---

[18] Some elements in the resource rich province of Irian Jaya (West Papua) too have declared their desire for self-determination, as the indigenous people have been disappointed at the way the central government had dealt with the management and development of their region. With the autonomy law now in place, it is expected that participatory governance will take precedence over exploitative practices of the central government authorities.

[19] One of the reasons for the success in the peace negotiations could be related to the post-September 11 political atmosphere that may have affected much of GAM's options amid international public opinion and pressure imposed upon by the war on terrorism.

tions.[20] The most crucial consequence of this relates to the upsurge of inter-religious conflict namely in the Spice Islands of Maluku (or Moluccas), which later spilled over to Poso (Central Sulawesi). Although the real trigger of the conflict remains sketchy, the conflict has decidedly been between local Muslim and Christian communities. A number of versions surfaced as to the question of how the conflict first started. Reliable reports suggest the conflict might have been triggered by a clash between Muslim and Christian *premans* (thugs) in the capital city of Ambon. Others have cited how scores of Christian thugs were deliberately shipped from Jakarta during one fasting month of Ramadhan to stir up trouble and intimidate the Muslims in Ambon. The conflict itself was stirred by local Protestant groups to replicate the East Timor-style of secession by reincarnating the defunct RMS (Republic of South Maluku) movement. With headquarters based in the Netherlands, the group attempted to agitate the local Muslim community to spur just enough violence and devastation to bring about a United Nations resolution to back its claim for "self determination". According to intelligence assessment, the nature of the conflict in Maluku was based more on religious grounds than on local politics, giving purportedly 7:3 in proportion.[21] Although official estimate of the death toll of the six-year-old conflict stands at 9,000, unconfirmed sources put it between 15,000 and 35,000.[22] Though conditions have greatly improved ever since the signing of the Malino Declarations, the region's islands are still very much divided between the Muslim and Christian communities. In the latter case of Poso, the conflict was sparked off by a killing spree at the Wali Songo Islamic traditional boarding school, where around 200 religious students, teachers as well as inhabitants were

---

[20] For references on post-Suharto Indonesia, see Donald K. Emmerson (editor), *Indonesia Beyond Suharto: Polity, Economy, Society, Transition* (New York: East Gate and Asia Society, 1999); Geoff Forrester (editor), *Post-Soeharto Indonesia: Renewal or Chaos?* (Singapore: Institute of Southeast Asian Studies, 1999); and Chris Manning and Peter Van Diermen (editors), *Indonesia in Transition: Social Aspects of Reformasi and Crisis* (Singapore: Institute of Southeast Asian Studies, 2000).

[21] Derived from a personal interview with an anonymous source close to the Maluku conflict.

[22] Idem.

massacred. Now and then, the security conditions remain on high alert, as skirmishes still occur in the divided region.[23]

With respect to Muslim politics, the *reformasi* supplied two major patterns. The first relates to the influx of Muslims going into mainstream politics, while the other is linked to the rise of militant Islam. The former can be witnessed in the 1999 general elections when over 200 political parties registered to the KPU (General Elections Commission). Out of all the registered parties, 48 were considered eligible to participate in the *pesta demokrasi*, as Indonesians would term it. And out of the all the eligible participants, almost twenty were considered Muslim-based political parties with only five able to pass the two percent electoral threshold.[24] In the 2004 parliamentary elections, the Muslim political parties again contested but lost yet again to the more secular parties of Golkar and PDI-P. Even in the direct presidential elections, Muslim running candidates such as Rais (from PAN) and Hamzah Haz (from PPP) gained fewer votes than those who had no religious background such as Susilo Bambang Yudhoyono (PD), Megawati (PDI-P) and Wiranto (Golkar). In the end, it was Yudhoyono who won the first ever direct presidential balloting after a runoff to the second round with Megawati as the runner up. These recurring losses without doubt raised the question of political efficacy of the Muslim-based political parties. Azyumardi Azra, rector of the state-owned Islamic University in Jakarta, succinctly put it, "Islamic leaders and political elites only want seats more than anything else".[25] This indeed highlights the reality about what Roy (1994) earlier calls the politicization of religion in Indonesia.[26]

---

[23] For more on the latter issue, see "Indonesia Backgrounder: Jihad in Central Sulawesi" by International Crisis Group (ICG) (Jakarta/Brussels), published on February 3, 2004.

[24] Although some of these parties claim to be of nationalist character (e.g. PKB and PAN), they rely on Muslim constituents belonging to two of Indonesia's giant organizations i.e. NU and Muhammadiyah.

[25] Derived from Azra's statement made to a closed audience in a discussion entitled "Government Responses to Islamic Resurgence in Southeast Asia" held by Center for Contemporary Islamic Studies (CCIS) in Singapore in the first quarter of 2002.

[26] Roy, op. cit.

Indonesian Mode of Jihad

The other issue at hand when dealing with Muslim politics in Indonesia is the reassertion of militant Muslims following the downfall of the authoritarian government.[27] If previously these groups were operating clandestinely due to the state's policy of intimidation and suppression, democracy has provided them with the constitutional platform to function freely just like any other civil society organizations. Prominent among the country's militant groups are Laskar Jihad (LJ),[28] Front Pembela Islam (FPI) and Majelis Mujahidin Indonesia (MMI).[29] The following section will briefly profile what these groups stand for, and how they operate.

Although formally defunct now, LJ obtained media limelight throughout the region for a number of years owing to its palpable role in the prolonged inter-religious conflict in Maluku. In the view of its leader, Ja'far Umar Thalib, once an obscure preacher from East Java and a jihad veteran of Afghanistan, the deployment of jihad warriors in Ambon and Poso was merely to protect Muslims and prevent what he claims as a "*konspirasi* to follow the footsteps of East Timor [to secede] and build a separate state".[30] LJ claimed that had the government been able to secure and defend the Muslims, the existence of the group would not have been necessary. Organizationally, LJ is highly disciplined with members, who are well trained and prepared for jihad. Harold Crouch, a keen Indonesian military

---

[27] The same argument can be found in Khamami Zada, *Islam Radikal: Pergulatan ormas-ormas Islam garis keras di Indonesia* (Jakarta: Teraju, 2002).

[28] Formally, the name of the group is actually "Forum Komunikasi Ahlussunnah wa al-Jamaah", abbreviated as FKASW. For the sake of brevity, however, I will continue to use LJ.

[29] There are indeed other militant Muslim groups in Indonesia beside the three. Groups such as NII and Hizbut Tahrir Indonesia (HTI), for instance, are significant but not so relevant to our current discussion. For instance, NII has disintegrated into at least nine splinter groups, each claiming to be the 'real' NII. Meanwhile HTI, though highly assertive and insists on the imposition of the *syariah* as well as the resurrection of the caliphate, still operates within the corridors of the law. Often, it raises socioeconomic issues such as the privatization of water, high cost of education and the interventionist role played by the International Monetary Fund (IMF).

[30] "Indonesia's Dirty Little Holy War" in *Time Asia*, 158 (24) 2001.

observer from the Australian National University, lamented, albeit exaggeratingly, "They've got real organization and they've got reasonably capable people. You might find an airline pilot or two in LJ, but in the others, I doubt it very much."[31] During the pinnacle years of 1999-2001, membership of the group stood at an estimated ten thousand, where at least three thousand rotating members were deployed in the Maluku province at any given time throughout the conflict.[32] Membership comprises mostly young, militant men between the ages of 20 and 35. The group was formally disbanded in late 2002 based on a *fatwa* issued by two Saudi religious scholars, who decreed that the organization was no longer maintaining its Salafi, an ultra conservative Sunni ideology and outlook. In reality, the disbandment was a result of a political concession made in return for Thalib's release from custody for sanctioning the stoning to death of one of his followers found to be committing adultery while on his tour of duty in Maluku.[33]

Meanwhile, FPI is led by less-than 40-year-old Habib Muhammad Rizieq Shihab. Its existential goal is to primarily rid the country of social vices. In doing so, the Jakarta-based group regularly deploys members to seek and destroy *pusat-pusat kemaksiatan* (dens of evil) such as karaoke lounges, bars, discotheques and red-light districts, which they perceive as an affront to Islam and undermining the *syariah*. FPI activities, which often reach peak season during the holy month of Ramadhan, have become somewhat an annual jihad ritual supposedly to wipe out morally repugnant activities in society. It has been alleged that the group often extorts money from illicit business owners as premiums for 'security insurance'. FPI, which

---

[31] "Indonesia's Osama" in *The Straits Times* (Singapore), published on March 30, 2002: A1.

[32] Derived from a personal interview with an anonymous informant, who observed the conflict at close range.

[33] According to an anonymous informant interviewed in early 2003, the LJ leader was at first reluctant to enforce the law and insisted that the already married transgressor repented. However, Thalib later obliged when the transgressor himself demanded the application of the *rajam* (stoning) in the belief that God would forgive him.

frequently stage anti-American and Israel demonstrations, claims to have millions of registered members across various provinces. A more realistic assessment, however, suggests the group enjoys not more than five thousand militant supporters. Before becoming an FPI member, one must consent to a "martyr's contract" (*kontrak siap mati syahid*). In Shihab's words, "*Masuk FPI berarti siap jihad*" [Being an FPI member means being ready at all times to undertake jihad].[34] Shihab, who has had many run-ins with the police, euphemistically maintains that the U.S.-led military campaign in Afghanistan was "not in line with the domestic aspiration".[35] For him, anti-Western protests are spontaneous reactions to showcase the Islamic community's resentment toward America's "arrogant foreign policy".[36]

Out of the three groups, the most prominent and emerging militant group today is the MMI. Established in 2000, MMI aims to formally turn Indonesia into a *negara Islam* (Islamic state) with the *syariah* being the sole basis for state Constitution and legal system. Various prominent Muslim figures attended MMI's inauguration, including Rais of Muhammadiyah. MMI holds frequent mass demonstrations and religious gatherings denouncing the U.S. and Israeli policies toward Muslim nations. Its *amir* (leader) is a 65-year-old Muslim preacher named Abu Bakar Ba'asyir, who heads a traditional Islamic boarding school called Al-Mukmin at Ngruki-Sukardjo in Central Java. For his zealous insistence on the comprehensive application of the *syariah*, Ba'asyir went into self-exile for 15 years in Malaysia to avoid the wrath of Suharto's state apparatus. It was in Malaysia that he allegedly developed his network comprising young militant Muslims.

Upon his return from exile, Ba'asyir established and developed the MMI with the hope to marshal young Muslims to venture into

---

[34] "Siapa suruh datang ke Ambon" [Who told you to come to Ambon], *Gatra* (Jakarta), published on January 22, 2000: 25-26.

[35] "Al-Habib Muhammad Rizieq Shihab: Ini jelas pelanggaran berat" [This is surely a major transgression] in *Forum* (Jakarta) 29 (X) October 22, 2001.

[36] Ibid.

political activism and push for the Islamic agenda.[37] The cleric is currently wanted by a number of foreign governments, particularly the U.S., Australia and Singapore, which in addition to Israel was considered "terrorist governments".[38] The allegation charged against Ba'asyir is his role as the suspected spiritual leader of JI, a regional, shadowy terrorist network said to have close ties with Al-Qaidah. On September 2, 2003, an Indonesian court ruled that there was no real evidence pointing to Ba'asyir's leadership in JI. In spite of the ruling, the court sentenced him to four years in jail for being involved in the recent spate of bombings in the country, a serious charge, which he vehemently denied until today. The allegation includes the spate of bombing at the Bali nightclubs (2002), the J.W. Marriott Hotel (2003) and more recently the Australian Embassy (2004) in Jakarta. Ba'asyir, who once characterized Bin Laden as a "true hero", stated, "There is no value in life without the struggle to uphold the *syariah* in Indonesia."[39]

In the eyes of the international community, the mushrooming of such groups as above point to increasing militancy among the Indonesian Muslims. However, whether or not the political phenomenon proves to be a significant indicator to the level of militancy among Indonesian Muslims remains ambiguous. What's clear is that these groups, however small they may be, have inadvertently molded the international public opinion to conceive Indonesia as being a safe haven for militant Muslims or more harshly a seedbed for Islamic terrorism. Such sweeping generalizations, however, are problematic in two ways. One is that it amplifies the groups' diminutive but noisy existence to an extent in which they themselves might not have achieved on their

---

[37] See Fauzan al-Anzhari, *Saya Terroris?: Sebuah Pledoi* [Me Terrorist? A Defense] (Jakarta: Penerbit Republika, 2002).

[38] Reference by Ba'asyir to each government is often followed by the phrase "*la'natullah*" (May Allah's curse be upon you).

[39] Derived from Ba'asyir statement during a long-distance live sermon at a *Tabligh Akbar* (religious public gathering) in Bandung, Indonesia, on November 2, 2002 in which the author personally attended.

own. The other is that such an assessment is more likely than not to touch upon the sensitivity and sensibility of the generally moderate and largely secular Indonesian Muslim community. At any rate, the passing of such predisposed judgment will not help reign in the militants but in turn enhance the credibility of their argument and promote their cause by bringing sympathy as well as solidarity even to the nominal Muslims.

Aside from the external pressures, the militant Muslims themselves confront at least three major difficulties of their own. The primary challenge to their existence is the palpable intellectual hollowness, which renders much of their movements shallow, shortsighted and hence intolerant. This deficiency in intellectualism has not only deflected participation among the burgeoning, highly educated middle class, but also effectively entrapping the militant Muslims in a medieval mindset, where the forces of good ("us", the Muslims) is in perpetual war against the evil ("them", the infidels). When such constraining binary logic is maintained, the groups' prospect for survival becomes fairly bleak, as members would quickly exhaust the groups' capacity to renew themselves. As former JIL coordinator Ulil Abshar-Abdalla contends, "Islamic militant groups do not have the intellectual capacity needed to build a sustaining movement".[40]

The second problem relates to organizational shortcomings. Most of these militant groups are subject to infiltration and penetration by the intelligence community, much like the experience held by the then PLO (now PA) and Hamas, which carry out harsh punishments to those accused of being "Israeli collaborators". The trouble lies intrinsically in the Islamic universal etiquette code on *husn adh-dhan* (positive thinking) that prohibits Muslims to hold suspicion of their own fellow religionists. This, according to one informant, was one of the reasons for FPI's dismantlement and subsequent revamping in

---

[40] Derived from private conversation with Abdalla on January 7, 2003, in Singapore. Abdalla was invited to Singapore to share his views on liberal Islam in the "ISEAS Regional Forum Outlook 2003".

2002.[41] Cohesion within the rank and file is therefore difficult to achieve, compelling them to opt for a "less-for-more" strategy. For this reason, one finds most militant religious groups to be small, yet effective when it comes to mobilizing members to engage in direct actions. In addition to their learned prudence, clandestine militant groups operate in tiny cells comprising three to five members. The method of communication is also unique, as information is often transmitted by a single, trusted courier acting as the instructional gatekeeper and connector to the higher or lower cell. To enhance the effectiveness of the chain of command and increase the level of *esprit de corps* within these groups, a system of *bay'at* (pledge of allegiance) is enforced, entailing strict obedience to and submission of will before the leader. Normally, this would necessitate group members swearing on their lives to defend the interest of the group and uphold the code of silence. Similar to the worldwide practice of intelligence, before any real initiation takes place, prospective members undergo a long process of spotting and vetting.

Apart from the internal problems faced by these militant groups, there is also an inherent problem confronted by the wider community of Islamic groups regardless of size and politico-religious orientations. This relates to the collective action problem, where rivalry, more than camaraderie, is the name of the game. Often times, it degenerates into a less than elegant strategy in vying for media attention and recognition from the state and public. The long-held tradition of contestation between NU and Muhammadiyah, for instance, has effectively made them eternal adversaries, especially prior or during election times. Logically, if the two major Islamic anchor movements in Indonesia, with a combined membership of more than sixty million, were to set aside their differences and converge, their combined voting block would surely be the envy of other political groups. The non-cohesive nature of the Muslim body politic has become the primary

---

[41] Derived from personal interview with Umar of DDII on November 29, 2002, in Jakarta.

reason for the failure of political Islam in Indonesia, which in turn breeds distrust, suspicion and enmity among and within themselves. As Abdalla succinctly explains, "LJ cannot cooperate with FPI, while MMI is not seeing eye-to-eye with Hizbut Tahrir Indonesia (HTI)."[42] Hence, the collective action problem exists not only at the individual but more so at the group level. In such a competitive environment, the optimum strategy for each group is to continuously remain visible by staging noisy protests and demonstrations. As for the more extreme clandestine militant groups, widespread mayhem and terror in society would seem to be the likely and most viable option to consider. Much of the recent terror attacks occurring in Indonesia have mostly, if not all, been blamed on the secretive JI terrorist network.[43]

The next section details the findings derived from the individual level survey conducted in six major cities in Indonesia. The section looks specifically at the determinants to Indonesian Muslims' level of willingness to participate in jihad. The presentation comprises chi square tests and crosstabulations, while also highlighting the matrix of correlations provided in Appendices 2 and 3.

Participation in Jihad among Indonesian Muslims

Looking at the current state of affairs in Indonesia and in many developing Muslim countries, it is difficult to maintain the argument that jihad is an anachronistic form of political action. Appendix 4 provides highlights of the demographic characteristics and attributes of the respondents in Indonesia, which will then be analyzed against the dependent variable on participation.

---

[42] Derived from private conversation with Abdalla on January 7, 2003, in Singapore.

[43] For more, see *White Paper: The Jemaah Islamiyah Arrests and the Threat of Terrorism* (Singapore: Ministry of Home Affairs, January 7, 2003); Bilveer Singh, "The Emergence of the Jemaah Islamiyah Threat in Southeast Asia: External linkages and influences", paper presented at a workshop on *International Terrorism in Southeast Asia and Likely Implications for South Asia* organized by the Observer Research Foundation, New Delhi, India on April 28-29, 2004; and Kumar Ramakrishna, *"Constructing" The Jemaah Islamiyah Terrorist: A preliminary inquiry*, Working Paper No.71 (Nanyang Technological University, Singapore: Institute of Defence and Strategic Studies, October 2004).

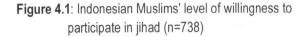

Figure 4.1: Indonesian Muslims' level of willingness to participate in jihad (n=738)

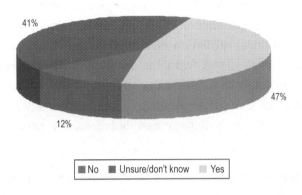

Figure 4.1 offers a univariate data analysis on the dependent variable using the Indonesian dataset. Data reveals that out of 738 Indonesian respondents, 92 (12.5%) responded negatively to the question on participation in jihad. Those who were undecided (answering "unsure/don't know") comprise 301 (40.8%) respondents. This leaves a total of 345 (46.7%) respondents, who stated their willingness to participate in jihad. The 46.7% figure is indeed high, but whether or not this militant inclination is caused by the respondents' demographic characteristics or religiosity requires further investigation.

To do this, data on the dependent variable is analyzed against the respondents' demographic characteristics. Aside from observing the matrix of correlations as a guide to determine the strength of association between the demographic and participation variables, crosstabulations are provided to determine whether or not demography significantly affects the Indonesian Muslim participation in jihad. Appendix 2 (under the category of "Indonesia") informs us that the only two demographic factors having significant measures of association (within the $p \leq .05$ level) with participation are racial/ethnic identity and political affiliation, as indicated by the asterisk next to the coefficient values. This study finds that while racial/ethnic identity is significant at .012 level, its relationship with the dependent variable is a fairly weak one with the coefficient value standing at a mere .109. In a nutshell, this figure indicates "to what degree, on a zero-to-one scale, two variables are linked".[44] An almost similar inference can be derived from looking at the case of political affiliation and its measure of association with participation in jihad. Thus, with the *Kendall tau-b* coefficient value of .098, one can safely assert that the strength of association between political affiliation and participation in jihad is also a weak one. To further reinforce these findings, crosstabulations are provided below.

Figure 4.2: Crosstabulation between racial/ethnic identity and participation in jihad (valid *n*=738)

Racial/ethnic identity	Participation in jihad			Total
	No	Unsure/ Don't know	Yes	
Minority	40 (9.7%)	163 (39.7%)	208 (50.6%)	411 (100%)
Majority	52 (15.9%)	138 (42.2%)	137 (41.9%)	327 (100%)

x^2 statistic: 8.806; *p*-value: .012

Observing Figure 4.2, one can say that respondents from minority racial/ethnic groups (in this case, the non-Javanese) tend to be more assertive in their politico-religious behavior, which in this case denotes their higher level of willingness to participate in jihad than respondents from the majority racial/ethnic group (or the Javanese). It is also apparent in the case of Indonesia that minority respondents have a greater willingness to participate in jihad (50.6%) as opposed to those

---

[44] See Michael S. Lewis-Beck, *Data Analysis: An introduction* (Thousand Oaks, California: Sage Publications, 1995), 41. A simpler method to assess the figure is to convert it into percentage, which in this case is just less than 11%. The closer the figure gets to the one scale (or 100%), the stronger the measure of association is between the two tested variables.

from the majority racial/ethnic group (41.9%). Moreover, respondents from the minority group are less likely to say "no" when it comes to participation in jihad (9.7%) compared to those from the majority (15.9%). One explanation for this may perhaps be that respondents from the majority racial/ethnic group as explained earlier in this chapter tends to be more easygoing when it comes to religion and politics. This is in line with the known fact that the Javanese people tend to be subtle and indirect in their political attitude and cultural behavior, as translated into their less than thrilled attitude toward participation in jihad. Predictably, most Javanese respondents, owing possibly to their religious syncretism, find comfort in being undecided about the whole issue of participating in jihad (42.2%), more so than their minority compatriots.

Figure 4.3: Crosstabulation between political affiliation and participation in jihad (valid *n*=738)

Political affiliation	Participation in jihad			Total
	No	Unsure/ Don't know	Yes	
Unaffiliated	75 (13.2%)	244 (43.0%)	249 (43.8%)	568 (100%)
Affiliated	17 (10.0%)	57 (33.5%)	96 (56.5%)	170 (100%)

x^2 statistic: 8.396; *p*-value: .005

Meanwhile Figure 4.3 informs us that politically affiliated Indonesian Muslims are somehow more likely to be willing to participate in jihad (56.5%) as opposed to those who are unaffiliated (43.8%). Presumably, this is associated with the higher degree of political consciousness on the part of those affiliated with political organizations or parties. The crosstabulation also indicates that the number of those who are politically unaffiliated and simultaneously undecided (43.0%) are almost equally high compared to those who are unaffiliated and willing to participate in jihad (43.8%). A more important finding suggests that the socioeconomic status of the respondents i.e. gender, age, marital and employment statuses, income and educational levels are insignificant when it comes to participation in jihad. Thus, variations in SES bear almost no effect on participation in jihad, statistically speaking.

Religiosity and Jihad in Indonesia

This section will discuss some of the relevant findings with respect to religiosity and its relationship with the variable on participation. Appendix 5 provides a brief overview of the measures of religiosity among the Indonesian respondents. Again, analyzing first the measure of religiosity against the dependent variable using the matrix of correlations, eight measures of religiosity have significant correlations (having p-values of $\leq .001$) with participation in jihad.[45] These measures of religiosity include: informal Islamic studies, Quranic recitation, books read, media publications, religious exposure, sacrifice, self-sacrifice and solidarity. However, looking closely at the *Kendall tau-b* coefficients of the above measures indicate that those higher than .200 (denoting relatively strong measures of association) are media publications (.231) and all the measures under the dimension of religious affection i.e. religious sacrifice (.263), self-sacrifice (.293) and solidarity (.355). Hence the four measures provide a better predictor when it comes to Indonesian Muslims' participation in jihad as compared to demographic characteristics and attributes. Examining this issue using crosstabulations would expectedly bring to light a clearer account.

Figure 4.4 shows the correlation between media publications and one's tendency to participate in jihad. As seen in the crosstabulation, the arrow in the "no" column is pointing toward north, which represents a tendency that the less subscription to Islamic media publications, the more likely one is to be unwilling to participate in jihad. Meanwhile the arrow in the "yes" column suggests the more one

---

[45] See Appendix 3 under the "Indonesia" column.

Figure 4.4: Crosstabulation between media publications and participation in jihad (valid n=738)

Media publication(s)	Participation in jihad			Total
	No	Unsure/ Don't know	Yes	
None	56 (22.9%)	108 (44.1%)	81 (33.1%)	245 (100%)
1 Publication	25 (10.8%)	96 (41.6%)	110 (47.6%)	231 (100%)
>1 Publications	11 (4.2%)	97 (37.0%)	154 (58.8%)	262 (100%)

x^2 statistic: 55.650; p-value: .000

subscribes to Islamic media publications, the higher likelihood for one to participate in jihad. This is marked by the increasing trend in percentage in subsequent rows. Indeed this finding confirms a statement made to the author by an aspiring jihad participant. Asked why he was inclined to answer the call for jihad, he said, "I was very much influenced by my habit of reading Islamic newsmagazines such as *Sabili*."[46] It is therefore conceivable that when one subscribes and regularly reads Islamic media publications, especially those arousing the Muslim politico-religious sensitivity and sensibility, there is a higher likelihood that one will be inclined to participate in jihad. However straightforward this may seem, the pattern is far from perfect, as the middle column ("unsure/don't know") provides no clear indication of any neat, orderly patterns except that the percentages in the cells are more or less the same. It would thus be more meaningful if patterns of the overall crosstabulations were to be compared with ones involving measures under the dimension of religious affection namely religious sacrifice, self-sacrifice and solidarity. Figures 4.5, 4.6 and 4.7 below

---

[46] *Sabili* is a popular hard line politico-religious newsmagazine that is widely read by Muslims throughout Indonesia. The statement was made to the author by an anonymous interviewee on November 1, 2002, in Bandung. He is a university student from Central Java, and teaches Arabic in his spare time. He applied for jihad in Maluku but was rejected on health grounds, as he wore a pair of spectacles. In hindsight, he later explained, "I would not know what would become of me if I did really go." Nevertheless, he still reads *Sabili* on a weekly basis.

illustrate the relationship between the three measures and the variable on participation.

Figure 4.5: Crosstabulation between religious sacrifice and participation in jihad (valid *n*=735)

Religious Sacrifice	Participation in jihad			Total
	No	Unsure/ Don't know	Yes	
Strongly disagree/ Disagree	**19 (42.2%)**	13 (28.9%)	13 (28.9%)	45 (100%)
Indifferent/ Don't know	25 (15.0%)	**100 (59.9%)**	42 (25.1%)	167 (100%)
Agree/ Strongly agree	48 (9.2%)	187 (35.8%)	**288 (55.1%)**	523 (100%)
T o t a l	92 (12.5%)	300 (40.8%)	343 (46.7%)	735 (100%)

x^2 statistic: 84.429; *p*-value: .000

Figure 4.6: Crosstabulation between religious self-sacrifice and participation in jihad (valid *n*=735)

Religious self-sacrifice	Participation in jihad			Total
	No	Unsure/ Don't know	Yes	
Totally unwilling/ Unwilling	**13 (25.5%)**	17 (33.3%)	21 (41.2%)	51 (100%)
Unsure/ Don't know	41 (20.9%)	**115 (58.7%)**	40 (20.4%)	196 (100%)
Willing/ Totally willing	38 (7.8%)	168 (34.4%)	**282 (57.8%)**	488 (100%)
T o t a l	92 (12.5%)	300 (40.8%)	343 (46.7%)	735 (100%)

x^2 statistic: 89.747; *p*-value: .000

Figure 4.7: Crosstabulation between religious solidarity and participation in jihad (valid *n*=738)

Religious solidarity	Participation in jihad			Total
	No	Unsure/ Don't know	Yes	
Indifferent	**14 (46.7%)**	11 (36.7%)	5 (16.7%)	30 (100%)
Concerned	49 (16.4%)	**167 (56.0%)**	82 (27.5%)	298 (100%)
Very concerned	29 (7.1%)	123 (30.0%)	**258 (62.9%)**	410 (100%)
T o t a l	92 (12.5%)	301 (40.8%)	345 (46.7%)	738 (100%)

x^2 statistic: 122.656; *p*-value: .000

Simply using eyeballing technique, the persistence and consistency of the diagonal pattern of the shaded cells in all three crosstabulations reveal an unmistakable inference, which clears doubts about the effects of these measures on Indonesian Muslims' participation in jihad. It indicates that the more one approves of religious sacrifice and self-sacrifice, the more one is willing to participate in jihad. In the technical sense, the more one "agrees" to the notion of sacrifice and also "willing" to sacrifice oneself, the more likely it is for one to want to participate in jihad. Similarly, the more one displays solidarity (through statement of concern) with Muslims at large, the greater likelihood it is for one to be willing to participate in jihad. In short, the dimension on religious affection plays a significant role in determining Muslim participation in jihad, at least in the Indonesian context.

The next chapter will focus on the Iranian Muslims. A more or less similar structure for the chapter is imposed for the sake of fairness and easier comparison.[]

5

Revisiting
Revolutionary Iran

Following the discussion on the Indonesian Muslims, this chapter will now focus its attention on their counterparts in Iran. Similar topics of discussion brought forth in the previous chapter will be highlighted to enable us to draw comparisons between the two different Muslim communities. While the first section provides a brief elaboration on the ideology of Shia Islam and its role in the state, it will be followed by a discussion on the survey findings on the Iranian Muslims.

Shia Islam, many believe, was first established as a byproduct of the Islamic community's political crisis, which occurred right after the demise of Prophet Muhammad.[1] The leadership crisis surfaced following the deadlock concerning the pertinent issue of political succession. At that specific juncture, the pressing question was who had the right to replace Muhammad, the Messenger of God, as leader

---

[1] For an introductory exposition on the political history and evolution of Shia thought, see Moojan Momen, *An Introduction to Shi'i Islam: History and doctrines of Twelver Shi'ism* (New Haven: Yale University Press, 1985) and Syed Hussein M. Jafri, *The Origins and Early Development of Shi'a Islam* (Qum, Iran: Ansariyan Publication, undated).

of the *ummah*. For the Sunnis of course, the brief deliberation among the Prophet's companions held at Bani Saqifah and the subsequent appointment of Abu Bakar ash-Shadiq as caliph was a legitimate, if not necessary, political solution to resolve the vacuum of power. While the Shias (derived from *Shi'atu Ali* or Ali's party), the question was more of religious doctrinaire than political protest.[2] According to the proponents of Shia Islam, the Imams had already been 'appointed' by Allah and hinted accordingly by His Messenger. This connotes that Ali—undoubtedly part of the *Ahl al-Bayt* (People of Prophet's Household) and thus bearing the infallible quality—had more rights than anyone else to assume the task of leadership in the Islamic community. *Ahl al-Bayt* is a Quranic term, which refers to the Prophet's household.[3] Although controversy looms over who exactly are included and excluded in this exalted category, most Shia Muslims maintain that it does not incorporate the wives and companions of the Prophet. In addition, as Shia Muslims believe themselves to be the transmitters of the so-called *resaleh* (true Islamic message), it follows that Shiaism, in the eyes of the Imams, is the one and only straight path in Islam.

A large part of Shia Islam's political ideology rests on the politico-religious leadership of the infallible Imams. Correspondingly, the belief in the combined temporal and spiritual leadership embodied in the Imamate constitutes an essential article of faith in Shia Islam.[4] The Shia Muslims' doctrine on politico-religious leadership is said to be based on a Prophetic tradition, stipulating the requirement for all Muslims to minimally recognize and maximally pledge allegiance to the Imam of the time. The usual logic being extended has to do with the notion of comprehensiveness in Islam. The oft-cited reason is that Islam has provided everything that mankind will ever want and

---

[2] For a contending view on this issue, see Juan R.I. Cole and Nikki R. Keddie (editors), *Shi'ism and Social Protest* (New Haven, Connecticut: Yale University Press, 1986).

[3] For further reading, see commentaries on Quran 33:33.

[4] To learn more about the faith of Shia Islam, see for instance: Muhammad Rida al-Muzaffar, *The Faith of Shi'a Islam* (Qum, Iran: Ansariyan Publication, 1982); and Yann Richard, *Shi'ite Islam: Polity, ideology and creed* (translation) (Cambridge, Massachusetts: Blackwell, 1995).

need in terms of Divine guidance. For that matter, Shia Muslims maintain that it would be totally incomprehensible, if not illogical, for Allah to overlook the most important aspect in the development and management of the *ummah*, which relates to the principal leadership of the Islamic community. This is essentially where the divergence in political doctrines surfaces between the Sunnis and the Shias. As Algar (2001) puts it:

> [Shiis and Sunnis] differ in their theory of the succession, not merely in the identity of the successor, but also in the functions of the successor. The functions of the successor, the Imam, in Shi'i beliefs, include the authoritative explanation of the text of the Qur'an, the authoritative interpretation and even extension of the Islamic law, the guidance of the individual in his spiritual life in a fashion somewhat akin to the role of the *murshid* in Sufism, and the role of the sole legitimate leader of the entire Muslim community—the *ummah*.[5]

For most Iranians, they prescribe to *Itsna Asyariyah* or the Twelver form of Shia Islam, which alludes to their faith in the 12 infallible Imams, with Ali being the first one. The school of thought is also called the Ja'fari creed, as its followers prescribe to the jurisprudence developed and systematized by the sixth Shia Imam Ja'far ash-Shadiq. In Iran, Shia Ja'faris constitute around 90% of the country's aggregate number of Muslims. According to their belief, the last Imam, Muhammad al-Mahdi, is said to be hidden from the physical world, and is currently working in the spiritual plane in preparation to redeem the world one, last time. Contemporary Shia Muslims are thus living in the period of *entezar*, waiting for the Mahdi to resurface from his major occultation (*ghaybat al-kubra*) during which the world would be filled with justice, but only for a short period of time until the coming of the *Qiyamah* (Judgment Day). Meanwhile, the minor

---

[5] Hamid Algar, *Roots of the Islamic Revolution in Iran* (Oneonta, New York: Islamic Publications International, 2001), 14-15.

occultation (*ghaybat al-shughra*) supposedly took place more than ten centuries ago when the Mahdi opened channels of communications to his four trusted deputies. Following this line of thinking, Shia Muslims consider any and all worldly powers exercising power and authority "must *ipso facto* be illegitimate" until and unless proof is offered to indicate that they are executed "on behalf of the absent Imam".[6] In the mean time, while awaiting the re-advent of the Mahdi, Shia Muslims are obligated to defend what is known to be "*Islam-e vaqi'i*" (the essentially true Islam) with all means necessary whether minimally by way of *taqiye* (prudential dissimulation) or maximally by jihad. The strong conviction among the Shia Muslims in the re-advent of the Mahdi and the subsequent ultimate deliverance makes them seemingly more politically conscious and socially pro-active than their Sunni brethren. With such belief entrenched in their politico-religious consciousness, it is no wonder that Shia Muslims are less able to detach religion from politics.

In maintaining their ideology, Shia Muslims constantly reinvent tradition to instill a sense of heroism and mission in life, which revolves around the re-institutionalization of the Imamate. This tradition is maintained by the stirring up of emotions and the jolting of the hearts and minds of the believers. The custom found in many, if not all, Shia Muslim communities is *rauza* or the day of remembrance for Imam Hussein, the 'Prince of Martyrs', who occupies the third position in the politico-religious leadership chain of the Shia Imams. The *rauza* is an annual event commemorating the Karbala tragedy every tenth day of the Muslim month of Muharram, which is typically filled with recitations of elegiac verses to commemorate the martyrdom of Imam Hussein, son of Ali through the Prophet's daughter, Fatimah. In major cities of Iran, attendants of the *rauza* would often pour out onto the streets, parading their commiseration to Imam Hussein by self-flagellation. To this day, the political significance of the *rauza* cannot be underestimated, as was evidently proven to be a strong

---

[6] Algar, op. cit., 15.

mobilizing force during the 1978/1979 nationwide protests against the Shah of Iran.

According to Aghaie (2001), while the Karbala narrative "has served as one of the central sources for Shia symbols and rituals," the narrative itself has undergone a complex process of revisions affected by the sociopolitical transformation and "ending with a synthesis of a 'new' Karbala narrative".[7] The historical narrative of the *rauza* is set during the time of the notoriously crooked caliph Yazid bin Mu'awiyah of the Ummayah clan. The caliph, upon learning of Imam Hussein's ardent refusal to pledge allegiance to him, gave orders to persecute, and if need be kill, Imam Hussein, his family members and devoted followers. These orders were then executed, and resulted in the tragic drama that unfolded in the killing fields of Karbala (now Iraq),[8] leaving only a handful of Hussein's family members to tell others of their ordeal. Tragically, Hussein's head was decapitated, and later paraded like a trophy on the streets of Damascus. It is this hear-trending episode in the history of Islam that epitomizes the Shia Muslims' politico-religious thought, practice and ethos. The relentlessly emphatic remembrance of Imam Hussein henceforth provides not only the basic foundation for the Shia Muslims' appreciation of Islamic chivalry but a "self identification with Imam Hussein" in his "struggle for justice against the overwhelming powers of tyranny".[9]

As a consequence, Fischer (1980) argues that the life of Shia Muslims revolves around this "Karbala paradigm",[10] based on a popularly cited tradition that has long offered Shia Muslims a martyr's

---

[7] See Kamran Aghaie, "The Karbala Narrative: Shia political discourse in modern Iran in the 1960s and 1970s" in *Journal of Islamic Studies*, 12 (2) 2001: 151-176.

[8] From the perspective of Shia Muslims, the symbolism attached to Karbala can never be overrated. Even *turbahs*, a form of dried, carved up clays used for prostration in prayers, are more valuable if made from the clays of Karbala, as it is said to have been mixed with the blood of martyrs.

[9] Algar, op. cit., 16.

[10] See Michael M. J. Fischer, *Iran: From religious dispute to revolution* (Cambridge, Massachusetts: Harvard University Press, 1980).

ethos that reads: "Everyday is Ashura, and every land is Karbala".[11] Thus, similar to all Semitic religions, they regard martyrdom (*syahid*) or self-sacrifice for the sake of Islam as a genuine path to ultimate spiritual freedom and happiness in the Hereafter. Virtually all of the Shias' infallible Imams were martyred, either by way of assassination or food poisoning. This historicity has reinforced the imperative for Imam Mahdi's occultation as a means to prevent any harm imposed upon him by the enemies of Islam. Indeed, in Shia Islam, becoming a martyr captures the imagination of all those wishing to undertake the most desired form of religious observance.

In view of this backdrop, the Shia Muslims project the severe persecution against the *Ahl al-Bayt* as their own self-image. This is possibly one of the reasons why the tragedy of Imam Hussein is annually commemorated by the Shia Muslims around the world, including in some parts of Indonesia. In Pariaman, West Sumatra, the commemoration is known as "*tabui*", whereas in some parts of Aceh, the annual occasion is called "*Asan Osen*", a reference to the two venerable siblings i.e. Imams Hasan and Hussein. The next section discusses the place of Shia Islam in the state of Iran, which treads along the fine line between religion and politics.

Shia Islam and the State

Some scholars argue that Shia Islam "began partly as a protest".[12] Although to an extent true, the present author would only go as far as stating that protests, resistance, opposition, rebellion and revolution are all central to Shia Islam. Each of these politico-religious forms of collective action arguably represents a different Shia variant of *jehad-e Islam* (Islamic jihad), which precisely explains why laymen would perceive Shia Islam as a frenzied form of belief system. Even a large

---

[11] The tradition is attributed to Imam Ja'far ash-Shadiq, the great grandson of Imam Hussein, who was emphatically quoted as saying, "*Kullu yawmin ashura, wa kullu ardhin Karbala*".

[12] For instance, Cole and Keddie, op. cit., 4.

segment among their Sunni brethren considers Shia Islam doctrines and traditions as exceedingly filled with *bid'ah*, subjecting the Shia Muslim community to stereotyping, prejudice and religious discrimination. Such antipathy toward Shia Muslims and their supposedly heretical teachings are rampant in the mostly Sunni Arab Middle East, South Asia and the Malay archipelagos.[13] A cynical commentary in *Attadamon* (Solidarity), an Arab magazine, once describes a Shia Muslim as being a "mutineer by his very nature".[14] Furthermore:

> He is an uncapitalist antagonist. Opposition lurks in the essence of his faith and his thoughts. Perceiving himself as wronged in history, he is always ready to erupt or explode. His rights have been usurped; he may choose only between revolution and mutiny. It is said that the difference between a Shia and a Sunni is that the Sunni is born with his eyes on the throne, while the Shia is born with the Karbala complex gleaming in his eyes.[15]

Shia Islam was made into the official religion of Persia by the Safavid monarchy at the very turn of the 16th century. Echoing other scholars, Fischer (1980) argues that it was during the Safavids that "Shiaism was altered to be more nationalist and less universalist".[16] After more than four centuries, not only has Shia Islam stood the test of time as the country's official religion, but also evolved in many ways to become the essential basis for the state, governance and politics. The triumph of the 1979 Khomeini-led Islamic revolution in toppling Shahanshah Mohamed Reza Pahlevi gave further credence to Shia Muslims' notion on how the meek (or *mustadh'afin*, literally

---

[13] In Sunni-dominated Pakistan, violence against the minority Shia Muslim community is an almost weekly event involving the anti-Shia group known as Sepah-i Sahaba, often resulting in cycles of violence. In Malaysia, the Shia Islam ideology is formally banned. Meanwhile in Indonesia, efforts to ban Shia Islam have not been too successful, as the ideology remains influential, especially among Muslim intellectual circles and the traditionalist NU.

[14] Peter Theroux, *The Strange Disappearance of Imam Moussa Sadr* (London: Weidenfeld and Nicolson, 1987).

[15] Ibid, 9.

[16] See Fischer, op. cit., 29.

"the oppressed") would inherit the earth. It reinforced what Islamic traditional seminarians had said all along about how Allah favors them, and would grant the Kingdom of God in return for their perseverance and steadfastness.[17] Thus Iran was seen then—at least during the early days of the *mullahs'* victory over the autocratic monarchy—as being part of a Divine plan to regain Islam's stature in the world. While Cottam (1990) argues that "the revolution of Iran was one of the greatest populist explosions in human history",[18] others limit its effect only to the Muslim world. In an award winning article entitled "The Revolt of Islam: When did the conflict with the West begin, and how could it end?" in *The New Yorker* (published on November 19, 2001), Lewis maintains that Iran's Islamic revolution is "by far the most powerful and significant movement within the Islamic world for more than a century". For Ram (1997), Iran's Islamic revolution was a byproduct of the doctrine on "dynamic *entezar*", as a precursor to the second coming of the Mahdi.[19] Furthermore 'this "redeeming" role of the Islamic revolution was heralded by the Iranian leadership time and again'.[20] However, as far as the international community is concerned, the larger problem created by Khomeini relates to the contagion effect of the Islamic revolution. Hoveyda (2002) forthrightly contends that:

> [Khomeini] triggered in the Muslim world a new kind of aggressive militant Islamic fundamentalism and revived the idea of waging a jihad against the infidels ... Since Khomeini, terrorists have become bands of "believers" who devote their entire lives to the advancement of a cause. Such terrorists do not fear death: They have been taught

---

[17] Refer back to the section on "The mindset of militant Muslim" in Chapter 3.

[18] Richard Cottam, "Inside Revolutionary Iran" in R.K. Ramazani (editor), *Iran's Revolution: Search for consensus* (Bloomington, Indiana: Indiana University Press, 1990).

[19] Haggay Ram, "Exporting Iran's Islamic Revolution: Steering a path between pan-Islam and nationalism" in Bruce Maddy-Weitzman and Efraim Inbar (editors), *Religious Radicalism in the Greater Middle East* (London: Frank Cass, 1997).

[20] Ibid, 7.

that the sacrifice of their earthly existence will open for them the "gates of Paradise".[21]

Admittedly, the contagion effect of the Islamic revolution did enhance the standing of militant Muslims worldwide. However, to label all devout revolutionaries and militant Muslims "terrorists" is misleading, if not inaccurate, as their participation in politics does not necessarily entail violent or terror tactics. Green (1995), for instance, asserts, "Among the revolution's most notable characteristics was the fact that it was almost entirely peaceful".[22] In the eyes of Khomeini's followers, supporting, abetting and defending the revolution was a religious obligation not to be missed out, as it was equivalent to working in fulfillment of the interest of Islam. In effect, neglecting such obligation meant the dereliction of duty on their part *as* Muslims.[23] Thus if jihad were defined in the active sense of the word to mean struggle—and that participation is defined as an actor's attempt to change the polity—then the Islamic revolution of Iran would undoubtedly qualify as a form of collective action on the part of the Iranian revolutionaries. This would mean that participants who engage in street demonstrations, acts of civil disobedience and other forms of contentious politics against Pahlevi's monarchical state are amenable to jihad.

Another fallacy in Hoveyda's (2002) assessment is that Iranian 'terrorists' did not become instant "believers" because of Khomeini or the Islamic revolution. If the Assassins were anything to go by, then the Islamic revolutionaries were merely the permutated form of the earlier "religious terrorists".[24] But in no sense whatsoever did the revolution contribute to the sudden explosion in the number of terrorists

---

[21] Fereydoun Hoveyda, *The Broken Crescent: The "threat" of militant Islamic fundamentalism* (Westport, Connecticut: Praeger, 2002), 89-93.

[22] Jerold D. Green, "Terrorism and politics in Iran" in Martha Crenshaw (editor), *Terrorism in Context*, (University Park, Pennsylvania: Pennsylvania State University Press, 1995), 572.

[23] Refer back to Faraj's argument in his work entitled *Al-Faridah al-Ghaybah* in Jansen, op. cit.

[24] The term was adopted from Juergensmeyer, op. cit.

or terrorist activities worldwide. What is clear is that ever since the *mullahs* gained control of state affairs in Iran, the boundaries of politics turned abruptly expansive, encompassing the newfound policy on the exportation of the revolution, which undoubtedly contradicts the geopolitical interests of the American "Great Satan". As a result, the direction of Iran's foreign policy drastically changed from being a pro-American passivist under the Pahlevi regime to being an active supporter, helper and financier of various Islamic movements, most notably those in the Middle Eastern hemisphere. For Ayatollah Khomeini, "Iran's mission was about universal redemption—not the hell of economics and politics,"[25] denoting a political stance, which entailed the lending of generous support for the Hezbollah, the PLO (now PA), the Bosnians and the Chechens. Almost certainly, the *mullahs* also felt an urgent need to 'liberate' their neighboring brethren from Saddam Hussein and his ruthless Baathist party, which waged an eight-year (1980-1988) war—resulting in the death of more than one million people—against Iran. The so-called "Iraqi-imposed war" came about when Iraq unilaterally claimed sovereignty over a waterway called Shatt el-Arab or known in Iran as Arvand-Rood.

Of course, various facets of Iran's political activism at the regional and global front were expected in post-revolutionary Iran, especially with Khomeini at the helm of the republic as the *Fagheh*, which practically rendered him as the final arbiter on virtually all aspects of life in Iran. However, in spite of the mounting Islamic sentiment in Khomeini's Iran, the pride of Nationalism within the state had never exactly waned. The 'Iran for Iran' attitude apparently survived for the most part especially among the politically active segments of the population. Ram (1997) asserts:

> Islamic unity is thus defined as focusing on what all Muslims have in common—the Prophet of Islam, the Quran and the struggle against common enemies—*not* the merging of separate political entities or

---

[25] Daniel Brumberg, *Reinventing Khomeini: The struggle for reform in Iran* (Chicago: University of Chicago Press, 1997), 133.

the nullification of all distinctions among Muslims ... We see, then, that despite the *'ulama's* millenarianism and commitment to an Islamic world order, Nationalism has remained active in revolutionary Iran and continues as a major force in Iranian culture—its accommodation to religious teachings, notwithstanding.[26]

With the demise of Ayatollah Khomeini in 1989 and the rise to power of pragmatic leaders from among the clerical class, Iran's attitude toward international politics again shifted from being self-righteous, idealistic and assertive to a more engaging, approachable and compromising state. As an indicator, there are far less militant clergies calling for Muslims to put up armed struggle against the oppressors (*mustakbirin*) of the world. Such transformation represents the fact that "even when a revolutionary regime coming to power proves to be religion-based and initially nonconformist, its inability to change the system eventually forces it to reach an accommodation with the existing order."[27] The supposed revolutionary inertia was caused chiefly by the change in leadership, which subsequently led to questions of political accountability and legitimacy. The main challenge was associated with the towering figure of the exceedingly charismatic Khomeini, who became too much to bear for any successor to emulate. This somewhat created a psychological quandary to Khomeini's successor in terms of fulfilling the public's expectations and meeting the needs in terms of leadership of the Iranian clerical class.

The next problem touches upon the very foundation of the Iranian state or the concept of *Velayat-e Fagheh*. Apparently, when designing the foundation for the *hokumat-e Islami* (Islamic government) during his years of exile, Khomeini did not seem to mind that nobody except himself would suitably fit to occupy the immensely powerful office of the *Fagheh*. Evidently, neither Ayatollah Ali Khamenei nor

---

[26] In Maddy-Weitzman and Inbar, op. cit., 16.

[27] Anoushiravan Ehteshami, "Islamic Governance in Post-Khomeini Iran" in Abdel Salam Sidahmed and Anoushiravan Ehteshami, *Islamic Fundamentalism* (Boulder, Colorado: Westview Press, 1996), 150.

anyone else was suitable enough to don the oversized and heavy mantle of the late Ayatollah Khomeini. It was discovered that during the vetting period to find Khomeini's successor, a number of prominent and influential senior clerics including Ayatollah Shariat Madari and Ayatollah Ali Montazeri were short-listed. However, due to major differences of political opinions with Khomeini on some crucial aspects of Islamic governance, they were both dismissed. This evidently had led to the significant decline in the confidence that Iranians had in their leadership, leading them to believe that their system of government was far from being politically competitive. The condition was further exacerbated when the Islamic republic was seen to have failed to deliver economic development, triggering high rates of unemployment and cost of living, which in the end facilitated the increasing sociopolitical tensions in the already restless country. It also does not help that around three quarters of Iran's population comprise people below the age of 35. Obviously, the demographics does not lend much help to Iran's passionate revolutionaries, as the majority of the Iranians were either unborn at the time of the Islamic revolution or they were simply too young to reminisce about the wrongs committed by the *ancięn regime*. Thus the clash of ideals and competing visions of the state, largely emanating from the intergenerational gap that separates the old revolutionary guards and the *MTV*-oriented young cohorts, becomes almost unavoidable. Today, the young generation living in urban centers throughout Iran surreptitiously use banned satellite dishes to watch *MTV*, *HBO*, *CNN*, etc. Student activists and dissidents moreover make use of satellite technology to gain access to California-based Persian channels airing liberal, if not anti-government, views of the Iranian exiles in the U.S. and Europe.

The initial step toward reform took place when Hojjatoleslam Hashemi Rafsanjani assumed in the late 1980s the executive power as president of the republic. In his dealings with Khomeini, Rafsanjani laid out the groundwork for the expansion of the presidential power, while abolishing the prime minister's office, which he thought was a surplus to the requirements of the intended new republic.[28] The atmosphere of change came to a more dramatic turn when the reform-minded Mohammed Khatami came into office, after a landslide win in the 1997 general elections. During his tenure, president Khatami fought at the political front against the conservative segment of the Iranian society led essentially by Khamenei, who became the successor *Fagheh* after Khomeini's demise. Efforts by president Khatami and his supporters were primarily directed at limiting the power of the unelected *Fagheh*, who has veto powers on virtually any and every significant aspect confronted by the state and nation. With such inherited power, it no doubt gave Khamenei and his revolutionary followers much political leverage in setting the agenda for the nation, making reform an even more arduous task.

A prominent case involved a previously obscure history professor at the Tehran-based Teachers' Training College, Hashem Aghajeri. His case, extending all the way to Iran's Supreme Court and attracting international attention, sprung in mid 2002. It was sparked by Aghajeri's political speech at his left-wing party, the Organization for Islamic Mujahedeen of the Revolution, where he questioned why Iranians should blindly follow fallible religious leaders. Aghajeri's main defense was that the Iranian people are *not* "monkeys", who are obliged to follow orders unquestioningly. Aghajeri, who lost a leg in the Iran-Iraq war and an ardent supporter of Khatami, also called for "Islamic Protestantism", a recurring theme introduced to the Iranians by the revolutionary ideologue, Syariati. As a result, Aghajeri was condemned to death with subsidiary sentencing of an eight-year jail term, 74 lashes and a 10-year ban on teaching.[29] Indeed the sentencing of the professor did not sit well with the country's pro-democracy activists, who were increasingly frustrated with the slow progress of reforms promised by Khatami during his election campaigns. Undeniably,

---

[28] For more on the subject, see Anoushiravan Ehteshami, *After Khomeini: The Iranian second republic* (London: Routledge, 1995).

[29] "Iran sentences reformist to death for insult to Prophet Muhammad" in *New York Times*, published on November 8, 2002: 8.

Aghajeri's message was seen as a stake piercing through the heart of Iran's most sensitive political issue, which pertained to the legitimacy of clerical rule and specifically the incontestable authority of the *Fagheh*. After two years of legal battle, domestic fracas and international pressure, the death penalty was eventually revoked, and hard line conservatives had to concede after receiving a nod from Khamenei, who eventually saw the case as a self-defeating strategy on the part of the religious establishment.

Aghajeri's case somewhat revealed the quintessential predicament and vulnerability faced by a regime unwilling to bow to the dictates of the changing political realities. The fact remains that a great portion of the Iranian population demands real change, and aspires to have a genuinely lively political atmosphere in the country. The above-cited case is evidence that the majority of the Iranian population has become increasingly weary of the relentless revolutionary zeal that ultra conservative elements have been fruitlessly trying to instill. Even prior to the emergence of the Aghajeri case, Milani (2001) has hinted that what had actually been going on was "a debate of Islam against Islam ... where one Islam attempts to embrace modern ideas; [while] the other is confident that its Divine regulations transcend time and space".[30] This point takes us back to Watt's argument on the militant Muslims' perception of reality that has seemingly entrapped them in a state of "unchangingness",[31] driving some of them to resort to radical solutions.

Another twist to Iran's political fate occurred in mid 2005, when a university lecturer-turned-politician Mahmoud Ahmadinejad won the presidential elections. Ahmadinejad, the previously little known mayor of Tehran, for sure seems to know how to grab international media attention. Since becoming president on August 3, 2005, he has made international headline news for his bold statements about

---

[30] Mohsen Milani, "Reform and resistance in the Islamic Republic of Iran" in John L. Esposito and R. K. Ramazani, *Iran at the Crossroads* (New York: Palgrave, 2001), 29-56.

[31] Refer back to the section on "Religion as a tool of resistance" in Chapter 3.

the "myth" of the Jewish Holocaust as well as Iran's unyielding policy on the nuclear standoff. Predictably, Ahmadinejad's statements and policies have irked much of the Western powers, namely the U.S., Israel and its European allies. However, in contrast to the typical Western response,[32] Ahmadinejad's figure has drawn supporters, especially in Muslim countries, including Indonesia. Right or wrong, to many Muslims, Ahmadinejad symbolizes David, the ordinary-looking, yet righteous, Prophet going up against Goliath.

Iranian Mode of Jihad

The history of jihad in Shia Islam probably goes back to the first generation supporters of Imam Ali, whose fundamental task was to retrieve what they thought rightfully belonged to the *Ahl al-Bayt*, namely the Prophet's mantel of leadership over the *ummah*. Almost similar to the larger history of the *ummah*, the saga of Shia Islam is satiated with political dissension, discord and excesses. The earliest form of disintegration emerged when a splinter group was poised to turn Shia Islam into a cult-like movement to idolize Imam Ali. The so-called Al-Ghulat movement, however, was instantly eliminated by its supposed God reincarnate, Ali, himself for fear that the Muslim community would be swayed by the deviant teachings. "Al-Ghulat" itself literally means 'those who hyperbolize', referring to how some followers of Imam Ali went overboard in their love and devotion for their leader. Even after the purging of Al-Ghulat, schisms within the Shia Muslim community continued with some remaining to be active and influential such as the Ismaili and Zaydi sects.[33] One of the most violent groups, which used assassination and intimidation as a political tool was the Khawarij or Kharijites, once a powerful ally of Imam Ali.

---

[32] At the time of writing, three permanent members of the United Nations Security Council namely the U.S., Britain and France are pushing the political agenda for sanctioning Iran. However, two others, China and Russia, have rejected the proposal, while calling for further diplomacy and negotiations.

[33] The labeling of these groups is usually based on the name of the leaders, which members of the group consider as the 'rightful Imam'.

It was this group that broke the rank, mutinied and ultimately murdered the first Imam of Shia Islam.

Unfortunately, such extreme politico-religious behavior in Shia Islam persisted well into the 11th century when the reign of the so-called *Hashashin* (hence the English term, "Assassin") sprung into history. The legend pertaining to the Assassins, which incidentally started in the highlands of Iran, involved stories of young men and women engaging in Hashish smoking, political intrigue, lovemaking and murder-cum-suicide. The Assassins originated as a splinter group, an offshoot from the Ismaili sect of Shia Islam, led by a certain 'Old man of the mountain' bearing the name of Hassan-i Sabbah. Together with his disciples, Sabbah engaged in self-exile and excommunicated himself from mainstream society, building his own citadel on a hilltop. When undertaking operations, the group acted more like a modern-day hit squad, which engages in covert activities such as reconnaissance, infiltration and assassination of influential figures in the society. The *modus operandi* entailed a hit-and-run tactic, which was usually done by stabbing the victim in public while the perpetrator then disappears into the crowd. The weapon of choice was a traditional dagger, concealable beneath the perpetrators' robe.[34] As deviant as the sect may seem to be, members of the group perceive themselves, like all religious-inspired terrorists, as transformers of society supposedly working for the sake of Allah.

The allure of membership in the *Hashashin* entailed lavish indulgence in pure pleasure involving maidens, whose main task is to entertain the young men prior to any undertaking of mission. The sumptuous scheme was apparently devised by the 'Old man' intentionally to create, in the subconscious minds of the Assassins, the illusion of Paradise. This illusion was reinforced by the Quran, which guarantees the supply of virgins for the 'martyrs', effectively creating the 'rush' among the young recruits to their death. What came out of

---

[34] For further reading, see Bernard Lewis, *The Assassins: A radical sect in Islam* (New York: Octagon Books, 1980).

this legendary tradition was the emergence of various militant groups within Shia Islam, which tried to imitate the art of political persuasion from the Assassins. Green (1995) even went as far as to assert that the Assassins are "the precursors to modern terrorists".[35] For others, the Assassins' underground philosophy, secret hideouts and covert operations could have easily captured the imagination of those interested in going all the way to look for 3Gs (god, guns and guts). The first and foremost group that should be highlighted here is the Fedayeen-e Islam, which—like many Islamic groups worldwide—strove to uphold the *syariah*, and demanded the state to conform to Islamic principles. Its leader, Navab Safavi, was viewed largely as "a half-educated fanatic".[36] Established in 1946, the group comprised young Shia Muslim men willing to kill for their perceived notions of Islam. Like its historic predecessor, assassination became a common tool for the group to express its politico-religious ideals. The Fedayeen's activities reached its peak in the 1950s. The first victim of assassination was Ahmad Kasravi, a liberal poet and thinker, who was known to have rather outspoken attitude toward Shia Islam in general and the religious circles in particular. Kasravi was gunned down in execution style within the premises of the Ministry of Justice in Tehran. Apart from Kasravi, successful assassinations by the Fedayeen include: former Iranian prime ministers Abdel Hussein Hazhir, Ali Razamara and Hassan Mansur. Numerous other attempts were unsuccessful, contributing to the eventual demise of the Fedayeen.

Such a violent history cannot without doubt be overlooked. Though the Fedayeen may have relinquished its movement, its legacy still exists today. It has been said, with much reservation, that Safavi had, to an extent, influenced Khomeini. This is relatively difficult to confirm, especially if Khomeini's politico-religious thought, practice and ethos are used as a basis for evidence. Granted Khomeini viewed martyrdom as a "blessing", "secret of success" and "source of tran-

---

[35] Green in Crenshaw, op. cit., 554.

[36] Ibid, 561.

quility,"[37] and that such views coming from a leader of a nation was somewhat problematic, given the impression that the state itself condoned reactionary forms of political actions. Furthermore, Khomeini's self-styled leadership often annoyed secular Western states, which were predisposed to labeling Iran as a state that 'sponsors and harbors terrorists'.

During the height of the Islamic revolution, one of the pillar organizations ardently supporting Khomeini was a group known only as the Students Following the Line of Imam (Khomeini). With the young *tolabehs* (religious seminarians) and university students serving as its core members, SFLI's greatest exploit was the American Embassy hostage taking, which caused the biggest ever diplomatic rift between the U.S. and Iran, which still reverberates until today. Khomeini's tacit approval of the hostage taking, which lasted for 444 days but claimed no lives, also seemed to prove to the outside world how the Supreme Leader of Iran would defend the revolutionary interests *at all cost*. The episode also revealed how determined and desperate the Iranian militants were to prove American complicity in the 'crimes' committed by the Pahlevi regime. Although the hostage crisis did not result in any deaths, the precedence set in motion a political move by the U.S. to force Iran into the ranks of the pariah states alongside North Korea and Cuba, which the Bush administration has now labeled "the Axis of Evil".

A more recent militant group increasingly gaining prominence is the Ansar-e Hezbollah, an ultra rightwing group having branches in many provinces and cities throughout Iran. Its leader, Saeed Asgar, is a quintessential *agent provocatéur*. In 2000, Asgar attempted an assassination on a Tehran city councilor, Saeed Hajjarian, landing him in a two-year jail term, which he was only to serve half of his sentence. Although the group projects itself as being independent of the state, Ansar-e Hezbollah has been quietly supported by the *mullah* regime. This anti-reformist group essentially comprises militant Mus-

---

[37] Algar, op. cit., 161.

lims, who act as vigilantes and would go to all extent to defend the Islamic republic and its revolutionary ideals, even if it meant crossing the boundaries of Iran's (already Islamic) law. In parallel to Indonesia's FPI, Ansar-e Hezbollah often employs thugs to intimidate perceived enemies of Islam. A case in point emerged in mid 2003 when university students demonstrated nationwide for almost ten nights demanding the government to reform. During that time, students frequently demonstrated within the compounds of their universities or in the vicinity of their dormitories. However, instead of the usual "*Margbar Amrika!*" (Death to America!), they chanted "*Margbar Khamenei!*" (Death to Khamenei!) and "*Margbar Khatami!*" (Death to Khatami!), which signified the aggravation felt by the young generation toward the leadership and government.

In June 2003, as students of Daneshgha-e Tehran (Tehran University) spilled over onto the streets in front of the male dormitory demanding reform, plainclothes vigilantes belonging to the Ansar-e Hezbollah arrived at the dormitory with batons to take the law into their own hands. After arriving earlier at the scene to cordon off the busy area, the police arrested over 500 people, whom officials described as "enemies of the (Islamic) revolution".[38] At the time of the nationwide unrest, members of the Ansar-e Hezbollah also stormed Tehran's Allameh Tabataba'i University, and reportedly assaulted at least 80 students, and destroyed their properties. The government's official statement pertaining to the rioting was rather enigmatic. Speaker of the *Majlis* (Parliament) Mehdi Karoubi ascertained that there were "very few students among rioters".[39] While defending the *status quo*, Karoubi further stated, "The students you saw are the children of the Islamic revolution. They might have problems with certain officials or state institutions, but they do not have a problem with the Islamic

---

[38] "Official pledges use of force against troublemakers: 520 Arrested in Tehran unrest" in *Iran News* (Tehran), published on June 23, 2003: 3.

[39] "Karrubi says 'very few' students among rioters" in *Tehran Times* (Tehran), published on June 23, 2003: 2.

system."[40] However, such an explanation does not in any way expose the true "instigators" of the riots, which seemed to persistently point to "plainclothes men" working in the interests of "foreign elements".[41] The nationwide rioting was a tricky predicament for the establishment, which accused Washington of illicit involvement. The alleged U.S. involvement in the unrest apparently referred to the unremitting broadcast of Persian-language television channels based in Los Angeles, agitating Iranian middle class, who had access to satellite dishes, to hold demonstrations against the government. Analysts indeed saw the unrest as the latest visible signs of the crack within the Islamic regime and a strong measure of the declining popularity of the political ayatollahs. What is more, the fact that conservative elements within the government had used the Ansar-e Hezbollah to crush the student movement further dented the credibility of the administration and proved to some degree the government's inability to reposition itself amid the rising tide of reform. Although the rationale for the use of vigilante groups to undermine and attack political oppositions should hardly be surprising, it nevertheless demonstrated the fact that even an Islamic government, supposedly operating on religious and ethical principles, can be tempted to use oppressive, Machiavellian tactics.

Again, such method used against the perceived enemies of the state demonstrates how the culture of jihad still prevails in a state strongly bounded by historical and religious imperatives. In view of this, the logic follows that the armed forces, police, civil defense as well as the Pasdaran (Revolutionary Guards) can always be relied upon for the purposes of jihad in defense of the state from both foreign invasion and internal security disturbances. In addition to the traditional arms of the state, the Iranian government also sponsors a militia called the Basij. With an estimated membership of five million,

---

[40] "Information ministry, police to deal with instigators: Protesting students meet Karoubi" in *Iran Daily* (Tehran), published on June 23, 2003: 1-2.

[41] "Caution against foreign provocations: 166 MPs condemn plainclothes men" in ibid, 1.

the voluntary force consists of 1800 male "Ashura Battalions" and 400 female "Az-Zahra Battalions". Data derived from a confidential report on Iranian defense suggest that although Khamenei initially expected the volunteers to reach 10 million, only about half the targeted number of people signed up for the service. The final assessment of the report states that this fact may well be another indicator of the decreasing level of political support among the populace for the Islamic regime. The Basij operates within the boundaries of the formal system of the law, and acts as an early warning system against internal corruption of the Islamic state. Like the Pasdaran, the Basij is loyal to the Islamic revolutionary ideals and is under the full command of the *Rahbar*. Following the 2003 nationwide student unrest, the Basijis, anxious about the nation's instability and wanting to deter the 'enemies' of the Islamic republic, issued a statement "to renew their allegiance with the founder of the Islamic Revolution of Imam Khomeini, the martyrs, and the Commander in Chief of the Armed Forces (Ayatollah Ali Khamenei)".[42] They also "pledged to struggle to defend the sacred Islamic establishment and its achievements just like we do to save our lives, and will never cease this sacred battle even for one moment".[43]

The next section labors on the empirical findings based on the survey of Iranian Muslims, while attempting to establish the connection that ties demography, religiosity and jihad.

Participation in Jihad among Iranian Muslims

Using frequencies and valid percentages, Appendix 6 highlights the Iranian respondents' demographic characteristics and attributes. The small number of female respondents (18.7% out of the aggregate number of Iranian respondents) was largely due to refusal in participating in the survey, stemming most likely from the socio-cultural

---

[42] "Basijis pledge to protect Islamic system" in *Iran Daily* (Tehran), published on June 21, 2003: 1.

[43] Ibid.

and legal constraints related to the demarcation of gender, which is regulated by the Islamic law.[44]

The univariate data analysis on the dependent variable is provided in the Figure 5.1 below. It shows that a staggering 61% of the total 258 Iranian respondents indicated their willingness to participate in jihad, a figure that is significantly higher than the 49% of the Indonesian respondents.[45] A possible explanation for their high inclination to participate in jihad is that Iranian Muslims are more used to assertive politico-religious behavior than their Sunni brethren. For the former, the Shia Islam history and ideology supplies a strong reference point in determining their choices in regard to politico-religious actions. During the face-to-face interviews in Iran, it was predictably revealed that all respondents working as state security *apparatchiks* such as police officers, armed forces personnel and members associated with either the Pasdaran or Basij fervently stated their willingness to participate in jihad.

Figure 5.1: Iranian Muslims' level of willingness to participate in jihad (*n*=258)

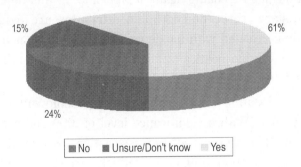

Meanwhile respondents who were unwilling amounted to 15%, and those who said "unsure/don't know" comprise 24% of the total

---

[44] While the interviewers in Iran happen to be all male, the survey was conducted on street pavements at city centers, further enhancing the possibility of rejection by female respondents.

[45] Refer back to Chapter 4.

number of respondents. Many of the respondents who answered "unsure/don't know" shared more or less the view that Muslims were only obliged to participate in jihad under the auspices of the Imam Mahdi as the Ultimate Redeemer. Some explained that in the absence of the Imam, only "defensive jihad" can be waged and not the offensive one. This latter group of respondents considered that both the Iraqi-imposed war and the 'looming' American invasion would qualify for a call for defensive jihad. Meanwhile, respondents who declined to participate clearly mentioned their dislike toward either the current administration of the establishment as a whole. Most of these respondents who opted for non-participation were unconvinced about the government's insistence on the infallibility of the Islamic regime. They argued that jihad was only intended for the purposes of defending or furthering the interest of *Islam-e vaqi'i.* Sounding the collective sentiment, one respondent said, "What the government is promoting is *not* actually the true form of Islam."

As in the Indonesian survey, demographic characteristics will now be analyzed against the respondents' level of willingness to participate in jihad. Looking again at Appendix 2, this time under the "Iran" category, three demographic attributes are evidently and significantly correlated with the dependent variable i.e. marital status, educational level and political affiliation. Each of these attributes will be analyzed below using crosstabulations.

On marital status, it is clear that its relationship with participation is a positive one. With a significance level of .009 and a contingency coefficient of .187, the measure of association between one's marital status and participation in jihad is relatively strong. Figure 5.2 informs us that respondents who are either married or divorced with dependent(s) are more likely to participate in jihad (71.1%) than those who are single (52.6%). This is somewhat counter intuitive, as it would be expected that an individual having a spouse and dependent(s) would be less inclined to participate in jihad, considering the risks involved in such decision and the burden that one would impose on the family should any fateful tragedy occurs as a result of their participation. Another interesting fact, still in relation to marital status, is that single respondents are more likely (28.5%) to say "no" to the question on willingness to participate in jihad, as opposed to others who are married or divorced with dependent(s) (18.2%). A possible explanation for this phenomenon is due to religious emotional maturity, which supposedly is brought forth by the responsibility borne out of marriage.

Figure 5.2: Crosstabulation between marital status and participation in jihad (valid n=258)

Marital status	Participation in jihad			Total
	No	Unsure/ Don't know	Yes	
Not married	39 (28.5%)	26 (19.0%)	72 (52.6%)	137 (100%)
Married/Divorced with dependent(s)	22 (18.2%)	13 (10.7%)	86 (71.1%)	121 (100%)

x^2 statistic: 9.355; p-value: .009

Figure 5.3 underlines the relationship between educational level and participation. The p-value of .003 level indicates a significant relationship between the two variables. Unlike the case in Indonesia, where educational level is *not* significantly correlated with participation, the Iranian sample data informs us otherwise. According to the matrix of correlations in Appendix 2, the measure of association between education and participation stands at -.170 (*Kendall tau-b* coefficient). The negative notation of the coefficient, in principle, denotes a negative relationship i.e. the decrease of something denotes the increase of something else, and vice versa. Here, the pattern of relationship can be seen through the directions of the arrows under the "no" and "yes" columns. As expected, the arrow in the "no" column informs us that there is a tendency for the highly educated respondents to state their unwillingness to participate in jihad, with the highest valid percentage located at the bottom, far left cell. In the mean time, the less educated one is, the greater the likelihood is for one to be willing to participate in jihad (see the "yes" column). In this respect, educational level may help us to better understand who among Iranian Muslims would be more likely to participate in jihad. This finding obviously contradicts the Indonesia case, which saw educational level being significantly uncorrelated to participation. In sum, if education is associated with one's measure of cool-headedness (and therefore rationality), our intuition has served us right, at least in the case of Iran, that the promotion of education would predictably decrease the likelihood of one's tendency to participate in jihad.

Figure 5.3: Crosstabulation between educational level and participation in jihad (valid *n*=255)

Educational Level	Participation in jihad			Total
	No	Unsure/ Don't know	Yes	
Low (no school-primary school)	1 (6.3%)	2 (12.5%)	13 (81.3%)	16 (100%)
Medium (secondary-high schools)	23 (18.9%)	17 (13.9%)	82 (67.2%)	122 (100%)
High (polytechnic/ academy/ university)	35 (29.9%)	20 (17.1%)	62 (53.0%)	117 (100%)

x^2 statistic: 8.776; *p*-value: .003

Figure 5.4: Crosstabulation between political affiliation and participation in jihad (valid *n*=256)

Political affiliation	Participation in jihad			Total
	No	Unsure/ Don't know	Yes	
Unaffiliated	60 (23.9%)	39 (15.5%)	152 (60.6%)	251 (100%)
Affiliated	0 (00.0%)	0 (00.0%)	5 (100%)	5 (100%)

x^2statistic: 3.216; *p*-value: .023

Meanwhile Figure 5.4 above brings to light the association between political affiliation and participation. Although the sample merely netted five politically affiliated Muslim respondents (or those who confessed to being politically affiliated), it confirms the previous findings in Indonesia that the level of political consciousness may have some bearing to one's willingness or unwillingness to participate in jihad. Technically speaking, 100% of the politically affiliated respondents stated their willingness to participate in jihad. However, due to the minutiae number of those claiming to be politically affiliated, the finding is hardly decisive, as there are no variations in the lower row of the crosstabulation. Interestingly, although the survey was conducted in city centers, only five Iranians claim to have some form of political affiliation. The clearest possible reason that may contribute to this phenomenon may relate to the earlier discussion on revolutionary inertia, which has turned citizens to become apathetic toward the whole business of politics in the country. Another explanation may relate to the suspicious minds of the Iranian respondents, who may have some level of distrust toward the survey and/or interviewers, making them reluctant to tell the truth about their political affiliation.

Based on casual conversations held with ordinary Iranians on the streets, there seemed to be a perception that the state has become increasingly intransigent, especially during the tense period following the U.S.' invasion and subsequent occupation of Afghanistan and

Iraq, two countries directly bordering Iran. It is also apparent that Iranians have become somewhat disheartened by the stifling political system, which has done little in sociopolitical and economic reforms. Anxiety and mistrust toward the government are conceivably on the rise, especially after the 2003 nationwide unrest. As an illustration, upon my arrival in Iran, a student of politics in Daneshgha-e Tehran cautioned me on this matter. He explained, "There are a lot of spies everywhere. Some people say they are *against* the state, but in actual fact, they are *with* the state. I cannot trust anybody nowadays."[46] Indeed such an environment would inadvertently breed the culture of fear. Thus, while Iranian Muslims are innately and consciously political, the ordinary people on the streets today are probably more suspicious than excited at being asked about their political views and inclinations, especially by a *khareji*. Otherwise, a higher level of political affiliation would have been at play.

Religiosity and Jihad in Iran

This section discusses the relationship between religiosity and participation in jihad. As elaborated in the earlier section of this chapter, Islam is a fact of life in Iran and cannot be detached from its politics. Compared to other Muslims living in 'secular' states, Iranian Muslims should logically find it much easier to observe their religion, and maintain, if not increase, their level of religiosity. This is due to the constant promotion and propagation of Islam by the state. Appendix 6 provides descriptive statistics on the level of religiosity among Iranian Muslim respondents. This is done by dissecting the variable on religiosity while establishing various measures to see the overall picture of Islamic religiosity in Iran.

Analyzing the measure of religiosity against the dependent variable using the matrix of correlations, one should consult Appendix 3.

---

[46] A statement made to the author during a conversation within the compounds of Tehran University in late May 2003. Later in the day, I was fortunate to be introduced to one of the grandsons of the late Ayatollah Khomeini, who happened to be studying in the same Faculty of Law and Political Sciences.

Out of the 12 measures of religiosity, nine are significantly correlated (having p-values of d".009) with participation. They include: informal Islamic studies, Quranic recitation, books read, religious exposure, daily prayers, visits to place(s) of worship, religious sacrifice, self-sacrifice and solidarity. A close observation of the *Kendall tau-b* coefficients of the nine measures indicates that those higher than .300 (denoting strong measures of association)[47] would only include: religious exposure (.325), daily prayers (.379), religious sacrifice (.513), self-sacrifice (.564) and solidarity (.436). Again, examining the relationship between these measures of religiosity and participation in jihad using crosstabulations will hopefully bring about a much clearer pattern.

Figure 5.5: Crosstabulation between religious exposure and participation in jihad (valid n=248)

Religious exposure	Participation in jihad			Total
	No	Unsure/ Don't know	Yes	
Never	50 (40.3%)	17 (13.7%)	57 (46.0%)	124 (100%)
Medium (< 2 hours)	5 (10.4%)	8 (16.7%)	35 (72.9%)	48 (100%)
High (>1 hours)	4 (5.3%)	12 (15.8%)	60 (78.9%)	76 (100%)

x^2 statistic: 38.753; p-value: .000

The crosstabulation provided in Figure 5.5 above is relatively self understood. As depicted by the directions of the two arrows, it is apparent that a clear relationship is at play between religious exposure and participation in jihad. Being an Islamic state, it should not be surprising at all to find how Muslims' exposure to religious messages and propagation can affect their attitude toward jihad. Ever since the triumph of the revolution, Iranian press, more so the

---

[47] Although the determination on the threshold of the coefficients may seem arbitrary (Indonesia's case was .200), it is nevertheless based on common sense and comparative valuation of the different measures of religiosity.

broadcasting media, have found it difficult to report on anything deemed by the government to be against the interests of the state, Islam and the *ummah*. In view of that, there is a very thin line that divides the true Islamic messages from government propaganda. As an example, poem recitation of the likes of Saadi's *Golestan* (Rose Garden)[48] may be voiced over a documentary clip of the late Khomeini leading prayers before his followers or giving speeches to an attentive audience on the virtues of the Islamic republic. In such an instance, it is really hard to judge whether or not such programs are religious, as the subliminal message is clear and the political psychological implications are fairly obvious. Notwithstanding, the crosstabulation, as depicted in Figure 5.5, indicates a strong relationship between religious exposure and participation in jihad, which means that the more one is exposed to religious messages, the more one is inclined to participate in jihad. The reverse is also true. The less religious propagation one regularly receives, the less likely one would be willing to participate in jihad.

Figure 5.6: Crosstabulation between daily prayers and participation in jihad (valid *n*=257)

Daily Prayers	Participation in jihad			Total
	No	Unsure/ Don't know	Yes	
Never/hardly	23 (79.3%)	1 (3.4%)	5 (17.2%)	29 (100%)
At least once	37 (16.2%)	38 (16.7%)	153 (67.1%)	228 (100%)

x^2 statistic: 57.220; *p*-value: .000

Figure 5.6 above tests the relationship between daily prayers and participation. The assumption is that daily prayers affects Muslim

---

[48] The masterpiece was created by Syaikh Musleh al-Din Sa'adi Shirazi, a 13th century Persian love poet and mystic from Shiraz. The masterpiece is one of the monumental products of Persia's rich mystical tradition.

participation in jihad. According to Islamic legal doctrines, daily prayers are considered as a pillar of the faith ("*imad ad-din*"), distinguishing a Muslim from an infidel. Hence, daily prayers often serve as a religious partition and ultimately the pinnacle of Islamic ritual practices. If a Muslim does not conduct the daily prayers, then he or she may not justifiably be called a true believer. From the above crosstabulation and the matrix of correlations as depicted in Appendix 3, it can be asserted that daily prayers do have a relatively strong measure of association with one's willingness to participate in jihad. Simply put, one who prays daily is more likely to participate than those who do not. When the issue of congregational prayers such as the *nemaz-e jum'eh* (Friday prayers) is taken into consideration, the relationship would expectedly be further enhanced due to its multiplier effects. As can be observed weekly through Iranian media, the *nemaz-e jum'eh* serves not only to aggrandize the regime and its accomplishment, but also to instill the values and perspectives of militant Islam. One of the main features before the actual prayer entails a politico-religious sermon, which would intermittently be followed by the chest-beating congregation chanting "*Margbar Amrika!*"

Figures 5.7, 5.8 and 5.9 essentially showcase the measure of association between religious affection and participation. They delve into issues pertaining to religious sacrifice, self-sacrifice and solidarity, and measure their association with participation in jihad. Out of the three crosstabulations under the dimension of religious affection, only self-sacrifice (Figure 5.8) shares the similar shaded diagonal pattern, which, like the Indonesian case, means that willingness to sacrifice one self denotes the propensity to also participate in jihad. Although seemingly tautological, it should be noted here that jihad is defined as armed struggle, which does not automatically, or even necessarily, correspond to any form of self-sacrifice.

Figure 5.7: Crosstabulation between religious sacrifice and participation in jihad (valid *n*=254)

Religious Sacrifice	Participation in jihad			Total
	No	Unsure/ Don't know	Yes	
Strongly disagree/ Disagree	**31 (72.1%)**	2 (4.7%)	10 (23.3%)	43 (100%)
Indifferent/ Don't know	14 (31.1%)	15 (33.3%)	**16 (35.6%)**	45 (100%)
Agree/ Strongly agree	13 (7.8%)	21 (12.7%)	**132 (79.5%)**	166 (100%)
T o t a l	58 (22.8%)	38 (15.0%)	158 (62.2%)	254 (100%)

x^2 statistic: 100.829; *p*-value: .000

Figure 5.8: Crosstabulation between religious self-sacrifice and participation in jihad (valid *n*=251)

Religious self-sacrifice	Participation in jihad			Total
	No	Unsure/ Don't know	Yes	
Totally unwilling/ Unwilling	**38 (70.4%)**	4 (7.4%)	12 (22.2%)	54 (100%)
Unsure/ Don't know	8 (29.6%)	**11 (40.7%)**	8 (29.6%)	27 (100%)
Willing/ Totally willing	11 (6.5%)	22 (12.9%)	**137 (80.6%)**	170 (100%)
T o t a l	57 (22.7%)	37 (14.7%)	157 (62.5%)	251 (100%)

x^2 statistic: 116.612; *p*-value: .000

Figure 5.9: Crosstabulation between religious solidarity and participation in jihad (valid *n*=257)

Religious Solidarity	Participation in jihad			Total
	No	Unsure/ Don't know	Yes	
Indifferent	**38 (58.5%)**	7 (10.8%)	20 (30.8%)	65 (100%)
Concerned	23 (15.1%)	30 (19.7%)	**99 (65.1%)**	152 (100%)
Very concerned	0 (0.0%)	2 (5.0%)	**38 (95.0%)**	40 (100%)
T o t a l	61 (23.7%)	39 (15.2%)	157 (61.1%)	257 (100%)

x^2 statistic: 70.621; *p*-value: .000

Granted the contemporary form of jihad has employed suicide bombing, but the jihad repertoire comprise more than just self-sacrificing modes of struggle. As explained at considerable length in Chapter 3, jihad can take numerous politico-religious forms of collective action. What is more, having to carry the burden of the "Karbala complex",[49] self-sacrifice to a militant Shia Muslim may indeed be second nature, which in turn further reinforces their "self identification with Imam Hussein".[50] Interestingly, data suggests that this identification does not go beyond the self, as evidently proven in the case concerning religious sacrifice in Figure 5.7. The ambiguity lies in the non-diagonal pattern of the shaded cells on the crosstabulation (specifically regarding the cell located at second row under the "yes" column). The question to pose here is why some would be willing to participate in jihad but be simultaneously "indifferent" toward the sacrifice by their brethren for the defense of Islam and/or Muslims. The plausible answer to this may be associated with the Shia Muslims' disapproval over the contemporary utilization of jihad by Bin Laden's

---

[49] Refer back to the section on "Political Ideology of Shia Islam" in the beginning of this chapter.

[50] Algar, op. cit.

Al-Qaidah and the likes of other Sunni militant groups. Hence, although mainstream Shia Muslims may conceivably share the motives behind such extreme exploit, their politico-religious mindset is difficult to be diverted from the redemption that would be ultimately delivered by the Mahdi. Furthermore, in situations where power relations are exceedingly lopsided and Muslims have no rational means to attain victory, Shia Islam permits, if not urges, its followers to resort to *taqiye* for the sake of survival. This, according to one Iranian survey respondent, would thus constitute "*siyaasi-e vaqi'i*" (true politics). Such logic suggests that to agree on the sacrifice of others would be almost tantamount to endorsing the actions of others, which in fact may be harmful to the general interest of Muslims at large. Thus, the seemingly 'misplaced' shaded cell may well explain this ambiguity.

An almost similar ambiguity applies to Figure 5.9. Like Figure 5.7, the shaded cells on the crosstabulation do not form the expected diagonal pattern, as in all the Indonesian crosstabulations on religious affection.[51] For many Iranian respondents, the question on religious solidarity mentioning "the plight of Muslims of Palestine, Bosnia and Iraq" was decidedly problematic.[52] According to them, the question on Iraq should have been separated, as it posed a major reservation on their part. While epitomizing the politico-religious sentiment of many Iranians, one respondent in Tehran said unabashedly, "Let the Iraqis suffer under the Americans. They waged war on us for eight whole years! They surely had it coming." Although the sentiment may seem overly nationalistic and therefore 'unIslamic', the allusion is unambiguous. The Iranian Muslims' sense of solidarity failed to overcome their Nationalism, especially when it comes to their longtime archenemy and competitor.

Chapter 6 will subsequently deal with the larger picture on how religiosity affects Muslim participation in jihad. Based on the aggregate dataset, it will also highlight the theoretical implications of this study.[]

---

[51] Refer back to the section in Chapter 4 on "Religiosity and Jihad".

[52] See the whole wording and coding in Appendix 1A on "Religious solidarity" (Question t).

6

Comparing
Islamic Religiosity,
Political Expression
and Jihad

This chapter delves into comparative religiosity in Islam, political expression and their relationship with jihad. The first section consists of descriptive analyses and statistical inferences on the aggregate Muslim sample. This will be followed by the different aspects of Islamic religiosity practiced in the two communities under investigation. The second part details the evidence on how religious affection—denoting identity, affinity, solidarity and sense of attachment to the *ummah*—, constitutes the most significant among the three dimensions in affecting Muslim participation in jihad.

Analyzing Aggregate Data

As done in Chapters 4 and 5, demography will be measured against participation in jihad. As can be viewed from Appendix 8, the demographic characteristics of the aggregate sample is a combined dataset gathered from Indonesia and Iran. Looking at the aggregate dataset, the matrix of correlations between demographic and participation variables shows that gender, employment status and political affiliation are significantly correlated (within the $p \leq .05$ level) with participation in jihad.[1] However, coefficients of demography—standing merely above .080—reveal that the strength of association between these factors and the participation variable is fairly weak.

To begin with, gender and participation variables do significantly correlate (with p-value at .038). However, there seemed to be very little indication of gender bias when it comes to Muslim participation in jihad, as indicated in the 15.8% of females, compared to the 15.1% of males, who were unwilling to participate. Furthermore, female respondents willing to participate in jihad stood a little lower (at 45.8%) than their male counterparts (at 53.6%). This slight discrepancy along with its coefficient value of .081 has led me to infer that although gender matters, its measure of association with participation is weak. This can only mean that in terms of willingness to participate in jihad, the variable on gender does not affect much of the outcome. However, when the variable is measured against participation, using the dichotomous variable on nationality as an interaction effect, gender becomes insignificant.

Figure 6.1: Crosstabulation between employment status and participation in jihad (valid N=995)

Employment Status	Participation in jihad			Total
	No	Unsure/ Don't know	Yes	
Unemployed	53 (13.0%)	158 (38.6%)	198 (48.4%)	409 (100%)
Employed/ Self-employed	100 (17.1%)	181 (30.9%)	305 (52.0%)	586 (100%)

x^2 statistic: 7.511; p-value: .023

The same goes with employment status in which the weakness of the measure of association is illustrated by Figure 6.1. With a

---

[1] See Appendix 2 under the "Aggregate" column.

coefficient value of .087, inference can be derived to show that partici-pation in jihad is not much affected by whether one is employed or not. Although differences are noticeable in the figures of the valid percentages, hardly any lucid pattern can be configured. This is rather counter intuitive, as one tends to think that having a steady job, and therefore income, would suffice to deter a person from participating in any high-risk form of collective action. Yet, empirical evidence suggests otherwise.

In addition, the same inference is also obtained by analyzing the correlations between political affiliation and participation in jihad. Here, a person's level of political awareness and activism is significantly correlated with his or her level of willingness to participate in jihad. Again, however, looking at the coefficient value of .082 (with a p-value=.036) the strength of association is no doubt a weak one. A likely explanation for this may lie in the intrinsic nature of jihad being a political form of collective action based on religious grounds. Hence, political activists such as those involved in pushing for reforms in both Indonesia and Iran, who may not necessarily have any substantial religious incli-nations, would most probably think twice before participating in jihad. In fact, it is conceivable that jihad may not have crossed their minds at all or simply is not even a personal option. An alternative rational explanation is that jihad involves considerable risks to the activists, resulting in the participants to opt for less riskier, more legitimate forms of collective action such as joining a political party or participating in street rallies.

This suggests that demographic factors do to some degree affect Muslim participation in jihad. However, as indicated in the analyses on gender, employment status and political affiliation, the effects of these measures are not strong. Given these findings, one can safely conclude that SES only remotely determines Muslim participation in jihad, undermining previous studies that place too much emphasis on the relationship between SES and participation. Thus, this brings us to another possible determination that may help explain Muslim participation in jihad, which is religiosity.

Dimensions of Islamic Religiosity and Participation in Jihad

Does the level of a person's religiosity matters when considering whether or not to participate in jihad? If so, to what extent can religiosity be measured? Can it be a strong predictor to one's willingness or unwillingness to participate in a politico-religious form of collective action? Then what aspect of religiosity mostly determines the outcome of participation? These are just some of the questions that I will later address. As explained in the very beginning of Chapter 1, Islamic religiosity in this study is essentially measured on the basis of three religious dimensions familiar to all Muslims: religious knowledge, ritual practices and religious affection.[2] Appendix 9 portrays the religious characteristics and attributes of the aggregate sample.

Looking at the aggregate dataset, the level of religiosity among Muslims in Indonesia and Iran seems relatively high, despite (or because of) the current hostile sociopolitical circumstances that emanated from the September 11 tragedy and the subsequent worldwide war on terrorism. Here, the comparative analyses between Indonesia and Iran would hopefully avoid any and all variants of essentialism. "This strategy," according to Cole (1992), "clarifies the manner in which we are confronted not with a monolithic phenomenon, Islam, but with a range of exceedingly diverse societies in which a variety of peoples has adopted a Muslim identity through editing the Great Tradition and combining it with elements of local traditions."[3] One obvious similarity between Indonesia and Iran lies in the very fact that they are Muslim countries having over 85% of their populations professing Islam. The other corresponding fact is that the two states and societies are at a somewhat similar level of development with both

---

[2] Refer to Chapter 1 on the sampling survey and Appendices 1A, 1B and 1C on the survey questionnaire's wording and coding.

[3] Juan R. I. Cole, *Comparing Muslim Societies: Knowledge and the state in a world civilization* (Ann Arbor, Michigan: University of Michigan Press, 1992), Introduction.

still coming to grips with modernization and all their excesses. Lastly, due to their richness in natural resources and strategic geopolitical location, Indonesia and Iran have had their share of being colonized and subjugated for centuries by foreign powers, which often provide significant contextual nuances to their prevailing mode of politico-religious thought, practice and ethos.

Figure 6.2: Comparison between Indonesia and Iran

	Indonesia	Iran
Geographic location	Southeast Asia	Middle East
System of government	Quasi-Secular Republic	Theocratic Republic
Leadership structure	President	Spiritual Leader & President
Legal system	Based on Roman-Dutch Law	Islamic Constitution based on Ja'fari creed
Aggregate population	218 million	66 million
Muslim population	87%	98%
Major school of thought	Sunni	Shia

Apart from the above-mentioned linkages, however, the two countries probably have more differences than similarities. The contrast can perhaps be best viewed from Figure 6.2. Beyond the formal distinctions shown in the table above, sociopolitical and cultural differentials also exist when analyzing the two states and societies, making the task of comparison more intriguing. A primary consideration that must be taken seriously into consideration and also tied to the subject matter of this study encompasses the differentiation between the Sunni and Shia Muslims. The distinction, as elaborated in earlier chapters, provides the very basis for the divergence in the Muslims' political thought, practice and ethos. As a consequence, their attitude toward jihad becomes understandably dissimilar.

Figure 6.3: Column chart on aggregate frequencies and valid percentages of Muslim participation in jihad (N=996)

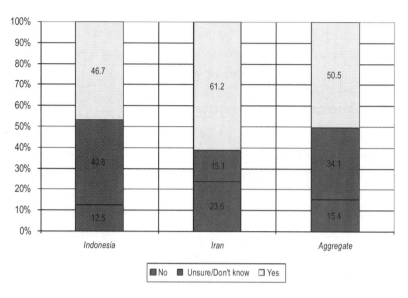

Question: Would you be willing to participate in jihad?

x^2 statistic: 60.399; p-value: .000

Figure 6.3 above shows that more than half of the aggregate Muslim respondents (50.5%) stated their willingness to participate in jihad. For the Indonesians, although the 46.7% said "ya", the percentage figure did not differ much from those conveying their indecisiveness (40.8%). As for the Iranian survey, while most respondents (61.2%) answered "*baleh*", the number of those who were unwilling to participate is comparatively higher than that of the Indonesians (by 11.1%). From the above, one can confirm the existence of a high level of willingness among Muslims in Indonesia (46.7%) and Iran (61.2) to participate in jihad. The p-value of .000 denotes that nationality does matter when considering the variation in the responses between respondents in Indonesia and Iran. The substantial variation in the figures between Indonesia and Iran (within a margin of 14.5%) can be explained by a number of reasons. *First*, Indonesia is geographically distant from the Middle East, which has been the epicenter of conflict with the West. To some degree, the geographic fragmentation of the *ummah* may play an offsetting role in fostering Islamic religious affection among Muslims. A survey respondent from Bandung, Indonesia, for instance, commented on the question pertaining to religious solidarity by saying, "Why should we bother too much about the things going on over there [in the Middle East]? We have enough problems of our own in Indonesia." Echoing a similar sentiment in Iran, he went further by stating his willingness to participate in jihad "only if the U.S. were to invade Indonesia".[4] What this may entail is that geographical interconnectedness plays a role in determining the level of Muslim consciousness in relation to 'the sacred Muslim land', as discussed in Chapter 3. Although many Indonesians may find it hard to conceive any of their state territory as being part of the larger sacred land, the reverse perception exists in the subconscious mind of a Middle Easterner, who considers Mecca, Medina and Jerusalem as the holiest cities in Islam. Notably, at least two million pilgrims from all corners of the world converge annually in Mecca and Medina. As for the Iranian Shia Muslims, the role of land sacredness is more complex because the land they see as holy has expanded over the centuries to include more contemporary *harams* (forbidden places) such as Mahshad and Qum. It is worth noting that Shia Muslims hold Najaf and Karbala (in Iraq) also their main holy sites, which Iranian pilgrims frequently visit.

Second, a major political disparity is at play between Indonesia and Iran in terms of state sponsorship of jihad. Being a quasi-secular state, Indonesia formally considers participation in jihad within the country as extra judicial. As former president Wahid once cynically lamented, "I do not necessarily care if they want jihad or *jahit* (to sew). However, any activity that threatens the security of the state must be dealt with accordingly."[5] The statement was an apparent attempt

---

[4] Interview conducted with respondent on November 1, 2002.

[5] "Siapa suruh datang ke Ambon" [Who told you to come to Ambon] in *Gatra* (Jakarta), published on January 22, 2000: 26.

to deter Muslims from undertaking jihad to Maluku, where religious, sectarian violence had erupted, resulting in the breakdown of civil order and the partitioning of the local communities. In reality, thousands of Muslims did participate in jihad in places such as Maluku and Poso. This phenomenon, however, must not quickly be dismissed as political acquisience on the part of the state or the reformed government. Rather, it merely displayed the state's failure in upholding the rule of law. As explained in Chapter 4, one of the causes for this failure has been the liberalizing effects of *reformasi* in which much of the power and authority, including in the field of domestic law and order, has been relinquished from the military.

Contrary to the Indonesian case, the Iranian state has the Islamic Constitution on its side to mobilize citizens in the waging of jihad, whether within the country (to root out "internal corruption of the system") or abroad (to "export the revolution" and strive against "oppressive" regimes). In spite of this, for jihad to be effective, the call must be sanctioned by way of the issuance of a *fatwa* by the *Rahbar* as the country's final arbiter. As one business manager working for a Tehran-based political journal puts it, "If the *Rahbar* issues a *fatwa* on jihad, then every Shia Muslim should ideally follow."[6] Of course, in Indonesia, such conferment by the head of state (to promote and wage a jihad) would be almost inconceivable, if not next to impossible. What is conceivable post-*reformasi*, which has occurred on a number of occasions, is if the MUI—being the country's highest authority over Islamic religious affairs—, would sanction the waging of jihad either to Palestine, Afghanistan or Iraq. Although elements within the MUI did support jihad in Maluku and Poso, the *fatwa* never came to fully represent the influential body.

Third, due to the differentiation in politico-religious thought, practice and ethos, Muslim devotees in Indonesia and Iran have shown distinctive levels of participation in jihad. What can be genereally inferred from the dataset is that Indonesian Muslims are less assertive than

---

[6] Based on a conversation held in his office in Tehran in mid June 2003.

their Iranian brethren, especially when it comes to participation in a politico-religious form of collective action. This may be caused by the problem of the multiple identities attached to the Indonesian Muslims i.e. Javanese, Indonesian and Muslim, as discussed in Chapter 4. Furthermore, religious syncretism, which tends to naturally enhance one's level of tolerance toward others, may also play a neutralizing effect in reducing the willingness to participate in jihad.

Looking at it from the Iranian perspective, it is conceivable to think that the Shia Islam ideology plays a role in determining the high level of participation in jihad. Thus, due to the Shia consciousness attached to the "Karbala complex", Iranian Muslims have been prone to a range of militant forms of collective action i.e. protest, revolution or jihad. Simply put, Shia Islam by its very own nature is a militant movement, requiring Muslims to manifest their faith and conviction in politics and religion. Recounting what Syariati once said, "Islam is the religion of militant individuals who are committed to truth and justice. It is the religion of those who desire independence. It is the school of those who struggle against imperialism."[7]

Statistically, as seen in Appendix 3, the matrix of correlations on religiosity is based on the *Kendall tau-b* coefficients, which are useful in identifying measures of association between and among ordinal variables. Observing the matrix under the "Aggregate" column, there are nine highly significant ($p \leq .001$ level) measures, which cuts across the boundaries of the three religious dimensions. The measures with such p-values under the two dimensions of Knowledge of Islam and ritual practices are: informal Islamic studies, Quranic recitation, religious books read, subscription to religious-oriented publications, religious exposure and visit(s) to places of worship. However, looking at the coefficient values of these religious factors (averaging .128), one can infer that the measure of association between the first two dimensions (knowledge of Islam and ritual practices) and participation is not altogether strong. Out of these six measures, publications

---

[7] In Watt, op. cit., 135.

read (measured in terms of how much an individual subscribes to reading Islamic publications) and religious exposure (measured by way of a respondent's overall exposure to religious messages) hold the strongest level of association with the participation variable.

Figure 6.4: Crosstabulation between media publications read and participation in jihad (valid *N*=996)

Publications read	Participation in jihad			Total
	No	Unsure/ Don't know	Yes	
None	104 (24.4%)	135 (31.7%)	187 (43.9%)	426 (100%)
One Publication	29 (11.2%)	98 (37.8%)	132 (51.0%)	259 (100%)
More than one Publications	20 (6.4%)	107 (34.4%)	184 (59.2%)	311 (100%)

x^2 statistic: 51.897; *p*-value: .000

Figure 6.5: Crosstabulation between religious exposure and participation in jihad (valid *N*=986)

Religious exposure	Participation in jihad			Total
	No	Unsure/ Don't know	Yes	
None	66 (32.7%)	55 (27.2%)	81 (40.1%)	202 (100%)
≤ 2 hours per week	35 (11.2%)	126 (40.4%)	151 (48.4%)	312 (100%)
> 2 hours per week	50 (10.6%)	157 (33.3%)	265 (56.1%)	472 (100%)

x^2 statistic: 15.260; *p*-value: .000

Figures 6.4 and 6.5 inform us of a glaring pattern in which the percentage for the "no" column steadily goes bottom-up, while the "yes" column moves top-down. For Figure 6.4, this means that the less the number of Islamic publications subscribed, the less likely the individual would be willing to participate. In contrast, the more publications subscribed, the more likelihood that one is willing to participate in jihad. A similar pattern is found in Figure 6.5 pertaining to religious exposure.

Hence, if knowledge of Islam and ritual practices are showing relatively weak measure of association with the participation variable, then the other dimension, religious affection, should be further analyzed in greater detail.

Religious Affection, Nationality and Jihad

Observing Appendix 3 under the "Aggregate" category, the dimension on religious affection—operationalized using measures of religious sacrifice, self-sacrifice and solidarity—seems to be showing an unambiguous pattern. This is indicated by the display of persistent patterns of all the significance levels, which all stand at .000. In addition, all measures of religious affection have coefficient values of more than .300, which, generally speaking, is relatively high for individual-level surveys. Based on the overall picture of the statistical inferences derived from the compiled religious attributes of the respondents, religious affection may indeed be the most significant determinant to Muslim participation in jihad.

To get a sense of the general picture, Figure 6.6 provides descriptive statistics on the religious affection dimension, which is divided into three separate columns based on the segregation of the dataset i.e. Indonesia, Iran and Aggregate. Next in line are crosstabulations on the dimension on religious affection. Figures 6.7, 6.8 and 6.9 depict the relationship between religious affection (i.e. sacrifice, self-sacrifice and solidarity) and the dependent variable on participation in jihad.

Figure 6.6: Frequency and valid percentage data on religious affection (N=996)

	Indonesia	Iran	Aggregate
	Frequency (%)	Frequency (%)	Frequency (%)

Religious sacrifice
Some people would give up their lives for the defense of Muslims and/or Islam.
Do you agree with these people?

	Indonesia	Iran	Aggregate
Strongly disagree/Disagree	45 (6.1)	43 (16.9)	88 (8.9)
Indifferent/Don't know	167 (22.7)	45 (17.7)	212 (21.4)
Agree/Strongly agree	523 (71.2)	166 (64.3)	689 (69.7)

Self-sacrifice
Would you be willing to sacrifice your own life for the sake of Muslims and/or Islam?

	Indonesia	Iran	Aggregate
Totally unwilling/Unwilling	51 (6.9)	54 (21.5)	105 (10.6)
Unsure/Don't know	196 (26.7)	27 (10.8)	223 (22.6)
Willing/Totally willing	488 (66.4)	170 (67.7)	658 (66.7)

Religious solidarity
How do you feel toward the plight of Muslims in Palestine, Bosnia and Iraq?

	Indonesia	Iran	Aggregate
Indifferent	30 (4.1)	65 (25.3)	95 (9.5)
Concerned	298 (40.4)	152 (59.1)	450 (45.2)
Very concerned	410 (55.6)	40 (15.6)	450 (45.2)

The persistent diagonal shading of the cells in the Figures above indicates the fairly consistent effect of these measures on the participation variable. This suggests that as the level of measure in religious sacrifice, self-sacrifice and solidarity increases, the level of willingness to participate in jihad among Muslim respondents also increases. This translates into the following: the more religious affection that a Muslim has for his or her brethren, the greater likelihood it is for the individual to be willing to participate in jihad.

Analyzing further the matrix of correlations on religiosity and participation (see Appendix 3), and comparing results from Indonesia

Figure 6.7: Crosstabulation between religious sacrifice and participation in jihad (valid *N*=989)

Religious Sacrifice	Participation in jihad			Total
	No	Unsure/ Don't know	Yes	
Strongly disagree/ Disagree	**50 (56.8%)**	15 (17.0%)	23 (26.1%)	88 (100%)
Indifferent/ Don't know	39 (18.4%)	**115 (54.2%)**	58 (27.4%)	212 (100%)
Agree/ Strongly agree	61 (8.9%)	208 (30.2%)	**420 (61.0%)**	689 (100%)
T o t a l	150 (15.2%)	338 (34.2%)	501 (50.7%)	989 (100%)

x^2 statistic: 203.563; *p*-value: .000

Figure 6.8: Crosstabulation between religious self-sacrifice and participation in jihad (valid *N*=986)

Religious self-sacrifice	Participation in jihad			Total
	No	Unsure/ Don't know	Yes	
Totally unwilling/ Unwilling	**51 (48.6%)**	21 (20.0%)	33 (31.4%)	105 (100%)
Unsure/ Don't know	49 (22.0%)	**126 (56.5%)**	48 (21.5%)	223 (100%)
Willing/ Totally willing	49 (7.4%)	190 (28.9%)	**419 (63.7%)**	658 (100%)
T o t a l	149 (15.1%)	337 (34.2%)	500 (50.7%)	986 (100%)

x^2 statistic: 221.401; *p*-value: .000

Figure 6.9: Crosstabulation between religious solidarity and participation in jihad (valid *N*=995)

Religious solidarity	Participation in jihad			Total
	No	Unsure/ Don't know	Yes	
Indifferent	**52 (54.7%)**	18 (18.9%)	25 (26.3%)	95 (100%)
Concerned	72 (16.0%)	**197 (43.8%)**	181 (40.2%)	450 (100%)
Very concerned	29 (6.4%)	125 (27.8%)	**296 (65.8%)**	450 (100%)
T o t a l	153 (15.4%)	340 (34.2%)	502 (50.5%)	995 (100%)

x^2 statistic: 184.408; *p*-value: .000

and Iran, one can see that wide variations occur in many of the measures of religiosity with respect to coefficient values as well as the significance levels. In the Indonesian case, for instance, publications read is the next most important measure after the three measures under religious affection. As for the Iranian data, the measure of daily prayers seems to be the most influential measure following religious sacrifice, self-sacrifice and solidarity. Others such as religious exposure and visit to places of worship are also significant but fall behind in terms of salience in relationship to the participation variable.

The dimension on religious affection in the Iranian case clearly underscores its salience, especially with the display of coefficients as high as .564 (with a *p*-value of .000).[8] The high coefficient values of the dimension on religious affection in the Iranian data and the apparent discrepancy between the aggregate and Indonesian data called for "nationality" to be further scrutinized and tested on the model of participation. This was done by way of employing binary logistics regression, which requires the dependent variable to be dichotomous.

---

[8] See Appendix 3 under the "Iran" column.

For this, a recoding was therefore conducted to transform survey answers into {0} for "no" and "unsure/don't know" and {1} for "yes". The primary focus is on establishing a regression model of participation based on the dimension on religious affection with the inclusion of nationality in the logistic regression. The main reasons for the inclusion of nationality as a dummy variable is due to its relatively high measure of association with the dependent variable (with $r=.239$ and p-value at .000). Apart from that, as explained earlier and more so in Chapter 5, nationality seems to have a strong bearing on religious affection, notably with the measure of solidarity. Appendix 10 shows the "variables in the equation" resulting from the binary logistic regression. Using the Backward Stepwise (Wald) Method, the table indicates that seven steps were undertaken to achieve the final regression model.[9] Observing the regression outcome, the effect of nationality in the model is thus additive, and should therefore not be treated as an interaction effect. Thus, if the basic regression model is the following:

$$Y = a_0 + b_1 x_1 + b_2 x_2 + b_3 x_3 + b_4 x_4 + e$$

where:

a_0 : -3.838

b_1 : 1.734 x_1 : Nationality

b_2 : .469 x_2 : Sacrifice

b_3 : .653 x_3 : Self-Sacrifice

b_4 : 1.192 x_4 : Solidarity

The model being offered here is thus:

$$Y = -3.838 + 1.734x_1 + .469x_2 + .653x_3 + 1.192x_4 + e$$

---

[9] For the sake of brevity, the author did not include the in-between steps, and only included the first and last ones.

The Nagelkerke R Square of .287, derived from the final step of the logistic regression, indicates that the model can explain a relatively high degree of variation in responses.[10] While the goodness-of-fit test, whose significance level stands at .492,[11] signifies the fact that the above model quite adequately fits the aggregate dataset of the survey.

Following this, I will conclude this study, and make assessments on the hypothesis offered in the outset of this book. Based on the research findings, I will also elaborate on the theoretical implications of his study in the hopes to further our understanding on Muslim participation in jihad.[]

---

[10] See Appendix 11.

[11] Ibid.

7

Concluding Remarks

This chapter will conclude the study. It incorporates discussions on the previously stated working hypothesis, theoretical and practical implications of the study as well as research limitations.

Rethinking about Participation

The notion of participation, as this study has shown, cannot and should not by all means be configured as "brute facts" (Schwartz 1984) delineated by clear-cut conceptual demarcations in the real world. Any and all forms of participatory acts, put simply, are ways for participants to gain access to a polity that would otherwise have been inaccessible to them. From the perspective of the participants, jihad is the only plausible alternative to correct the perceived wrongs in society. Accordingly, most participants view jihad as the only recourse to undo the Muslim fate in current history. Although observers looking in perceive jihad as an illegitimate, if not repugnant, form of politico-religious expression, the participants themselves conceive the act as a primary method to prove one's worth as a true Muslim believer as opposed to being a hypocrite or infidel. In effect, jihad has become the perfect litmus test for the militant Muslims, who view it as a "sacred ideal in the world of the profane" (Schwartz 1984). Of course, this is still in view of the fact that some Muslims assume the non-existence or ineffectiveness of legal, peaceful and constitutional means to articulate their interests and redress grievances, as in the case of Iran's Islamic revolution.

Despite the reality that often showcases jihad as being somewhat "an atavistic reaction against modernity" (Euben 2002), the subjective interpretation by the participants, who regard it essentially as a struggle to expand the *dar al-Islam* and diminish the *dar al-Harb*, will continue to stubbornly play an important role in determining the level of Muslim participation in jihad. This assertion does not in any way necessitate scholars and moderate Muslims to succumb to the participants' multi-subjective interpretation. Nor is it to necessarily conceal an attempt to valorize jihad. The fact remains that jihad is embedded in the teachings of Islam, and that militant Muslims, In relation to religiosity, there is obviously some truth in the assumption that only participants have "privileged access to their own intentions and belief" (Wallis and Bruce 1986). Hence, any form of action undertaken, whether perceived by others as religious or otherwise, become amenable to their own subjective notions of what Islam *is* and *is not*. The onus therefore lies not with the participants, but rather on those who strive to clarify, explain and understand the participatory act under examination. In this regard, Schwartz (1984) was right on the mark when he established the direct correlations between Muslim participation in the Iranian revolution and the participants' perception of their conformity to the Islamic religious tenets. Based on the collected data and statistical inferences, a certain pattern has emerged in the way Muslims (more so the militant Muslims) perceive jihad. For the latter, participation in jihad is equivalent to the fulfillment of a religious duty *as* Muslims, rendering their actions to be a mode of expression or a method to convey their Muslim*ness*, regardless of how they define the term. Consequently, participation in jihad is one way of making claims about their religiosity, whether they refer to the self or collective.

In view of the above, the expressive choice model offered by Schuessler (2000), as argued in Chapter 2, has meaningfully helped to put personal identity and collective attachment in context with the question on why Muslims participate in jihad. Rational choice thus becomes the lesser of the two models to be appropriately employed in dealing with participation in politico-religious forms of collective action. The reason is that while rational choice revolves around the costs and benefits of participation, expressive choice model entails participating individuals to be able to accrue the benefits. In other words, returns to participation can only be attained via the individual undertaking the act of participation despite the risks involved. Free riding in jihad therefore becomes a dilemma because as individuals refrain from participation, the transcendental benefits consequentially become out of bounds for them. As elaborated in Chapter 2, the individuals then are left with the secular benefits, and are excluded from attaining the ultimate reward in the transcendental realm, whereas if the individuals were to participate, there is very little likelihood for them to simultaneously attain the secular as well as the transcendental benefits. This brings us to the issue of symbolic returns to participation, which for individuals opting to participate in politico-religious forms of collective action may be more desirable than other types of incentive. It is therefore safe to conclude that Muslims, like other religionists, are prone to expressive or symbolic returns to participation.

Due to this 'logic', there is less regard for the success of the outcome to the collective endeavor, as compared to the one found in rational choice models. Why? Because unlike the poor people's movement (Hall 1995), the ultimate goal is not to win the battle (in *this* world) but rather the ultimate war (in the Hereafter), which is much reflected in the militant Muslims' twin perspectives in life. Indeed, in that context, participation is not a matter of fact, which thereby requires the deconstruction of partitions separating the two major traditions in political science research i.e. explanation and interpretation.

From the numerous statistical findings, it can be concluded that the SES model, which "nearly all empirical studies of political participation rely on" (Leighley 1996), is insufficient to explain participation in politico-religious forms of collective action. If so, one palpable contribution of this study is that no demographic characteristics and superficial attributes can meaningfully be used to predict a Muslim's level of willingness to participate in jihad. This suggests that the overall measure of association between demography as an independent variable and participation in jihad as the dependent variable is a fairly weak one. For that matter, this study may serve as a rebuttal to those insisting that socioeconomic marginalization causes individuals to resort to seemingly pathological and extreme forms of collective action. However, as stated in the outset and discussed in great detail, jihad takes various forms. The fact that the jihad participants are not necessarily a unique group of people in and of themselves begs the corollary question of how different are these jihad participants from the 'ordinary' Muslims. No doubt, such a question is valid, given the fact that most people are often trapped into thinking in terms of patterned behaviors (King et. al. 1994), hence oversimplifying the complexity that abounds in the decisions that some Muslims make when considering to participate in any high risk collective endeavor.

Religiosity Matters

As implied in Chapter 1, Islamic religiosity has yet to be paid due attention from political scientists. Unlike religiosity in other Semitic religions namely Christianity and Judaism, political research on Islamic religiosity is far from reaching its critical mass. Consequently, when it comes to the determination on the various measures of Islamic religiosity, the playing field becomes almost inclusively open to various possibilities. The three dimensions of Islamic religiosity being offered in this study are therefore products of the author's own invention based on a combination between life-long experiential learning and observation. Thus any shortcomings in the model of Islamic religiosity presented here can be said, to some extent, caused by the lack of existing body of research as normally provided in other subject matters.

Put simply, religiosity means "a quality of spiritual being" (Simmel 1997) or "commitment to religion" (Secret et. al. 1990). From all of the studies on the effects of religiosity, it can be easily determined that commitment to a religion influences one's political outlook, attitudes, behaviors and actions. As articulated in Chapters 1 and 2, there is strong reason to believe that a certain degree of religiosity is likely to move people toward a particular position in politics. The higher the level of religiosity, the more likely it is for one to adopt a conservative political stance. In line with that, the lower the level of one's religiosity, the more likely that he or she would endorse liberal political agenda.

At varying degrees, religiosity plays a unique role in the life of a Muslim. Although at first instance religiosity may determine one's professed attachment to God, it can also serve as a potent ingredient for identity, affinity, solidarity and sense of attachment to a community of believers or, as in the Muslims' case, the *ummah*. However, it would be a major fallacy to think that only Islamic religiosity can provide its believers with the collective sense of attachment. What is evident is that the Islamic universal body politic, the *ummah*, has in many ways provided a convenient manifesto for the militant Muslims to seek the necessary support, if not community endorsement, from their brethren. The fact that Muslim politicians, activists, militants and jihad participants often employ the *ummah* to frame their political discourses, activities and movements indicate the usefulness of retaining the time-honored collective consciousness and imagination. It is for the same reason that these people can mobilize resources to help their cause.

In answering the central question on why Muslims participate in jihad, the present author has come to conclude that the hypothesis presented in Chapter 1 has strong reason to be affirmed. Religiosity does matter when Muslims contemplate on whether to participate in jihad or not. However, as discussed at great length, Islamic religiosity should not in any way be conceived as a monolithic phenomenon, able to be measured using one or two measures. This study has also found that Islamic religiosity is indeed an overloaded variable with essential dimensions proving to be less useful than others. The three religious dimensions employed in this study—knowledge of Islam, ritual practices and religious affection—are evidently useful to grasp at the different components of religiosity, which has empirically been proven to affect one's political outlook, attitude and behavior. This is particularly salient when one analyzes the effects of religiosity on the level of willingness to participate in a politico-religious form of collective action.

To be more specific, knowledge of Islam and ritual practices apparently turned out to be less than significant in determining the variation in the level of willingness to participate in jihad. Evidently, willingness to participate in jihad is foremost affected by the level of religious affection that one holds. Cross-national empirical evidence suggests that the higher one's religious affection, the greater the likelihood for the individual to participate in jihad. Here, the dimension on religious affection is operationalized using three measures i.e. sacrifice, self-sacrifice and solidarity. In line with the research findings, it is now apparent that religious affection hinges on the Muslims' proclivity to the ideology of martyrism, entailing personal inclination and community endorsement on sacrificial struggle. Indeed this re-inforces the hypothesis on the Muslims' expressive choice and sense of who they are and their attachment to the *ummah*, which ultimately beseeches the questions associated with personal and collective identity. So clearly, religiosity serves as an essential ingredient to personal identity and collective attachment. Despite the differences between Indonesian and Iranian Muslims in terms of race/ethnicity, sociopolitical history, geographic location and Islamic school of thought, religiosity (as in religious affection) positively affects their willingness to participate in jihad. This is even more pronounced when looking at the measure of religious solidarity.

In spite of the above, nationality also affects the way Indonesian and Iranian Muslims feel about the plight of their brethren in Palestine, Bosnia, Iraq or possibly elsewhere. In the case of Indonesia, the *reformasi* movement no doubt helped ushered in the religious re-assertion among many from within the Islamic community. The mush-rooming of militant groups such as LJ, FPI and MMI unmistakably indicates that the angry proponents of political Islam are still a force to be reckoned with. Although they are in constant short supply of membership, as compared to the mainstream Muslim organizations such as NU and Muhammadiyah, their presence in the political scene has somewhat proven to have a major bearing on the political discourses and processes at the national and even international levels. With the fast paced political liberalization occurring in the country, militant Muslims have taken bolder measures to call for an Islamicized state than previously when Indonesia was still under Suharto's autocratic rule. This trend apparently has increased in spite of the overwhelming pressures brought upon them by the authorities following the September 11 event and the October 2002 Bali bomb blasts. Yet, despite the seemingly worrying trend, it should be reiterated that cohesion among the militant Islamic groups has yet to materialize. In large part, this has been due to competing strategies and organizational rivalry.

Iran's case somewhat differs, as it is a confessional state led by a Spiritual Leader, who practically acts as the final arbiter in all matters pertaining to religion and politics. Due to this, unlike in Indonesia, where the state often quietly endorses the activities conducted by militant groups, the Iranian leadership often openly engages and patronizes these groups. The case of Aghajeri, as detailed in Chapter 5, is a prime example of how competing visions of the state, notably between the old revolutionary guards and the majority of Iran's young generation, would often times result in alienation and political apathy, as was revealed in the analysis of the survey data. Interestingly, although

Islam holds sway in the country, nationalistic sentiments are similarly strong. The Iranians' less than "very concerned" attitude toward the plight of the Iraqis, generated by the long war that occurred two decades ago, proves to be a deep wound that will not simply go away.

The implications of this study are unambiguous. If previously Islam had rarely been conceived as a global, transnational political force— due to overemphasis placed on the specificities of Muslim cultures in different regions of the world—it is high time that scholars concede to the universal appeal proffered by the religious affectionate values in Islam. With regard to Islamic religiosity, one must come to terms with the intrinsic nature of Islam being a poignant religion with potentially strong emotive pleas, which transcends the traditional political boundaries and geographic territories of the nation-state. Based on the findings of the survey, disparities are prevalent in terms of the Muslim religious conduct and attitudes toward *this* world. However, when it comes to their religious identity, affinity, solidarity and sense of attachment to the *ummah*, the difference merely lies in the degree to which they attend to their expressive needs and concerns. In other words, the survey data reveal that Muslims tend to have a high emotional attachment to their brethren, with the Iranians having some reservations toward their Iraqi neighbors.

It may be timely at this stage to ask: What can be done in light of the study's findings. Such a query can only be relevant if posed together with the following subsidiary questions: If the effects of religiosity were so significant, what is to be done with its excessive tendencies and damaging impacts? How can something as intrinsic as jihad be rooted out of a belief system that produced it? And how can the religious affectionate values in Islam be directed toward building a constructive engagement between the Muslims and the others? In this study, Islamic religiosity acts as the independent variable that significantly determines the Muslims' level of willingness to participate jihad, and that the most important dimension is religious affection. If the above questions imply that one should use all means necessary to deter Muslims from participating in jihad and thus preventing the so-called 'Islamic terrorism', it would be fair to also ask where the ultimate source of the problem lies. What exactly cause the various measures of religious affection to become so prominently influential that it can significantly affect Muslims to resort to extreme exploits? Why would, for instance, Muslims in this day and age still have passion for martyrdom? Then, how can compassion for other Muslims living in different parts of the world contribute to the radicalization of some segments within the Muslim world?

For the above questions, two things quickly come to mind. One relates to the nature and characteristic of Islam, which only Muslims can decide and make the changes necessary to emerge out of the current 'black hole'. For this to happen, Muslims need to get out of their 'state of unchangingness' and undertake not a retrogressive form of jihad but a progressive one in the hope to regain what had long been lost. And the first major task before Muslims is to recover the self confidence and esteem, which in effect will create the psychological boost needed to recapture the true essentialist Islam (*Islam-e vaqi'i*) that once reigned. Much of this can be achieved through rethinking and reinterpretation of the politico-religious doctrines set forth in the Quran, which would correctly place the *ummah* within the international political configuration.

Although many Muslims still abide by the ideology of martyrism, especially the Shia Muslims, one must also differentiate between the "men of words" and the "men of action", as cautioned by Scott (1985). Evidently, the majority of the Muslim respondents were almost equally positive toward religious sacrifice (69.7%) and self-sacrifice (66.7%), hence, signifying their implicit approval of the 'weaponization of death'. In view of the above, one should ask why the dictates of such circumstances prevailed in the first place. It is hard to deny the fact that the propensity for martyrism, among other things, is a sign of desperation. However, would not it be fair to ask further why they were so desperate or bitter toward their perceived enemy? When framed this way, it becomes almost conceivable that these people would choose to opt for extreme actions because their enemy is perceived to be persecuting *their* community or humiliating *their* brethren. If the literature on resistance is anything to go by, it is the unjust and exclusionary nature of today's global political configuration, which has failed to offer Muslims to 'sit on the table'. The incessant display of hypocrisy in Palestine, the aggressive American war on terrorism and the overbearing attitude toward Islam in sum provide a strong enough reason for militant Muslims to consider participating in extreme exploits. It is therefore imperative that the causes of these injustices and smugness be rooted out to foster the kind of identity, affinity, solidarity and sense of attachment that would breed creativity, productivity and, most importantly, tolerance of others.

As in many cases that employ similar lines of survey research, the limitation of this study relates to the data, which exclude Muslims from the Arab world, the one people most often associated with Islam. On this, the author is of the view that Arabs have been mistakenly considered as the standard bearer of the faith, even among Muslims. This erroneous view has been largely anchored in three facts: the Prophet of Islam was an Arab, the language of the Quran is Arabic and the holiest places on earth, according to the Muslim belief, are Mecca, Medina and Palestine, sites that are all located in the Arabian Peninsula. Inescapably, this brings the dichotomy between Arab and non-Arab Muslims. According to this binary framework, the latter are usually seen as 'lesser' Muslims compared to the former due mostly to the latter's linguistic handicap, supposedly preventing them to comprehend, transmit and teach the 'Word of Allah'.

What is more essential relates to the known fact that Indonesian as well as Iranian Muslims differs in terms of their politico-religious thought, practice and ethos when compared to their Arab brethren. Although they may share a sense of belonging to the Islamic heritage, their national predispositions may well overcome their attachment to the larger Muslim body politic or the *ummah*. In addition, their endowed racial/ethnic makeup too often determines their likes, dislikes, prejudices and preferences in life, which would understandably vary from their Arab counterparts. These differences may in turn result in divergent politico-religious attitudes, behaviors and actions. Thus, from the methodological point of view, the inclusion of Arab Muslims could have produced more consequential results and analyses, lending greater credence to the study in general.

The nature of the subject studied also posed some dilemmas. This mostly relates to the dual nature of jihad being both political and religious, effectively causing the analyses to oscillate between Islamic standard beliefs, doctrines, ideology and the Muslims' manifested attitudes, behaviors and actions. The problem in anatomizing jihad is that willingness to participate in such endeavor involves both worldly rationales and out-of-this-world moral justifications. While the former can be explained using rational and expressive choice models, the latter, from the political science perspective, can only be explained *as such*. It is therefore difficult to verify beyond reasonable doubt the true intentions or motivation of political actions based on religious grounds. As explained previously, only participants themselves have "privileged access to their own intentions and beliefs", rendering the study on religion and politics to demand basic understanding of, if not empathy for, the staunch believers. In other words, separating the truth from the subjective is indeed a very tough call to make, particularly when it concerns demarcating lines between religious doctrines and political actions.

In both the analytical and conclusion parts, it has been said that willingness to participate in jihad may not necessarily lead to *actual* participation. In an instant, such analytical predicament begs the question of the extent or usefulness of the given study. What this implies is that such an inquiry into something as important as jihad is useful and contributive only if the analyses and findings lead to an explanation or understanding regarding the Muslims' participation in jihad. Although the author may grant such repudiation, this study had never promised to provide any practical solutions to preventing Muslims from participating in what they call jihad, regardless of its consequences. Again, this stance obviously does not denote indifference toward the suffering that the sociopolitical action may entail, nor does it signify the valorization of jihad. It merely stands to demonstrate the author's commitment to neutrality, despite the fact that the subject matter itself may be multisubjective in nature.[]

Bibliography

Books

Abdalla, Ulil Abshar (editor). *Islam Liberal & Fundamental: Sebuah pertarungan wacana* [Liberal and Fundamental Islam: A discursive dispute] (Jogjakarta: Elsaq, 2003).

Abrahamian, Ervand. *The Iranian Mojahedin* (New Haven, Connecticut: Yale University Press, 1989).

Abu Sulayman, Abdulhamid. *The Islamic Theory of International Relations: New directions for Islamic methodology and thought* (Herndon, Virginia: International Institute of Islamic Thought, 1987).

Afandi, Arief. *Islam Demokrasi Atas Bawah: Polemik Strategi Perjuangan Umat Model Gus Dur dan Amien Rais* [Islamic Democracy High and Low: The polemic over the strategic models of resistance of Gus Dur and Amien Rais] (3rd edition) (Yogyakarta: Pustaka Pelajar, 1997).

Afshar, Haleh (editor). *Iran: A revolution in turmoil* (London: MacMillan, 1985).

Al-Anzhari, Fauzan. *Saya Terroris?: Sebuah Pledoi* [Me Terrorist? A Defense] (Jakarta: Penerbit Republika, 2002).

Ahmadi, Nader and Fereshteh Ahmadi. *Iranian Islam: The concept of the individual* (New York: St Martin's Press, 1998).

Ahmed, Akbar S. *Discovering Islam: Making sense of Muslim history and society* (revised edition) (London: Routledge, 2003).

_____. *Islam Under Siege: Living dangerously in a post-honor world* (Cambridge, England: Polity Press, 2003).

Ahmed, Ishtiaq. *The Concept of an Islamic State: An analysis of the ideological controversy in Pakistan* (New York: St. Martin's Press, 1987).

Al-Ahsan, Abdullah. *Ummah or Nation?: Identity crisis in contemporary Muslim society* (Leicester, UK: The Islamic Foundation, 1992).

Alam, M. Shahid. *Is There an Islamic Problem: Essays on Islamicate societies, the US and Israel* (Petaling Jaya, Malaysia: The Other Press, 2004).

Alexander, Yonah (editor). *Combating Terrorism: Strategies of ten countries* (Michigan: University of Michigan Press, 2002).

Algar, Hamid. *Roots of the Islamic Revolution in Iran* (Oneonta, New York: Islamic Publications International, 2001).

Almascaty, Hilmy Bakar. *Panduan Jihad Untuk Aktivis Gerakan Islam* [Jihad Handbook for Islamic Movement Activists] (Jakarta: Gema Insani Press, 2001).

Al-Muzaffar, Muhammad Rida. *The Faith of Shi'a Islam* (Ansariyan Publication, Qum, 1982).

Ansolabehere, Stephen and Shanto Iyengar. *Going Negative: How political advertisements shrink and polarize the electorate* (New York: Free Press, 1995).

Armstrong, Karen. *The Battle for God* (New York: Alfred A. Kopf, 2000).

Aronson, Elliot. *The Social Animal* (New York: Viking Press, 1972).

Barber, Benjamin R. *Jihad vs. McWorld: Terrorism's challenge to democracy* (New York: Ballantine Books, 2001).

Beinin, Joel and Joe Stork. *Political Islam: Essays from Middle East report* (London: I.B. Taurus, 1997).

Berger, Peter L. *Holy War Inc.: Inside the secret world of Osama bin Laden* (London: Weidenfeld & Nicolson, 2001).

Brumberg, Daniel. *Reinventing Khomeini: The struggle for reform in Iran* (Chicago: University of Chicago Press, 1997).

Brinton, Crane. *The Anatomy of Revolutions* (revised and expanded edition) (New York: Prentice-Hall, 1965).

Burke, Edmund and Ira M. Lapidus (editors). *Islam, Politics and Social Movements* (Berkeley: University of California Press, 1988).

Calhoun, Craig. *Neither Gods Nor Emperors: Students and the struggle for democracy in China* (Berkeley: University of California Press, 1995).

Chomsky, Noam. *Deterring Democracy* (London: Verso, 1991).

Clarke, Gerard. *The Politics of NGOs in Southeast Asia* (London: Routledge, 1998).

Clinton, Bennett. *In Search of Muhammad* (Washington, D.C.: Cassell, 1998).

Cole, Juan R.I. (editor). *Comparing Muslim Societies: Knowledge and the State in a world civilization* (Ann Arbor, Michigan: University of Michigan Press, 1992).

_____ and Nikki R. Keddie (editors). *Shi'ism and Social Protest* (New Haven, Connecticut: Yale University Press, 1986).

Crenshaw, Martha (editor). *Terrorism in Context* (University Park, Pennsylvania: Pennsylvania State University Press, 1995).

Dahl, Robert. *A Preface to Democratic Theory* (Chicago: University of Chicago Press, 1963).

Davidson, Lawrence. *Islamic Fundamentalism* (Westport, Connecticut: Greenwood Press, 1998).

Diamond, Larry and Marc F. Plattner (editors). *Nationalism, Ethnic Conflict and Democracy* (Baltimore: Johns Hopkins University Press, 1994).

De Bono, Edward. *The Happiness Purpose* (Harmondsworth, Middlesex: Penguin, 1990).

Edelman, Murray. *The Symbolic Uses of Politics* (Urbana, Illinois: University of Illinois Press, 1985).

Effendy, Bahtiar. *Islam and the State in Indonesia* (Singapore: ISEAS, 2003).

Ehteshami, Anoushiravan. *After Khomeini: The Iranian second republic* (London: Routledge, 1995).

Eickelman, Dale F. and James Piscatori. *Muslim Politics* (Princeton, New Jersey: Princeton University Press, 1996).

Ellul, Jacques (translation). *Propaganda: The formation of men's attitudes* (1st American edition), from French by Konrad Kellen and Jean Lerner (New York: Knopf, 1965).

Emmerson, Donald K. (editor). *Indonesia Beyond Suharto: Polity, Economy, Society, Transition* (New York: East Gate and Asia Society, 1999).

Engineer, Asghar Ali. *Religion and Liberation* (New Delhi: Ajanta Publications, 1989).

Esposito, John L. *The Islamic Threat: Myth or reality?* (Oxford: Oxford University Press, 1992).

_____ (editor). *Political Islam: Revolution, radicalism or reform?* (Boulder, Colorado: Lynne Rienner, 1997).

_____ and R. K. Ramazani. *Iran at the Crossroads* (New York: Palgrave, 2001).

_____. *The Unholy War: Terror in the name of Islam* (Oxford: Oxford University Press, 2002).

Euben, Roxanne L. *Enemy in the Mirror: Islamic fundamentalism and the limits of modern rationalism* (New Jersey: Princeton University Press, 1999).

Ferell, Jeff and Neil Websdale (editors). *Making Trouble: Cultural constructions of crime, deviance*, and control (New York: Aldine De Gruyter, 1999).

Firestone, Reuven. *Jihad: The origin of holy war in Islam* (New York: Oxford University Press, 1999).

Fischer, Michael M. J. *Iran: From religious dispute to revolution* (Cambridge, Massachusetts: Harvard University Press, 1980).

Forrester, Geoff (editor). *Post-Soeharto Indonesia: Renewal or Chaos?* (Singapore: Institute of Southeast Asian Studies, 1999).

Fromm, Erich. *The Sane Society* (London: Routledge, 1979).

Geertz, Clifford. *The Interpretation of Cultures: Selected essays* (New York: Basic Books, 1973).

Gill, Robin. *Theology and Sociology: A reader* (London: Cassell, 1996).

Gray, John. *Al-Qaeda and What it Means to be Modern* (London: Faber and Faber, 2003).

Gurr, Robert Ted. *Why Men Rebel* (Princeton, New Jersey: Princeton University Press, 1970).

Gunaratna, Rohan. *Inside Al-Qaeda: Global network of terror* (New York: Berkley Books, 2002).

Hafez, Mohammed M. *Why Muslims Rebel? Repression and resistance in the Islamic world* (Boulder, Colorado: Lynne Rienner, 2003).

Haliday, Fred. *Islam and the Myth of Confrontation: Religion and politics in the Middle East* (New York: I.B. Taurus, 1995).

Hall, Melvin F., *Poor People's Social Movement Organizations: The goal is to win* (Westport, Connecticut: Praeger, 1995).

Hefner, Robert W. *Civil Islam: Muslims and Democratization in Indonesia* (New Jersey: Princeton Review Press, 2000).

Hirschman, Albert O. *Exit, Voice, and Loyalty: Responses to decline in firms, organizations and states* (Cambridge, Massachusetts: Harvard University Press, 1970).

Hodgson, Marshall G.S. *The Venture of Islam* (Chicago: University of Chicago Press, 1974).

Hoveyda, Fereydoun. *The Broken Crescent: The "threat" of militant Islamic fundamentalism* (Westport, Connecticut: Praeger, 2002).

Hroub, Khaled. *Hamas: Political thought and practice* (Washington, D.C.: Institute for Palestine Studies, 2000).

Huntington, Samuel P. *The Clash of Civilizations and the Remaking of the World Order* (London: Touchstone Books, 1996).

———— and Joan M. Nelson. *No Easy Choice: Political participation in developing countries* (Cambridge, Massachusetts: Harvard University Press, 1976).

Ibrahim, Anwar. *The Asian Renaissance* (Singapore: Times Book International, 1996).

Ignatieff, Michael. *The Needs of Strangers* (London: Vintage, 1984).

Inayatullah, Sohail and Gail Boxwell (editors), *Islam, Postmodernism and Other Futures: A Ziauddin Sardar reader* (London: Pluto Press, 2003).

Ismail, Salwa. *Rethinking Islamist Politics: Culture, the state and Islamism* (London: I.B. Taurus, 2003).

Jackall, Robert. *Propaganda* (New York: New York University Press, 1995).

Jafri, Syed Husain Mohammad. *The Origins and Early Development of Shi'a Islam* (Oxford: Oxford University Press, 2000).

Jansen, Johannes J. G. (translator). *The Neglected Duty: The creed of Sadat's assassins and Islamic resurgence in the Middle East* (New York: Macmillan, 1986).

————. *The Dual Nature of Islamic Fundamentalism* (Ithaca, New York: Cornell University Press, New York: Macmillan, 1997).

Jowett, Garth S. and Victoria O'Donnell. *Propaganda and Persuasion* (3rd edition). (Thousand Oaks, California: Sage Publications, 1999).

Juergensmeyer, Mark. *Terror in the Mind of God: The global rise of religious violence* (Berkeley: University of California Press, 2001).

Keck, Margaret and Kathryn Sikkink. *Activists Beyond Borders: Advocacy networks in international politics* (Ithaca, New York: Cornell University Press, 1998).

Keddie, Nikki R. (editor). *Iran: Shi'ism from quietism to revolution* (New Haven, Connecticut: Yale University Press, 1983).

_____ and Rudi Matthee. *Iran and the Surrounding World: Interactions in culture and cultural politics* (Seattle: University of Washington Press, 2002).

Kepel, Gilles. *Jihad: The trail of political Islam* (Cambridge, Massachusetts: Harvard University Press, 2002).

Khomeini, Ruhollah. *The Last Message: The political and divine will of His Holiness Imam Khomeini (S.A.)* (The Imam Khomeini Cultural Institute, Tehran-Iran, 1992).

_____. *Hokumat-e Islam* [Islamic Government] (Tehran: Institute for the Compilation and Translation of Imam Khomeini's Work, 2002).

King, Gary, Robert O. Keohane and Sydney Verba. *Designing Social Inquiry: Scientific inference in qualitative research* (New Jersey: Princeton University Press, 1994).

Kohl, Herbert. *The Age of Complexity* (New York: Mentor Books, 1965).

Kolocotronics, Jamilah. *Islamic Jihad: An historical perspective* (Indiana: American Trust Publications Indianapolis, 1990).

Kukis, Mark. *My Heart Became Attached: The strange journey of John Walker Lindh* (Washington, D.C.: Brassey's, 2003).

Lawrence, Bruce. *Shattering the Myth: Islam beyond violence* (England: Oxford University Press, 2000).

Lewis-Beck, Michael S. *Data Analysis: An introduction* (Thousand Oaks, California: Sage Publications, 1995).

Lewis, Bernard. *The Assassins: A radical sect in Islam* (New York: Octagon Books, 1980).

————. *The Political Language of Islam* (Chicago: University of Chicago Press, 1988).

————. *What Went Wrong? Western impact and Middle Eastern response* (Oxford: Oxford University Press, 2001).

————. *The Crisis of Islam: Holy war and unholy terror* (London: Weidenfeld & Nicolson, 2003).

Little, Daniel. *Understanding Peasant China* (New Haven, Connecticut: Yale University Press, 1989).

Maalouf, Amin. *In the Name of Identity: Violence and need to belong* (New York: Penguin Books, 2003).

Mackey, Sandra. *The Iranians: Persia, Islam and the soul of a nation* (New York: Dutton, 1996).

Maddy-Weitzman, Bruce and Efraim Inbar (editors). *Religious Radicalism in the Greater Middle East* (London: Frank Cass, 1997).

Majumdar, Suhas. *Jihad: The Islamic doctrine of permanent war* (New Delhi: Voice of India, 2001).

Marsch, David and Gerry Stoker (editors). *Theory and Methods in Political Science* (Basingstoke, Hampshire: Macmillan, 1995).

Maududi, Abul A'la. *Towards Understanding Islam* (Beirut: IIFSO, 1980).

Manning, Chris and Peter Van Diermen (editors). *Indonesia in Transition: Social Aspects of Reformasi and Crisis* (Singapore: Institute of Southeast Asian Studies, 2000).

McAdam, Doug. *The Political Process and the Civil Rights Movement* (Chicago: University of Chicago Press, 1982).

McAdam, Doug, John McCarthy and Mayer N. Zald. *Comparative Perspectives on Social Movements: Political opportunities, mobilizing structures, and cultural framings* (England: Cambridge University Press, 1996).

Mernissi, Fatima. *Islam and Democracy: Fear of the modern world* (London: Virago Press, 1992).

Momen, Moojan. *An Introduction to Shi'i Islam: History and doctrines of Twelver Shi'ism* (New Haven: Yale University Press, 1985).

Moslem, Mehdi. *Factional Politics in Post-Khomeini Iran* (Syracuse, New York: Syracuse University Press, 2002).

Moussalli, Ahmad S. (editor). *Islamic Fundamentalism: Myths and realities* (Reading, U.K.: Ithaca Press, 1998).

Napoleoni, Loretta. *Modern Jihad: Tracing the dollars behind the terror networks* (London: Pluto Press, 2003).

Noorani, A.G. *Islam and Jihad: Prejudice versus reality* (Reading, U.K.: Global Issues, 2002).

Olson, Mancur. *The Logic of Collective Action: Public goods and the theory of groups* (Cambridge, Massachusetts: Harvard University Press, 1965).

Padgett, Stephen. *Organizing Democracy in Eastern Germany: Interest groups in post-Communist society* (Cambridge: Cambridge University Press, 2000).

Peters, Rudolf (translation). *Jihad in Mediaeval and Modern Islam* (translation, *Bidayatul Mujtahid*) (Leiden, 1977).

_____. *Jihad in Classical and Modern Times: A reader* (Princeton, New Jersey: Markus- Wiener, 1996).

Pipes, Daniel. *Path of God: Islam and political power* (New York: Basic Books, 1983).

Popkins, Samuel L. *The Rational Peasant: The political economy of rural society in Vietnam* (Berkeley: University of California Press, 1979).

Qutb, Syed. *Ma'alam fii al-Thariiq* [Milestone] (Himpunan Belia Islam, undated).

Rahman, Fazlur. *Approaches to Islam in Religious Studies* (Tucson, Arizona: University of Arizona Press, 1985).

Rais, M. Dhiauddin. *Teori Politik Islam* (Jakarta: Gema Insani Press, 2001).

Ramage, Douglas E. *Politics in Indonesia: Democracy, Islam and the ideology of tolerance* (London: Routledge, 1995).

Ramazani, R.K. (editor). *Iran's Revolution: Search for consensus* (Bloomington, Indiana: Indiana University Press, 1990).

Rashid, Ahmed. *Taliban: The story of the Afghan warlords* (Oxford: Pan Books, 2001).

Rawls, John. *Theory of Justice* (Cambridge: Harvard University Press, 1971).

Reeve, Simon. *The New Jackals: Ramzi Yousef, Osama bin Laden and the future of terrorism* (Boston: Northeastern University Press, 1999).

Renard, John. *Islam and the Heroic Image: Themes in literature and the visual arts* (Georgia: Mercer University Press, 1993).

Richard, Yann. *Shi'ite Islam: Polity, ideology and creed* (translation) (Cambridge, Massachusetts: Blackwell, 1995).

Robbins, Thomas and Susan J. Palmer. *Millenium, Messiahs, and Mayhem: Contemporary apocalyptic movements* (New York: Routledge, 1997).

Roy, Olivier. *The Failure of Political Islam* (translation) (Cambridge, Massachusetts: Harvard University Press, 1994).

Rusjd, Ibnu. *Bidajatul Mujtahid* (Volume V) (translation) (Jakarta: Bulan Bintang, 1969).

Said, Edward W. *Orientalism* (London: Penguin, 1978).

_____. *Culture and Imperialism* (London: Chatto & Windus, 1993).

_____ and Christopher Hitchens. *Blaming the Victims: Spurious scholarship and the Palestinian question* (London: Verso, 2001).

Salim, Arskal and Azyumardi Azra. *Shari'a and Politics in Modern Indonesia* (Singapore: Institute of Southeast Asian Studies, 2003).

Samudra, Imam. *Aku Melawan Teroris!* [I am fighting against Terrorists] (Solo, Indonesia: Jazera, 2004).

Sandler, Todd. *Collective Action: Theory and applications* (Ann Arbor, Michigan: University of Michigan Press, 1992).

Sardar, Ziauddin. *The Future of Muslim Civilization* (London: Mansell, 1987).

Schuessler, Alexander. *A Logic of Expressive Choice* (New Jersey: Princeton University Press, 2000).

Schwarz, Adam. *A Nation in Waiting: Indonesia's search for stability* (2nd edition) (Boulders, Colorado: Westview Press, 2000).

Scott, James C. *Moral Economy of the Peasant: Rebellion and subsistence in Southeast Asia* (New Haven, Connecticut: Yale University Press, 1977).

_____. *Weapons of the Weak: Everyday forms of peasant resistance* (New Haven, Connecticut: Yale University Press, 1985).

Shively, W. Phillips. *The Craft of Political Research* (4th edition) (New Jersey: Prentice Hall, 1998).

Sidahmed, Abdel Salam and Anoushiravan Ehteshami. *Islamic Fundamentalism* (Boulder, Colorado: Westview Press, 1996).

Simmel, Georg. *Essays on Religion* (New Haven, Connecticut: Yale University Press, 1997).

Skocpol, Theda. *States and Social Revolutions: A comparative analysis of France, Russia and China* (Cambridge, Massachusetts: Harvard University Press, 1979).

Spencer, William. *Islamic Fundamentalism in the Modern World* (Brookfield, Connecticut: Millbrook Press, 1995).

Sunhyuk, Kim. *The Politics of Democratization in Korea: The role of civil society* (Pennsylvania: University of Pittsburgh, 2000).

Taheri, Amir. *The Spirit of Allah: Khomeini and the Islamic Revolution* (Bethesda, Maryland: Adler and Adler, 1986).

Tarrow, Sydney. *Power in Movement* (2nd edition) (New York: Cambridge University Press, 1998).

Taylor, Philip M. *Munitions of the Mind: War propaganda from the ancient world to nuclear age* (England: P. Stephens, 1990).

Turner, Bryan S. *Weber and Islam: A critical study* (London: Routledge, 1974).

Turner, Ralph H. and Lewis M. Killian. *Collective Behavior* (3rd edition) (New Jersey: Prentice Hall, 1987).

Vas, Luis S.R. *Osama bin Laden: King of terror or saviour of Islam* (Dehli: Pustak Mahal, 2001).

Verba, Sydney and Norman H. Nie. *Participation in America: Political democracy and social equality* (Chicago: University of Chicago Press, 1972).

Jeffrey N. Wassertorm and Elizabeth O. Perry (editors). *Popular Protest and Political Culture in Modern China* (Boulder, Colorado: Westview Press, 1994).

Wallis, Roy and Steve Bruce. *Sociological Theory, Religion and Collective Action* (Belfast: Queen's University, 1986).

Ward, Keith. *Religion and Community* (Oxford: Clarendon Press, 2000).

Watt, William Montgomery. *Muhammad: Prophet and statesman* (Oxford: Oxford University Press, 1961).

_____. *Islamic Fundamentalism and Modernity* (London: Routledge, 1988).

Whitehead, Alfred North. *Science and the Modern World* (New York: Free Press, 1967).

White, Morton. *The Age of Analysis: 20th century philosophers* (New York: Mentor Books, 1956).

Zada, Khamami. *Islam Radikal: Pergulatan ormas-ormas Islam garis keras di Indonesia* (Jakarta: Teraju, 2002).

Zawati, Hilmi M. *Is Jihad a Just War?: War, peace and human rights under Islamic and public international law* (Lewiston, New York: E. Mellen Press, 2001).

Journal Articles

Aghaie, Kamran. "The Karbala Narrative: Shi'i political discourse in modern Iran in the 1960s and 1970s" in *Journal of Islamic Studies*, 12 (2) 2001: 151-176.

Andoni, Lamis. "Searching for Answers: Gaza's suicide bombers" in *Journal of Palestine Studies*, 26 (4) 1997: 33-45.

Barraclough, Simon. "Political Participation and Its Regulation in Malaysia: Opposition to the studies (Amendment) Act 1981" in *Pacific Affairs*, 57 (3) 1984: 450-461.

Bernstein, Mary. "Celebration and Suppression: The strategic uses of identity by the lesbian and gay movement" in *American Journal of Sociology*, 103 (3) 1997: 531-565.

Berejikian, Jeffrey. "Revolutionary Collective Action and the Agent-Structure Problem" in *American Political Science Review*, 86 (3) 1992: 647-657.

Billings, Dwight B. and Shaunna L. Scott. "Religion and Political Legitimation" in *Annual Review of Sociology*, 20, 1994: 173-202.

Bolce, Louis and Gerald De Maio. (a) "Religious Outlook, Culture War Politics, and Antipathy Toward Christian Fundamentalists" in *Public Opinion Quarterly*, 63 (1) 1999: 29-61.

_____. (b) "The Anti-Christian Fundamentalist Factor in Contemporary Politics" in *Public Opinion Quarterly*, 63 (4) 1999: 508-542.

Boroumand, Ladan and Roya Boroumand, "Terror, Islam and Democracy" in *Journal of Democracy*, 13 (2) April 2002: 5-20.

Brady, Henry E., Sidney Verba and Kay Lehman Schlozman. "Beyond Ses: A resource model of political participation" in *American Political Science Review*, 89 (2) 1995: 271-294.

Brockett, Charles D. "The Structure of Political Opportunities and Peasant Mobilization in Central America" in *Comparative Politics*, 1991: 253-274.

Brysk, Alison. "Turning Weakness into Strength: The Internationalization of Indian Rights" in *Latin American Perspectives*, 23 (2) 1996: 38-57.

Conell, Carol and Kim Voss. "Formal Organization and the Fate of Social Movements: Craft association and class alliance in the Knights of Labor" in *American Sociological Review*, 55 (2) 1990: 255-269.

Crowley, Stephen. "Barriers to Collective Action: Steelworkers and Mutual Dependence in the Former Soviet Union" in *World Politics*, 46 (4) 1994: 589-615.

Dale, Stephen Frederic. "Religious Suicide in Islamic Asia: Anticolonial terrorism in India, Indonesia and the Philippines" in *Journal of Conflict Resolution*, 32 (1) 1988: 37-59.

Davenport, Christian. "Multi-Dimensional Threat Perception and State Repression: An Inquiry into why states apply negative sanctions" in *American Journal of Political Science*, 39 (3) 1995: 683-713.

De Jong, Gordon F., Joseph E. Faulkner and Rex H. Warland, "Dimensions of Religiosity: Evidence from a cross-cultural study" in *Social Forces*, 54 (4) June 1976: 866-889.

Dingxin Zao. "Ecologies of Social Movements: Student Mobilization During the 1989 Pro-Democracy Movement in Beijing" in *American Journal of Sociology*, 103 (6) 1998: 1493-1529.

_____. "State-Society Relations and the Discourses and Activities of the 1989 Beijing Student Movement" in *American Journal of Sociology*, 105 (6) 2000: 1592-1632.

Entman, Robert M. "How the Media Affect What People Think: An information processing approach" in *Journal of Politics*, 51 (2) 1989: 347-370.

Euben, Roxanne L. "Killing (For) Politics: Jihad, martyrdom, and political action" in *Political Theory*, 30 (1) February 2002: 4-35.

Freedman, Paul and Ken Goldstein. "Measuring Media Exposure and the Effects of Negative Campaign Ads" in *American Journal of Political Science*, 43 (4) 1999: 1189-1208.

Gamson, William A., David Croteau, William Hoynes and Theodore Sasson. "Media Images and the Social Construction of Reality" in *Annual Review of Sociology*, 18, 1992: 373-393.

Gi-Wook Shin. "The Historical Making of Collective Action: The Korean peasant uprisings of 1946" in *American Journal of Sociology*, 99 (6) 1994: 1596-1624.

Green, John C., James L. Guth and Kevin Hill. "Faith and Election: The Christian right in congressional campaigns 1978-1988" in *Journal of Politics*, 55 (1) 1993: 80-91.

Harris, Fredrick C. "Something Within: Religion as a mobilizer of African-American political activism" (in articles) in *Journal of Politics*, 56 (1) 1994: 42-68.

Hercus, Cheryl. "Identity, Emotion and Feminist Collective Action" in *Gender and Society*, 13 (1) Special Issue: Gender and Social Movements (Part 2) 1999: 34-55.

Hetherington, Marc J. "The Media's Role in Forming Voters' National Economic Evaluations in 1992" in *American Journal of Political Science*, 40 (2) 1996: 372-395.

Hibbing, John R. and Elizabeth Theiss-Morse. "The Media's Role in Public Negativity Toward Congress: Distinguishing emotional reactions and cognitive evaluations" in *American Journal of Political Science*, 42 (2) 1998: 475-498.

Huntington, Samuel P. "Clash of Civilizations?" in *Foreign Affairs*, 72 (3) Summer 1993: 22-49.

Jones Jr., Oliver. "The Black Muslim Movement and the American Constitutional System" in *Journal of Black Studies*, 13 (4) 1983: 417-437.

Kahn, Kim Fridkin and Patrick J. Kenney. "Do Negative Campaigns Mobilize or Suppress Turnout? Clarifying the relationship between negativity and participation" in *American Political Science Review*, 93 (4) 1999: 877-889.

Karatnycky, Adrian. "Muslim Countries and the Democracy Gap" in *Journal of Democracy*, 13 (1) 2003: 99-112.

Kurzman, Charles. "Critics Within: Islamic scholars' protests against the Islamic state in Iran" in *International Journal of Politics, Culture and Society*, 15 (2) 2001: 341-359.

Layman, Geoffrey C. "Religion and Political Behavior in the United States: The impact of beliefs, affiliations, and commitment from 1980 to 1994" in *Public Opinion Quarterly*, 61 (2) 1997: 288-316.

Leighley, Jan E. "Group Membership and the Mobilization of Political Participation" in *Journal of Politics*, 58 (2) 1996: 447-463.

_____ and Arnold Vedlitz. "Race, Ethnicity, and Political Participation: Competing models and contrasting explanations" in *Journal of Politics*, 61 (4) 1999: 1092-1114.

Lichbach, Mark I. "What makes Rational Peasants Revolutionary?: Dilemma, paradox, and irony in peasant collective action" in *World Politics*, 46 (3) 1994: 383-418.

Liddle, R. William. "Soeharto's Indonesia: Personal Rule and Political Institutions" in *Journal of Asian Studies*, 58 (1) 1985: 68-90.

_____. "The Islamic Turn in Indonesia: A political explanation" in *Journal of Asian Studies*, 55 (3) 1996: 613-634.

Lijphart, Arend. "Unequal Participation: Democracy's unresolved dilemma" in *American Political Science Review*, 91 (1) 1997: 1-14.

Loveman, Mara. "High-Risk Collective Action: Defending human rights in Chile, Uruguay and Argentina" in *American Journal of Sociology*, 104 (2) 1998: 477-525.

Manza, Jeff and Clem Brooks. "The Religious Factor in U. S. Presidential Elections, 1960-1992" in *American Journal of Sociology*, 103 (1) 1997: 38-81.

Minkoff, Debra C. "Bending with the Wind: Strategic change and adaptation by women's and racial minority organizations" in *American Journal of Sociology*, 104 (6) 1999: 1666-1703.

Ostrom, Elinor. "A Behavioral Approach to the Rational Choice Theory of Collective Action" in *American Political Science Review*, 92 (1) 1998: 1-22.

Polletta, Francesca and James Jasper. "Collective Identity and Social Movements" in *Annual Review of Sociology*, 27, 2001: 283-305.

Posusney, Marsha Priptein. "Irrational Workers: The moral economy of labor protest in Egypt" in *World Politics*, 46 (1) 1993: 83-120.

Radcliff, Benjamin and Patricia Davis. "Labor Organization and Electoral Participation in Industrial Democracies" in *American Journal of Political Science*, 44 (1) 2000: 132-141.

Reese, Laura A. and Ronald E. Brown. "The Effects of Religious Messages on Racial Identity and System Blame among African Americans" in *Journal of Politics*, 57 (1) 1995: 24-43.

Riker, William and Peter Ordeshook, "A Theory of the Calculus of Voting" in *American Political Science Review*, 62 (1) 1968: 25-42.

Robnett, Belinda. "African-American Women in the Civil Rights Movement, 1954-1965: Gender, leadership, and micromobilization" in *American Journal of Sociology*, 101 (6) 1996: 1661-1693.

Schwartz, Joel D. "Participation and Multisubjective Understanding: An interpretivist approach to the study of political participation" in *Journal of Politics*, 46 (4) 1984: 1117-1141.

Schwartz, Shalom H. and Sipke Huismans. "Value Priorities and Religiosity in Four Western Religions" in *Social Psychology Quarterly*, 58 (2) 1995: 88-107.

Schlozman, Kay Lehman, Sidney Verba and Henry E. Brady. "Participation's Not a Paradox: The View from American Activists" in *British Journal of Political Science*, 25 (1) 1995: 1-36.

Secret, Philip E., James B. Johnson and Audrey W. Forrest. "The Impact of Religiosity on Political Participation and Membership in Voluntary Associations Among Black and White Americans" in *Journal of Black Studies*, 21 (1) 1990: 87-102.

Seul, Jeffrey R. "'Ours Is the Way of God': Religion, identity, and intergroup conflict" in *Journal of Peace Research*, 36 (5) 1999: 553-569.

Simpson, Miles E. and George H. Conklin. "Socioeconomic Development, Suicide and Religion: A test of Durkheim's theory of religion and suicide" in *Social Forces*, 67 (4) 1989: 945-964.

Smith, Christopher E. "Black Muslims and the Development of Prisoners' Rights" in *Journal of Black Studies*, 24 (2) 1993: 131-146.

Steensland, Brian, Jerry Z. Park, Mark D. Regnerus, Lynn D. Robinson, W. Bradford Wilcox and Robert D. Woodberry. "The Measure of American Religion: Toward improving the state of the art" in *Social Forces*, 79 (1) September 2000: 291-318.

Wald, Kenneth D., James W. Button and Barbara A. Rienzo. "The Politics of Gay Rights in American Communities: Explaining antidiscrimination ordinances and policies" in *American Journal of Political Science*, 40 (4) 1996: 1152-1178.

Williams, Rhys H. and N. J. Demerath III. "Religion and Political Process in an American City" in *American Sociological Review*, 56 (4) 1991: 417-431.

Media References

"Death rate in Iraq rises by 100,000 since war" in *The Irish Times*, October 29, 2004: 14.

"U.S. Pushes Upward its Estimate of Iraq Rebels" in *International Herald Tribune*, October 23, 2004: 1.

"A Growing Muslim Identity: Increasingly, Arabs define themselves in terms of Islam" in *Los Angeles Times*, July 11, 2004.

"Khamenei says U.S. uses war against terror as excuse to attack Islam" in *BBC Monitoring International Reports*, December 24, 2003.

"Omnipotent West suffers denial syndrome" in *New Straits Times* (Kuala Lumpur) October 23, 2003.

'Bush calls on the world to act with "moral clarity"' in *White House Bulletin*, September 23, 2003.

"Rebuilding an identity after September 11" (opinion) by Muqtedar Khan in *New York Times*, September 9, 2003.

"Indonesia calls on Muslims to drop conspiracy theories" in *The Straits Times* (Singapore), August 23, 2003.

"Suspect regrets Bali attack 'even though victims mostly white'" in *The Straits Times* (Singapore), August 23, 2003.

"Official pledges use of force against troublemakers: 520 Arrested in Tehran unrest" in *Iran News* (Tehran), June 23, 2003.

"Karrubi says 'very few' students among rioters" in *Tehran Times* (Tehran), June 23, 2003.

"Information ministry, police to deal with instigators: Protesting students meet Karoubi" in *Iran Daily* (Tehran), June 23, 2003.

"Caution against foreign provocations: 166 MPs condemn plainclothes men" in *Iran Daily* (Tehran), June 23, 2003: 1.

"Basijis pledge to protect Islamic system" in *Iran Daily* (Tehran), June 21, 2003.

"Menguntit pemindahan Imam" [On trail of Imam's relocation] in *Kompas* (Jakarta), November 26, 2002.

Sabili, 14 (X) (Jakarta), November 14, 2002.

"Iran sentences reformist to death for insult to Prophet Muhammad" in *The New York Times*, November 8, 2002.

"Bush Stresses Anti-Terror Resolve" in *Washington Post* (October 15, 2002).

"America's elusive minority: Muslims" in *Christian Science Monitor* (Boston) October 7, 2002.

"Hamas exploits Robin Hood image to its benefits" in *The Straits Times* (Singapore) August 2, 2002.

"Indonesia's Osama" in *The Straits Times* (Singapore) March 30, 2002.

"The Revolt of Islam: When did the conflict with the West begin, and how could it end?" (opinion) by Bernard Lewis in *The New Yorker*, November 19, 2001.

"Osama admits role in WTC attack" in *Daily News* (New York) November 11, 2001.

"Al-Habib Muhammad Rizieq Shihab: Ini jelas pelanggaran berat" [This is surely a major transgression] in *Forum* (Jakarta) 29 (X) October 22, 2001.

"Indonesia's Dirty Little Holy War" in *Time Asia*, 158 (24) 2001.

"Siapa suruh datang ke Ambon" [Who told you to come to Ambon] in *Gatra* (Jakarta) January 22, 2000.

Special References

Ahlul Bayt Digital Library (ABDL) at www.abdl.com/quran. All transliterations of the Quranic verses were derived from Pickthal.

"Constructing" The Jemaah Islamiyah Terrorist: A preliminary inquiry, by Kumar Ramakrishna, Working Paper No.71, Institute of Defence and Strategic Studies, Nanyang Technological University, Singapore, dated October 2004.

The Emergence of the Jemaah Islamiyah Threat in Southeast Asia: External linkages and influences by Bilveer Singh, paper presented at a workshop on "International Terrorism in Southeast Asia and Likely Implications for South Asia" organized by the Observer Research Foundation, New Delhi, India on April 28-29, 2004.

Indonesia Backgrounder: Jihad in Central Sulawesi, published by the International Crisis Group (ICG) (Jakarta/Brussels), dated February 3, 2004.

Dealing with Iran's Nuclear Program, published by ICG (Amman/Brussels), dated October 27, 2003.

Iran: Discontent and disarray, published as "Middle East Briefing" by ICG (Amman/Brussels), dated October 15, 2003.

Jemaah Islamiyah in South East Asia: Damaged but still dangerous, published by ICG (Jakarta/Brussels), dated August 26, 2003.

White Paper: The Jemaah Islamiyah arrests and the threat of terrorism, published by the Ministry of Home Affairs, dated January 7, 2003.

Iran: The struggle for the revolution's soul, published by ICG (Amman/Brussels), dated August 5, 2002.

Al-Qaeda in Southeast Asia: The case of the "Ngruki Network" in Indonesia, published as "Indonesia Briefing" by ICG (Jakarta/Brussels), dated August 8, 2002.

Indonesia Backgrounder: How the Jemaah Islamiyah terrorist network operates, published by ICG (Jakarta/Brussels), dated December 11, 2002.

"*Islam in Modern Indonesia*" conference proceeding, published by the United States-Indonesia Society and the Asia Foundation. The event was held in Washington, D.C. on February 7, 2002.

APPENDICES

Appendix 1A

A. Questionnaire (Wording and Coding)

Sample of 'Muslims on the streets' in Indonesia and Iran (*N=996*)

Demography

a. Gender

Coding: Female {0}; Male {1}

b. Age

Wording: *How old are you?*

Coding: 19 and below {1}; 20-39 {2}; 40-59 {3}; 60 and above {4}

c. Marital status

Wording: *Are you married?*

Coding: Not married {0}; Married/Divorced with dependent(s) {1}

d. Employment status

Wording: *Are you currently employed or self-employed?*

Coding: Unemployed {0}; Employed/Self-employed {1}

If "unemployed", please proceed to Question No. F!

e. Monthly income

Wording: *How much is your average monthly income?*

Coding: None/Low (0-1.000.000) {1}; Medium (1.000.001-3.000.000) {2}; High (3.000.001 and above) {3}

f. Educational level

Wording: *What is your level of education?*

Coding: Low (no schooling-primary school) {1}; Medium (secondary-high schools) {2}; High (polytechnic/academy/university) {3}

g. Racial/ethnic identity

Wording: *What would you consider yourself to be in terms of race and ethnicity,* for example ...?

Coding: Minority ethnic group (non-Javanese/non-Fars) {0}; Majority ethnic group (Javanese/Fars) {1}

h. Political affiliation

Wording: *Are you affiliated with any political organizations or parties? If so, which* organization or party?

Coding: Politically unaffiliated {0}; Politically affiliated {1}

Religiosity

Knowledge of Islam

i. Type of education

Wording: *Have you ever attended an Islamic school, academy, or university?*

Coding: Never attended Islamic formal education {0}; Had attended Islamic formal education {1}

j. Informal Islamic studies

Wording: *Have you ever attended any Islamic informal religious courses?*

Coding: Never attended {0}; Had attended {1}

k. Quranic recitation (per week)

Wording: *How many hours do you spend reciting the Quran per week?*

Coding: Never/Hardly {0}; Sometimes (0.01-1 Hour) {1}; Frequently (>1 Hour) {2}

l. Islamic books read (excluding the Quran)
Wording: *How many numbers of Islamic books, excluding the Quran, have you* read throughout your lifetime?
Coding: Never {0}; A few (1-10 books) {1}; Many (>10) {2}

m. Subscription to Islamic media publication(s) (per week)
Wording: *How many Islamic publications do you subscribe and read per week?*
Coding: None {0}; 1 Publication {1}; >1 Publications {2}

n. Religious exposure (per week)
Wording: *How many overall hours do you spend listening and watching religious* sermons and gatherings per week inclusive of programs on TV, radio, CD and cassette?
Coding: Never {0}; Medium (d"2 hours) {1}; High (>2 hours) {2}

Ritual Practice

o. Prayers conducted (per day)
Wording: *How often do you pray everyday?*
Coding: Never/Hardly {0}; At least once {1}

p. Visits to place(s) of worship (per week)
Wording: *How many times do you visit the mosque per week?*
Coding: Never/Hardly {0}; Sometimes (1-5 Times) {1}; Frequently (>5 Times) {2}

q. Alms giving
Wording: *How often do you pay the zakat, shadaqah, infaq or khums?*
Coding: Never {0}; Very seldom/Seldom {1}; Sometimes {2}; Often/Very often {3}

Religious Affection

r. Religious sacrifice

Wording: *Some people would give up their lives for the defense of Muslims and/or* Islam. Do you agree with these people?

Coding: Strongly disagree/disagree {0}; Indifferent/Don't know {2}; Agree/Strongly agree {2}

s. Self-sacrifice

Wording: *Would you be willing to sacrifice your own life for the sake of Muslims* and/or Islam?

Coding: Totally unwilling/Unwilling {0}; Unsure/Don't know {1}; Willing/Totally willing {2}

t. Religious solidarity

Wording: *How do you feel toward the plight of Muslims in Palestine, Bosnia and* Iraq?

Coding: Indifferent {0}; Concerned {1}; Very concerned {2}

Participation

u. Participation in jihad

Wording: *Would you be willing to participate in jihad?*

Coding: No {0}; Unsure/Don't know {1}; Yes {2}

Appendix 1B

B. Questionnaire (Bahasa Indonesia)

<u>Demografi</u>

a. Jenis kelamin

b. Umur
   Berapa umur Anda?

c. Status perkawinan
   Apakah Anda sudah menikah?

d. Status pekerjaan
   Apakah Anda bekerja?

e. Pendapatan bulanan
   Berapa rata-rata pendapatan Anda setiap bulan?

f. Tingkat pendidikan
   Apa pendidikan terakhir Anda?

g. Ras/etnisitas
   Anda aslinya orang mana (misalnya, Jawa, Sunda, Melayu, Batak, Bugis)?

h. Afiliasi politik

Apakah Anda berafiliasi dengan sebuah organisasi atau partai politik? Kalau ya, organisasi atau partai apa?

Religiusitas

Pengetahuan mengenai Islam

i. Tipe pendidikan

Apakah Anda pernah mengenyam pendidikan formal di sekolah, akademi, atau universitas Islam?

j. Studi Islam informal

Pernahkah Anda mengikuti kursus-kursus pendidikan Islam seperti pesantren kilat?

k. Membaca Al-Quran (dalam minggu)

Kira-kira berapa jam Anda membaca Al-Quran setiap minggu?

l. Buku-buku Islam yang pernah dibaca (tidak termasuk Al-Quran)

Sepanjang umur Anda, berapa kira-kira jumlah buku-buku Islam, selain Al-Quran, yang telah Anda baca?

m. Langganan media cetak Islam (dalam seminggu)

Berapa media cetak Islam yang Anda langgan dan baca rata-rata setiap minggu?

n. Eksposur terhadap publikasi keagamaan (dalam seminggu)

Berapa jam rata-rata per minggu Anda memerhatikan ceramah-ceramah agama di TV, radio, CD, kaset, dan lainnya?

Kegiatan ritual

o. Shalat (per hari)

Dalam sehari, seberapa sering Anda melakukan shalat?

p. Kunjungan ke tempat ibadah (per minggu)

Berapa kali Anda ke masjid setiap minggu?

q. Zakat, infak, dan sedekah

Seberapa sering Anda membayar zakat, infak, atau sedekah?

Afeksi dalam religiusitas

r. Pengorbanan religius

Sebagian orang rela mengorbankan nyawanya untuk membela Islam dan kaum Muslim. Apakah Anda setuju dengan sikap mereka?

s. Pengorbanan diri

Apakah Anda sendiri rela mengorbankan diri untuk membela Islam dan kaum Muslim?

t. Solidaritas keberagamaan

Bagaimana perasaan Anda melihat penderitaan kaum Muslim di Palestina, Bosnia, dan Irak?

Partisipasi

u. Partisipasi dalam jihad

Apakah Anda bersedia untuk berpartisipasi dalam jihad?

Appendix 1C

c. پرسش نامه (فا ر سي)

الف ـ جنسيت

ب ـ سن
شما چند سال داريد؟

پ ـ ازدواج
آيا ازدواج كرده ايد؟

ت ـ اشتغال
آيا شاغل هستيد؟ (دولتي / غير دولتي)

ث ـ درآمد ماهيانه
هر ماه چقدر درآمد داريد؟

ج ـ مدرك تحصيلي
سوابق تحصيلي شما چيست؟

چ ـ اصليت و نژاد

اصليت و نژاد شما چيست؟ (براي مثال : فارس ، كرد ، ترك ، عربي و غيره)

ح ـ سياسي

آيا با احزاب سياسي رابطه داريد؟

خ ـ تحصيلات مذهبي

آيا تحصيلات حوزوي داريد؟

د ـ كلاسهاي اسلامي

آيا جهت آموزشهاي اسلامي به كلاس هاي خاصي مي رويد؟

ذ ـ قرائت قرآن

هر هفته چند ساعت قرآن مي خوانيد؟

ر ـ خواندن كتابهاي اسلامي

تا به حال چند كتاب اسلامي مطالعه كرده ايد؟

ز ـ روزنامه و مجله اسلامي

هر هفته چند روزنامه و يا مجله اسلامي مي خوانيد؟

ژ ـ سخنراني مذهبي

در هفته چقدر به سخنرانيهاي مذهبي در مساجد يا تلويزيون و يا نوار گوش فرا مي دهيد؟

س ـ انجام مراسم مذهبي

آيا نماز مي خوانيد؟

ش ـ مسجد

هر هفته چند بار به مسجد مي رويد؟

ص ـ خمس و زكات

آيا هميشه خمس و زكات خود را مي پردازيد؟

محبت

ض ـ ايثار

اگر مردم بخواهند جهت حفظ و بقاي اسلام جان خود را فدا كنند ، آيا قبول مي كنيد؟

ط ـ از خود گذشتگي

آيا شما جهت حفظ و بقاي اسلام حاضريد جان خود را فدا نمائيد؟

ظ ـ احساس وحدت

نسبت به مسلمانان ساكن در فلسطين ، بوسني و عراق چه احساسي داريد؟

شركت كردن

ع ـ جهاد اسلام

آيا در جهاد اسلام شركت مي كنيد؟

Appendix 2

Matrix of Correlations Between Demographic and Participation Variables

	VARIABLES	INDONESIA	IRAN	AGGREGATE
a.	Gender	.036 (.616)	.131 (.108)	.081* (.038)
b.	Age range	.019[b] (.574)	-.001[b] (.990)	.018[b] (.527)
c.	Marital status	.024 (.811)	.187** (.009)	.073 (.068)
d.	Employment status	.086 (.063)	.076 (.471)	.087* (.023)
e.	Income level	.046[b] (.196)	.034[b] (.567)	.055[b] (.078)
f.	Educational level	.062[b] (.076)	-.170[b]** (.003)	-.002[b] (.953)
g.	Racial/ethnic identity	.109* (.012)	.111 (.197)	.064 (.133)
h.	Political affiliation	.098[b]** (.005)	.104[b]* (.023)	.082[b]* (.036)

[a] Phi coefficients; [b] Kendall tau-b; the rest are contingency coefficients

Figures in the parentheses are *p*-values (significance levels)

** $p \leq .01$; * $p \leq .05$ (2-tailed)

Appendix 3

**Matrix of Correlations (*Kendall tau-b*) Between Measures
of Religiosity and Participation Variable**

	MEASURES	INDONESIA	IRAN	AGGREGATE
i.	Type of education	.067 (.057)	.024 (.689)	.030 (.316)
j.	Informal Islamic studies	.129*** (.000)	.203*** (.000)	.115*** (.000)
k.	Quranic recitation	.117*** (.001)	.185*** (.001)	.121*** (.000)
l.	Islamic books read	.112*** (.001)	.154** (.009)	.121*** (.000)
m.	Islamic media publication(s)	.231*** (.000)	.075 (.175)	.162*** (.000)
n.	Religious exposure	.110*** (.001)	.325*** (.000)	.151*** (.000)
o.	Daily prayers	.039 (.541)	.379*** (.000)	.226*** (.000)
p.	Visits to place(s) of worship	.057 (.101)	.278*** (.000)	.100*** (.001)

q.	Paying of alms	.066	.059	.048
		(.055)	(.285)	(.109)
r.	Religious sacrifice	.263***	.513***	.334***
		(.000)	(.000)	(.000)
s.	Religious self-sacrifice	.293***	.564***	.374***
		(.000)	(.000)	(.000)
t.	Religious solidarity	.355***	.436***	.316***
		(.000)	(.000)	(.000)

Figures in the parentheses are *p*-values (significance levels)

*** $p \le .001$; ** $p \le .01$; * $p \le .05$ (2-tailed)

Appendix 4

Demographic Characteristics of the Indonesian Sample (*n*=738)

	Frequency	*%*[1]
Gender		
Female	356	48.2
Male	382	51.8
Age group		
19 and below	105	14.2
20-39	528	71.6
40-59	97	13.2
60 and above	7	0.9
Marital status		
Not married	443	60.0
Married/Divorced with dependent(s)	295	40.0
Employment status		
Unemployed	310	42.0
Employed or self-employed	428	58.0
Monthly income (in Indonesian rupiah)		
Low (0-1.000.000)	584	83.9

[1] The numbers in the data represent the valid percentage of each category, which considers and calculates missing information mostly due to respondents' reluctance to answer specific questions that they found to be too personal.

Medium (1.000.001-3.000.000)	95	13.6
High (3.000.001 and above)	17	2.4
Educational level		
Low (no schooling-primary schools)	43	5.8
Medium (secondary-high schools)	472	64.0
High (polytechnic/academy/university)	223	30.2
Racial/ethnic identity		
Minority (non-Javanese)	411	55.7
Majority (Javanese)	327	44.3
Political affiliation		
Politically unaffiliated	568	77.0
Politically affiliated	170	23.0

Appendix 5

Religious Characteristics of the Indonesian Respondents (*n*=738)

	Frequency	*%[2]*
Knowledge of Islam		
Type of education		
Never attended Islamic formal education	397	53.8
Had attended Islamic formal education	341	46.2
Informal Islamic studies		
Never attended	315	42.7
Had attended	422	57.3
Quranic recitation (per week)		
Never/Hardly	114	15.4
Sometimes (0.01-1 hour)	287	38.9
Frequently (>1 hour)	337	45.7
Islamic books read (throughout lifetime)		
Never	122	16.5
A few (1-10 books)	325	44.0
Many (>10 books)	291	39.4

---

[2] The numbers in the data represent the valid percentage of each category, which considers and calculates missing information mostly due to respondents' reluctance to provide answers to specific questions.

Subscription to Islamic media publication(s) (per week)		
None	245	33.2
1 Publication	231	31.3
>1 Publications	262	35.5
Religious exposure (per week)		
Never	78	10.6
Medium (≤ 2 hours)	264	35.8
High (>2 hours)	396	53.7
Ritual Practices		
Prayers conducted (per day)		
Never/Hardly	25	3.4
At least once	713	96.6
Place(s) of worship (per week)		
Never/Hardly	133	18.0
Sometimes (1-5 times)	394	53.5
Frequently (>5 Times)	210	28.5
Alms giving		
Never	7	0.9
Very seldom/Seldom	138	18.7
Sometimes	398	53.9
Often/Very often	195	26.4
Religious Affection		
Religious sacrifice		
Strongly disagree/Disagree	45	6.1
Indifferent/Don't know	167	22.7
Agree/Strongly Agree	523	71.2
Religious self-sacrifice		
Totally unwilling/Unwilling	51	6.9
Unsure/Don't know	196	26.7
Willing/Totally willing	488	66.4

Religious solidarity		
Indifferent	30	4.1
Concerned	298	40.4
Very concerned	410	55.6

Appendix 6

Demographic Characteristics of the Iranian Sample (*n*=258)

	Frequency	*%*[3]
Gender		
Female	48	18.7
Male	209	81.3
Age group		
19 and below	24	9.3
20-39	181	70.2
40-59	49	19.0
60 and above	4	1.6
Marital status		
Not married	137	53.1
Married/Divorced with dependent(s)	121	46.9
Employment status		
Unemployed	99	38.5
Employed or self-employed	158	61.5
Monthly income (in Iranian Riyals)		
Low (0-1.000.000)	151	59.2
Medium (1.000.001-3.000.000)	92	36.1
High (3.000.001 and above)	12	4.7

---

[3] The numbers in the data represent the valid percentage of each category, which considers and calculates missing information mostly due to respondents' reluctance to answer specific questions that they found to be too personal.

Educational level		
Low (no schooling-primary schools)	16	6.3
Medium (secondary-high schools)	122	47.8
High (polytechnic/academy/university)	117	45.9
Racial/ethnic identity		
Minority (non-Fars)	80	31.0
Majority (Fars)	178	69.0
Political affiliation		
Politically unaffiliated	251	98.0
Politically affiliated	5	2.0

Appendix 7

Religious Characteristics of the Iranian Respondents (*n*=258)

	Frequency	%[4]
Knowledge of Islam		
Type of education		
Never attended Islamic formal education	253	98.4
Had attended Islamic formal education	4	1.6
Informal Islamic studies		
Never attended	215	85.7
Had attended	36	14.3
Quranic recitation (per week)		
Never/Hardly	105	42.3
Sometimes (0.01-1 hour)	68	27.4
Frequently (>1 hour)	75	30.2
Islamic books read (throughout lifetime)		
Never	45	17.4
A few (1-10 books)	125	48.4
Many (>10 books)	88	34.1

[4] The numbers in the data represent the valid percentage of each category, which considers and calculates missing information mostly due to respondents' reluctance to provide answers to specific questions.

Subscription to Islamic media publication(s) (per week)		
None	181	70.2
1 Publication	28	10.9
>1 Publications	49	19.0
Religious exposure (per week)		
Never	124	50.0
Medium (≤2 hours)	48	19.4
High (>2 hours)	76	30.6
Ritual Practices		
Prayers conducted (per day)		
Never/Hardly	29	11.3
At least once	228	88.7
Place(s) of worship (per week)		
Never/Hardly	127	51.8
Sometimes (1-5 times)	90	36.7
Frequently (>5 times)	28	11.4
Alms giving		
Never	119	46.7
Very seldom/Seldom	27	10.6
Sometimes	59	23.1
Often/Very often	50	19.6
Religious Affection		
Religious sacrifice		
Strongly disagree/Disagree	43	16.9
Indifferent/Don't know	45	17.7
Agree/Strongly Agree	166	65.4
Religious self-sacrifice		
Totally unwilling/Unwilling	54	21.5
Unsure/Don't know	27	10.8
Willing/Totally willing	170	67.7

Religious solidarity		
Indifferent	65	25.3
Concerned	152	59.1
Very concerned	40	15.6

Appendix 8

Essential Demographic Characteristics of the Aggregate Sample (*N*=996)

	Frequency	*%*[5]
Gender		
Female	404	40.6
Male	591	59.4
Age group		
19 and below	129	13.0
20-39	709	71.3
40-59	146	14.7
60 and above	11	1.1
Marital status		
Not married	580	58.2
Married/Divorced with dependent(s)	416	41.8
Employment status		
Unemployed	409	41.1
Employed or self-employed	586	58.9

---

[5] The numbers in the data represent the valid percentage of each factor, which considers and calculates missing information mostly due to respondents' reluctance to answer specific questions that they found to be too personal.

Monthly income (in Rupiah/Riyals)[6]		
Low (0-1.000.000)	735	77.3
Medium (1.000.001-3.000.000)	187	19.7
High (3.000.001 and above)	29	3.0
Political affiliation		
Politically unaffiliated	819	82.4
Politically affiliated	175	17.6
Education level		
Low (no schooling-primary school)	59	5.9
Medium (secondary-high schools)	594	59.8
High (polytechnic/academy/university)	340	34.2

[6] At the time of the survey in Iran, conducted in mid 2003, the value of the Indonesian Rupiah and the Iranian Riyal was almost similar, around Rp.8,200 and IR.8,100 respectively to the US dollar. Although purchasing power parity points to discrepancy in cost of living, the monthly income category between Indonesia and Iran are still comparable.

Appendix 9

Religious Attributes and Characteristics of the Aggregate Sample (*N*=996)

	Frequency	*%*[7]
Knowledge of Islam		
Type of education		
Never attended Islamic formal education	650	65.3
Had attended Islamic formal education	345	34.7
Informal Islamic studies		
Never attended	530	53.6
Had attended	458	46.4
Quranic recitation (per week)		
Never/Hardly	219	22.2
Sometimes (0.01-1 hour)	355	36.0
Frequently (>1 hour)	412	41.8
Islamic books read		
Never	167	16.8
A few (1-10 books)	450	45.2
Many (>10 books)	379	38.1

---

[7] The numbers in the data represent the valid percentage of each category, which considers and calculates missing information mostly due to respondents' reluctance to provide answers to specific questions.

Subscription to Islamic media publication(s) (per week)		
None	426	42.8
1 Publication	259	26.0
>1 Publications	311	31.2
Religious exposure (per week)		
No/Low	202	20.5
≤2 Hours	312	31.6
>2 Hours	472	47.9
Ritual Practices		
Prayers conducted (per day)		
≤4 Times (Indonesia) or ≤2 (Iran)	54	5.4
5 Times (Indonesia) or 3 Times (Iran)	284	28.5
>5 Times (Indonesia) or >3 Times (Iran)	657	66.0
Place(s) of worship (per week)		
Never/Hardly	260	26.5
1-5 Times	484	49.3
>5 Times	238	24.2
Alms giving		
Never	126	12.7
Very seldom/Seldom	165	16.6
Sometimes	457	46.0
Often/Very often	245	24.7
Religious Affection		
Religious sacrifice		
Strongly disagree/Disagree	88	8.9
Indifferent/Don't know	212	21.4
Agree/Strongly Agree	689	69.7
Religious self-sacrifice		
Totally unwilling/Unwilling	105	10.6
Unsure/Don't know	223	22.6
Willing/Totally willing	658	66.7

Religious solidarity		
Indifferent	95	12.7
Concerned	450	45.2
Very concerned	450	45.2

Appendix 10

Binary Logistics Using Backward Stepwise (Wald) Method (valid *N*=984)

Step	Variables in the Equation	B	S.E.	Wald	Df	Sig.	Exp (B)
1	NITY	1.380	.688	4.022	1	.045	3.974
	SAC	.369	.495	.554	1	.457	1.446
	SSAC	.845	.520	2.635	1	.105	2.328
	SOL	1.311	.471	7.735	1	.005	3.710
	NITY by SAC	.207	.409	.256	1	.613	1.230
	NITY by SSAC	.110	.419	.069	1	.793	1.116
	NITY by SOL	-.114	.340	.113	1	.737	.892
	SAC by SSAC	-.057	.194	.086	1	.770	.945
	SAC by SOL	.060	.252	.056	1	.813	1.061
	SSAC by SOL	-.115	.253	.207	1	.649	.891
	Constant	-3.865	.805	23.076	1	.000	.021
7	NITY	1.734	.207	70.213	1	.000	5.665
	SAC	.469	.139	11.291	1	.001	1.598
	SSAC	.653	.128	25.863	1	.000	1.922
	SOL	1.192	.140	72.885	1	.000	3.292
	Constant	-3.838	.311	152.248	1	.000	.022

Legend: NITY=Nationality; SAC=Sacrifice; SSAC=Self-sacrifice; SOL=Solidarity

Appendix 11

Outcome of Binary Logistics Regression

Model Summary

Step	-2 Log likelihood	Cox & Snell R Square	Nagelkerke R Square
1	1122.880	.217	.290
7	1125.273	.215	.287

Hosmer and Lemeshow's Goodness-of-Fit Test

Step	df	Sig.
1	6	.400
7	6	.492

Classification Table

Step	Observed		Predicted Participation in jihad		Percentage Correct
			No-Unsure	Yes	
1	Participation in jihad (0-1)	*No-Unsure*	320	165	66.0
		Yes	134	365	73.1
	Overall Percentage				69.6
7	Participation in jihad (0-1)	*No-Unsure*	320	165	66.0
		Yes	133	366	73.3
	Overall Percentage				69.7

The cut value is .5

Index